Living Without the Screen

This book provides an in-depth study of those American families and individuals who opt *not* to watch television, exploring the reasons behind their choices, discussing their beliefs about television, and examining the current role of television in the American family. Author Marina Krcmar answers several questions in this volume: What is television? Who are those people that reject it? What are their reasons for doing so? How do they believe their lives are different because of this choice? What impact does this choice have on media research?

This volume provides a current, distinctive, and important look at how personal choices on media are made, and how those choices reflect more broadly on media's place in today's society.

Marina Krcmar is an Associate Professor in the Communication Department of Wake Forest University. Her research focuses on children, adolescents, and the media, and her most recent research has examined the effect of violent video games on adolescents and the role of media consumption in adolescent risk-taking.

LEA's Communication Series
Jennings Bryant/Dolf Zillmann, General Editors

Living Without the Screen

Causes and Consequences of
Life without Television

Marina Krcmar

Routledge
Taylor & Francis Group

NEW YORK AND LONDON

First published 2009
by Routledge
270 Madison Ave, New York, NY 10016

Simultaneously published in the UK
by Routledge
2 Park Square, Milton Park, Abingdon, Oxon OX14 4RN

Routledge is an imprint of the Taylor & Francis Group, an informa business

© 2009 Taylor & Francis

Typeset in Sabon by
HWA Text and Data Management, London

Printed and bound in the United States of America on acid-free paper by
Edwards Brothers, Inc.

Library of Congress Cataloging in Publication Data
Krcmar, Marina.
    Living without the screen / by Marina Krcmar. – 1st ed.
        p. cm.
    1. Television and family--United States. 2. Television viewers--United States. I. Title.
    HQ520.K73 2008
    302.23'450973--dc22   2008009109

ISBN10 HB: 0–8058–6328–1
ISBN10 PB: 0–8058–6329–X
ISBN10 EB: 1–4106–1781–5

ISBN13 HB: 978–0–8058–6328–4
ISBN13 PB: 978–0–8058–6329–1
ISBN13 EB: 978–1–4106–1781–1

To my father, Frantisek Krcmar, 1929–2004

Contents

Preface

I begin this book with a short confession; however, I will not go into great detail about it lest the story sound self-serving, or worse, dull. I live without a television. Although it may seem ironic that someone who studies the effects of mass media should live without TV, it is no more or less ironic than my colleagues who are single and study marital communication. I think it makes my perspective somewhat different, but no better or worse, necessarily. In fact, at a recent conference, I told a colleague that I did not have a television and her response was one of dismay. How, she asked, could a media effects researcher live without television? Although I bravely offered my reasons for doing so and my strategies for dealing with this aspect of my life, I was also struck, yet again, by the fact that there was no research on people like me. And yet I know there are others. I walked away from that conversation knowing there was research to be done.

Although all of my research has been quantitative social science, I believe that the best way to answer the questions I had about fellow nonviewers was to conduct interviews and to observe families in their homes. I needed to understand how nonviewers lived and why they had decided to forego television. I needed to understand their beliefs about television, politics, child rearing and family life. The problem, however, is that statistically so few people live without television, I was not sure how would I find them. A random sample of 200 homes might turn up two without television. Clearly, traditional survey methods were not the way to approach this. Instead, I employed a variety of strategies and ended up with what might best be called a convenience sample.

In the end, finding nonviewers was less difficult than I had feared. As I discovered, unlike participants in an experiment or randomly sampled respondents to a survey, people without television want to talk about their experiences. I posted online at various Web sites. I wrote a single line about wanting to interview families without television, and *they* e-mailed *me*. I was astounded. Here, I had spent a dozen years worrying over sample sizes and writing compelling letters to parents about the importance of allowing their children to participate in my studies. I defended what I did at PTA meetings and sat embarrassed and mute as a protective parent asked me if I let my own children participate in these studies. Now, participants were contacting me. I drove to their homes when I could and when it became clear that I couldn't drive to Indiana or California or Arkansas, I conducted phone interviews. I had interesting e-mail correspondences with people who signed off by saying, "Gotta run. The baby is awake and the 6-year-old is done with her blocks." I was honored that they fit me into the little free time they had. I also interviewed families with television and spent time in the homes of those with TV and without it. I talked to the children, hung out in their kitchens, and sat on their couches. Although this research is primarily based on interviews and some survey data, many observations came during times when I was silent, doing the ethnographic portion of the research.

From this process, I realized that these interviews were not only fascinating to conduct but that people cared about this issue. Television, and conversely not having one, matters. If television is really so intimately related to culture that "we really cannot isolate the role of media in culture because the media are firmly anchored into the web of culture" (Bird, 2003, p. 3), then what happens when we live without it? The individuals (72 nonviewing adults, 48 nonviewing children, 82 television viewing adults and 30 viewing children) who participated in this research provided invaluable information to help me address this question. Many participated in in-depth interviews, some filled out surveys and some also kept time-use diaries. Throughout the process I was repeatedly caught up in their stories, taken in by their perspectives, and compelled by their beliefs. If anything, my experience as a quantitative social scientist made it more, not less, difficult to conduct interviews in an unbiased way. Why do I say this? When conducting an experiment or a survey, an attempt at objectivity is built into the design. There are standard practices and procedures to minimize bias. By the time the study is underway, as much bias as possible has been identified and removed. But in the interview process, the interviewer is invited into the lives of the participants. The process is personal and I found myself drawn into the stories of people whose lives differed significantly from my own. Politics or age or social beliefs separated us and yet, in the end, these participants persuaded me. I was compelled by their points of view. Throughout this book then, one challenge has been trying to portray participants in their own voices while remaining objective in my own. I have attempted to discuss a family's moralistic stance about sex on television, for example, while remaining somewhat objective about it myself. I have been aided in this endeavor by the existing literature on television and the family. That literature often provided a counterpoint of objectivity to balance the subjective narratives of the families in this book. I can only hope I have been successful in this attempt at balance.

Research about television and the family has often examined TV as a medium that punctuates family life, allowing families to track time, to be entertained or informed. Television provides fodder for conversation or alternately, acts as a convenient screen to isolate family members from one another when that is what they desire (Lull, 1980). Television matters because, in many ways, it is integral to our lives. We watch it, as the uses and gratifications approach argues (and as will be discussed in greater depth in chapter 3), to be entertained, to pass time, to make social connections, to learn, and to escape (Rubin, 1984). It is the background noise, the accompaniment, and at times, the main étude of family life. When television is removed, the content is removed but a pseudo-social actor, a pseudo-social family member is removed, as well. What happens when television is no longer present in the home? This book attempts to address that question.

Acknowledgments

Creating this book has taken me from the very social and interactive experience of conducting interviews, to the intensely private experience of writing. However, in both phases, it could not have been possible without the input and assistance of many people. Their help was invaluable; however, remaining flaws are mine. First and foremost, I would like to thank the many fascinating people who welcomed me into their homes and patiently answered my questions, offered me tea and sandwiches and even dragged me along on family outings. Obviously, this book could not have been written without their generosity. Second, I would like to thank the two universities that supported me throughout the process. The University of Connecticut provided the much-needed sabbatical, and my colleagues provided a constant source of intellectual stimulation. Mark Hamilton, Kirstie Farrar, Karen Cornetto, Leslie Snyder and many others were always willing to talk with me about this project. Halfway through the process I moved to Wake Forest University; Steve Giles, Don Helme, Randy Rogan and Michael Hyde were always available for conversations about the mass media and have contributed to my thinking on the topic. I'd also like to thank Kathryn Beeler, also at Wake Forest, who has some of the keenest copy-editing eyes I've come across. Other colleagues have also helped me in my thinking over the years. Thanks are due to Dave Roskos-Ewoldsen, Kathryn Greene, Robin Nabi, Kris Harrison, Mary Beth Oliver, Art Raney, and Linda Keane for many wonderful conversations.

To others who have read chapters and versions of this manuscript, I'd also like to extend my sincere thanks: Lilly Krcmar, Mark Krcmar and Connie Gilbert contributed thoughtful comments about style and structure. Chantal Krcmar offered ideas from a sociological perspective that were both novel to me and infinitely helpful and Sally Milius offered observations about the content of the book and about being a nonviewer. I am infinitely lucky to have family and friends who have the wisdom to make insightful comments and the ability to do so graciously. And, of course, I am very lucky to have a cultural anthropologist for a husband.

Because I am trained as a quantitative social scientist, I shamelessly picked his brain for methodological ideas, theoretical direction and pragmatic concerns. Mark Cooke read and re-read chapter after chapter. From the stylistic to the theoretical, his ideas were always well thought out and on target. This book could not be what it is without him.

Finally, I thank my family for providing inspiration and joy. Mark, Maya, Georgia and Eve: thank you, thank you, thank you.

Part I
Introduction and Overview

The first portion of this book lays the groundwork for the research itself. I discuss the need for the research, the data collection process, and the sample both in the aggregate and in detail. I also discuss how nonviewers gave up television. In this first section of the book, we cover how nonviewers feel about living without television and their attitudes towards it. The final chapter in Part I presents three definitions of television: television as medium, content, and industry. These three definitions are then used to group the second, third, and fourth sections of the book. Much of the data for the first section of the book was gathered from the in-depth interviews.

Chapter 1

Living without Television

In this chapter, I begin by discussing why we need a book about families who do not watch television. I bring in the concept of negative space, a concept that emerged in the art world. Applying this to media research I ask if we can learn about television itself by studying those who purposefully do not watch it. I then discuss various definitions of television, emphasizing the importance of allowing television to be defined by audiences and by nonviewers, rather than by researchers. Last, I provide an overview of the chapters and give a brief summary of each one.

Why write a book about families who live without television? Perhaps for several reasons. First, from the available statistics, the number of families who live without television is likely to be somewhat larger than the actual numbers suggest. Whereas some 85% of American homes have cable (Ireland, 2005) and a whopping 98% have at least one television, these numbers do not paint a thoroughly accurate picture. Although almost all of the people I interviewed for this book consider themselves "TV-free,"(except those who participated in the control group) only one-third of the nonviewing families have no television set in their homes. In fact, some even subscribe to cable in order to access the Internet— although they do not have it hooked up to their television. In certain areas it is in fact cheaper to subscribe to a full spectrum of cable channels that get bundled in with Internet service than it is to have cable Internet service alone. And approximately two-thirds of this group have a television and VCR or DVD player that they keep in a closet and pull out to watch an occasional movie.

Second, and perhaps more importantly, media researchers, myself among them, have based their research agendas on a fairly straightforward assumption: people watch television. Preschool-aged children watch four hours per day (Comstock & Sharrer, 2001); the average adult watches three hours per day; elderly people watch upwards of six hours per day. In the average American household, the television is on for seven hours per day. However, there are those who truly watch none and we know little about them (see Foss & Alexander, 1996; and Zinsmeister, 1997 for exceptions). There is much to learn about television specifically and perhaps families more broadly by studying those who do *not* watch.

Negative Space

The metaphor of negative space has been used by some scholars (e.g., Daly, 2003) to understand how what we do *not* do, what we do *not* attend to, or what we do *not* study offers insights into our theories about topics that *do* garner our attention. In this book, I believe looking at families who do not watch television can tell us something about topics that have been researched time and time again: families and television.

The concept of negative space emerged initially in the study of art. Positive space in art refers to the images, the shapes, the forms that make up an image, a canvas or a frame. Negative space is simply that which is not taken up by the image. It is what is *not* the image or, phrased more positively, it is made up of the shapes and forms that are left when the object or image of attention is removed. In art, we are unaccustomed to looking at pictures, photographs, and drawings this way. We see things and objects, not the space and the shape of the space that surrounds objects. But as many artists argue, there is much to be learned by studying negative space. Daly (2003) has pointed out that "drawing and theorizing are parallel processes as both are concerned with representation...Our theorizing activity, like our everyday sensory experience, is always a matter of straddling the tensions between perception and imperception and attending to and ignoring" (p. 771). In other words, each theory is based on choosing certain variables and relationships and ignoring others. It is a process of focusing our attention, which, by definition, requires us to eliminate certain things from focus. Ultimately, then, if an understanding of art and a facility with drawing can be improved through attention to negative space—that which surrounds what we attend to and that which is *not there*—might our theories also benefit from studying what is not there? In the case of media research, might we learn something about television by studying those who actively and purposefully choose to avoid it?

Over five decades of research on the effects of media, or television more specifically, has made the implicit assumption that adults and children watch television. Television viewing is taken to be a universal activity—like eating or sleeping—which is, therefore, interesting to study not only in its effects, but more recently, in the way it is used (e.g., Rubin, 2002). It is certainly valuable to study the effects of mass media. It is equally important to study those who purposefully choose not to watch.

Something about the choice to avoid television, and about the home life that emerges from this choice, may help us come to understand the activity of watching television more thoroughly. We learn something about how individuals and families structure their time and their interactions with each other and how they come to hold the attitudes that they do. From this perspective, television in the home is not only moving images but something that affects families beyond the content presented. In other words, television is part of the social make-up of the household. Like another family member, it can interrupt a conversation, or provide fodder to start one. Therefore, it is possible that, socially speaking, homes without television may operate somewhat differently from homes with it.

Why might this be the case? Several researchers have considered the social aspects of television. Lull (1980) was one of the early researchers to examine the social uses of television. He argued that families use television not only as an entertainment medium, but for social uses as well. Although family members may watch particular content, how they watch, when they watch, and with whom they watch affects the social interaction in the family. He argues that families watch television to minimize conflict between arguing members or alternately, to provide an opportunity for two or more members to share physical proximity and contact. In other words, as early as 25 years ago, Lull emphasized that television has many functions.

Alexander (2001) has also suggested that television is more than an audio-visual technology. She has suggested that, examined in the context of the home, television is neither an object of perception nor of social cognition. It is neither an inanimate object, nor a social actor. Therefore, because it is neither inanimate nor quite interactive, Alexander views television as occupying an uneasy place in the American home, what she refers to as "contested space." Like Lull, Alexander has taken television to be an important part of the home not only because of what television presents on its screen, but also because of how television affects the patterns, rhythms, activities, and textures of family life. No other appliance seems to hold quite so much sway.[1] In both cases, the social uses of television and television as contested space, it is given an almost social power that it simply does not have in the homes explored in this book. If we remove the almost-family member of television, what is left in its place? Even a contested space leaves a void. What, if anything, fills the space?

---

1 Over the last decade, the family computer has begun to influence family life and family interaction in some of the same ways that television does (Jordan, 2002). However, for our purposes, we focus only on families without television because television is accessed by virtually all homes while family computer ownership is still influenced by factors such as socio-economic status.

Of the people who do not watch television, there is much we do not know. We do not know why they have made the choices they have, how they came to choose a life without television, what their ideas are or if those with children raise them in ways that differ from those who do have television. In fact, we do not even know if there is a stereotypical home without television, or if there are just many homes that for one reason or another, be it lack of time, interest or social ideology, do not watch television, sharing little else in common. Although Foss and Alexander (1996) argue that individuals who are heavy viewers and those who watch no television have similar conceptions of television (e.g., television has effects, television viewing can be an addiction), it is unclear from their research how nonviewers gave up television, why they did so or how their lives differ as a result. By studying them and by studying this negative space in media research, we can learn more about television and, I would argue, about families.

It is the goal of this book, then, to address some of those questions and to take a closer look at families who live without television. I will examine their motives for dropping television and their reasons for remaining without it. I will discuss their conceptions of television, their ideas about family life, and how they spend their time. I have interviewed single adults, couples without children, families with young or older children living in the home, and older couples, empty nesters whose children were raised without television and who now continue to live without it. In short, I will look at these individuals with the hope that they have something to offer our understanding of media consumption and, more broadly, to our understanding of families.

Defining Television

Although television itself seems a fairly straightforward entity, Andreasen (2002) describes how advances in technology have confounded our study of the medium. Perhaps the first technology that affected our study of television was the video cassette recorder. The VCR can be used to tape programs from broadcast and replay them at a time that is more convenient. The VCR can also be used to watch movies that originally played in the theaters or ones that were designed specifically for home use. Is this television? It may depend on the focus of the researcher. If I am interested in the effect of amount of screen time on children's reading skills, I may well count time spent with recorded material as television. However, if I am interested in the effects of commercials, I may be less likely to do so. So recorded programs are and are not television.

In addition, Andreasen (2002) has aptly asked, "If the rubric of *television viewing* appropriately includes the consumption of time-shifted programs, does it apply to those that, in addition, undergo a shifted *locus?*" (p. 4). Here, Andreasen explores how the Internet may or may not be television, depending on how the question is phrased and certainly depending on who you ask. She reports that Mark Cuban, president of Broadcast.com would argue that the Internet is not television, regardless of where the content appeared initially. Instead, he argued that it is a different medium. As we will discuss in this book, Cuban shares something in common with a subset of the nonviewers—those who consider television, by definition, a medium that provides a potentially continuous flow of stimulus, complete with programs and commercials. For these nonviewers, television is defined by its continuity and its omnipresence, not by its content (e.g., commercials, sex, violence) per se. Therefore, although it is not the purpose of this book to explore if new technologies still qualify as television, these debates do bring up yet another interesting question, one that was answered by those who participated in this study: What *is* television?

Although I began this research into nonviewing households with a fairly strict definition—a home with no television set in it—I began to take a more phenomenological approach and expanded the definition based on the families' own definitions. "Why do you consider yourselves TV-free?" I'd ask. "Because we don't watch television," they'd respond. Often, someone would pipe in "Didn't we watch the Super Bowl last year?" "No, that was two years ago. Remember, we still had that old brown couch of your mother's?" So, as I began to understand it, living without television is not a structural feature of the household, but a choice about what to do in it. So a family can consider themselves nonviewers, own a television that they keep in a closet, use it to watch movies and even, for some homes, rent a program that initially aired on broadcast television. But by their own definition, they do not "watch" television.

Therefore, the way we have defined television has been dominated by "positive space." We have defined television, first, by discussing the structural and technological features of the medium. Although Andreasen (2002) is certainly right in addressing how changes in technology have impacted the use of television in most American homes, a discussion of this nature still limits our understanding of television. Television is still perceived as an object with features, and those features then affect the use of television *by* families. It does not give us a chance to consider how families *define* television. Second, media researchers define television as it is used by families who watch it. They may have cable. They may have favorite programs that they watch in the evening or during meals. In other words, they see themselves as television viewers. They are the "positive space" in the landscape of media research. However, in the present study, two-thirds of the homes owned television sets yet identified themselves as nonviewers. It is very valuable here to consider what a television is, or what television watching is for these nonviewers. In exploring this negative space, we learn much about the use of television and we provide opportunity for people to define what it is.

Overview and Organization of the Chapters

In chapter 2, I describe the sample and method in detail. Overall, there were three main strategies for data collection for this project: interviews, surveys and time-use diaries. First, I explored the themes that emerge in the in-depth interviews and in-home observations. In total, I interviewed 120 nonviewers in 62 different families. Of these, 72 were adults and 48 were children. I also interviewed 20 adult viewers in 18 different families. Second, I had 63 of the adult nonviewers, and 29 of the child nonviewers keep time-use diaries and respond to surveys. I also had a matched sample of 62 adult viewers and 30 child viewers keep time-use diaries and respond to identical surveys. The survey questions asked about behaviors, attitudes, and beliefs concerning politics, consumerism, religion, education, and computer use. I will discuss these strategies in greater detail later in the book.

In chapter 3, I discuss the three main ways that people give up television: attrition, "kicking the habit," and environmental change. The first process is *attrition*. For those who eliminate television through attrition, television gradually stops having interest or meaning for them. This group stops watching television and then gets rid of it or stores it in the basement almost as an after-thought. The second process I refer to as *kicking the habit*. These individuals actually get rid of their set, sometimes in dramatic ways because they perceive it to have become a problem either for themselves or for their family in general. They may continue to desire it after it is gone, but perceive their viewing as a bad habit to be quit. Third, I discuss *environmental reasons*. When individuals give up television for environmental reasons, some outside factor such as a move or a divorce results in the loss of the television set; however, the set is never replaced because the individual or family comes to prefer living without it.

In chapter 3 I also introduce the uses and gratifications approach (Rubin, 2002). Here, I discuss Rubin's dimensions of television use motives (e.g., escape, information gain) and utilize these to interpret both viewers' and nonviewers' motivations for their behavior. Whereas both viewers and nonviewers discuss television in ways that are consistent with a uses and gratifications perspective, viewers see benefits to the various uses of television where nonviewers see drawbacks. For example, viewers may discuss the importance of keeping up with the news; however, nonviewers question the quality of information gained from television news. Also consistent with a uses and gratifications approach, nonviewers have replaced the uses of television with other stimulus. The "negative space" that is left when television is removed does not remain empty. Instead, the gaps left when television is absent are filled with human interaction, time spent in hobbies or reading the news on the Internet or in the newspaper.

Chapter 4 addresses attitudes towards living without television for adults and children. Although all adults in the sample are advocates of living without television, it is perhaps more surprising that children of all ages seemed to view it as a benefit as well. Although in families without television, adolescents sometimes complained about their loss of television as social capital, neither children nor adolescents seemed to miss television content. In this chapter I also discuss the importance of family attitudes and behaviors about television in relation to children's responses to nonviewing.

In chapter 5, I introduce the notion of television not as a technology that delivers audiovisual stimulus, but as a multi-faceted concept in the minds of nonviewers. In other words, I discuss what television *is* for nonviewers. Because about two-thirds of the people who participated in the study—and who thus consider themselves nonviewers—actually own a television set, I became interested in their own understanding of what is meant by television. Nonviewers work under the assumption that television is either television *content*, such as sex or violence; a *medium* that provides a potentially ongoing stream of content; or an *industry*, complete with producers, actors and advertisers. In this chapter, I begin discussing these various ways of perceiving television and how that conceptualization is related to the outcomes families expect from living without it. Overall, the research revealed that there is no unambiguous link between a given definition of television and how a family uses or does not use it. Rather, individuals' attitudes toward television and their discussion of it revealed a philosophy, or perhaps a working definition of television for themselves and their families that was incorporated into their approach to it, their reasons for rejecting it, and more broadly, into their approach towards their family life.

In this vein, chapter 5 also introduces the concept of family systems as a framework for understanding some of the ideas that emerge in the interviews. In general, systems theory is the study of the organization of phenomena, such as parts of a mechanical system, employees in an organization or members of a family. Systems are thought to be made up of regular interaction between phenomena (e.g., family members). Interdependent phenomena typically exhibit some coherent behavior. A system is also open to and interacts with its environment, including information in the environment. From a systems perspective, no one part can be studied independently. Rather, the relations between and arrangement of the phenomenon must be studied simultaneously. For example, an attitude about television in the home may best be understood concomitantly with attitudes towards family life. Using this systems perspective, we discuss how television and attitudes about it can be seen as part of the family system. Even in families without television, beliefs about it are often present in family discussions, in individuals' conceptions of their own family and in beliefs about decisions they make regarding their family. In fact, in nonviewing homes, the absence of television is often seen by members as an important defining feature of the family. Therefore, I argue that television is part of the family system even in, or especially in, families without it.

The remainder of the book is broken into three sections, reflecting the three definitions of television. Chapters 6–8 reflect television as content, chapters 9–12 reflect television as a medium and chapters 13–14 reflect television as an industry. In each of the three sections, the individual chapters reflect nonviewers' beliefs about what television *does* (e.g., it affects aggression, or it affects the way people use their time). In many cases, a link can be made between a particular definition of television and a particular objection. For example, nonviewers define content as that which is *on* television. The belief that television is mainly *content* is related to screening out sex, violence or commercials because individuals believe this content affects viewers' sexual behavior, aggression or consumerism. Alternately, nonviewers define the *medium* as the potentially on-going stimulus that makes its way into our homes. Concern over television as a medium is related to the belief that television interrupts time and the flow of family life. Those who believe this may avoid television because they want to engage more fully in what they refer to as their "real lives." Last, nonviewers define industry as those who produce, direct, and financially subsidize television. Concern about television as an industry is related to a rejection of the mass culture that television simultaneously represents and produces. Therefore, each section identifies a definition (i.e., television as content, medium or industry) and then various chapters in each section discuss individuals' beliefs about the effects of television viewed in this way. Individuals do not always hold a single definition of television; however, these three definitions do offer a framework for understanding what it means to live without television.

Section one, on television as content, discusses possible problems resulting from the actual messages of television. Chapter 6, "Keeping out Televised Sex and Violence," introduces Thomas and Charlotte Ford, a Midwestern family with 10 children. For them, avoiding television is a means of keeping out depictions of sex and, to a lesser extent, violence.

Literature on the effects of sex and violence in the media is briefly discussed as is the importance of religion in the lives of the Fords. Again, framed in a systems perspective, the importance of the Fords' beliefs about television and their beliefs regarding the benefits of not having it are discussed.

In chapter 7, I discuss the relationship between television and consumerism in children. Many parents mentioned their concern over consumerism both for themselves and for their children. Many nonviewers believed that their children are less materialistic and want less as a direct result of their lack of exposure to television commercials. Research on advertising that targets children is discussed, as is the research on the effects of television and commercials on children.

Chapter 8 introduces the close relationship between television and politics. For people like the Selridges, they believe that living without television allows them more political acuity and affords them a better, deeper, and more personal understanding of their political world. For Jonathan Selridge, who is in the U.S. Air Force, his attitudes about the policy decisions made by the United States government have particular relevance and power in his own life. His beliefs about television are tied to this. Like others who live without television, he worries that television has a direct, albeit unintended, effect on public policy. In this chapter, these ideas are addressed both in the voice of nonviewers and in the literature on television and politics.

Section two, which treats television as a medium, discusses the potential for television to interrupt family life and to provide continuous stimulus. In chapter 9, "Autonomous Children," the concept of perceived convenience is introduced. Natalie Carlson and her husband Mike discuss how television, as a babysitter and as a means of occupying bored children, may seem an easy solution initially but in the long run may cause more problems by encouraging children to require constant stimulation that is generated by someone or something else. In this chapter, I consider two possibilities. First, I discuss research on children, television, and attention span, and I look more closely at recent research on television exposure and attention deficit disorder. Second, I examine how family belief systems contribute to norms and affect behavior in the family. In this way, beliefs about television affect decisions to avoid television but may also fit into a larger network of beliefs for how children and families should act. I discuss how these beliefs about television, and not avoiding it per se, may influence the behavior of parents and ultimately children in the family. Mike and Natalie's own conception of family is considered as a particular example.

Chapter 10 grew out of the near unanimous mention of the idea of personal time. For many nonviewers, they believe television as a medium not only uses personal time, but also has the power to steal it against our will. Given the power that television is perceived to have, these nonviewers prevail in the power struggle by removing the screen. In doing so, they regain power in their home and secure control over their use of time. In this chapter I will also consider differences in time use by viewers and nonviewers, reporting on the time-use diaries and discussing the available literature on time-use studies in the United States.

In chapter 11, I review the literature on children, television, and creativity and also consider how nonviewing and the increased free time that results, could encourage creativity and imaginative play. A vast majority of the parents of nonviewing children mentioned that they believed that their children were more creative and imaginative because they are not exposed to television. In this chapter, parents report that the availability of uninterrupted free time has stimulated imaginative play in their children. Therefore, I introduce the concept of "flow," and the need for free time to achieve flow. I argue that the availability of free time, and the value that these parents place on creativity and imagination, may contribute to effects that are cited in the literature.

In chapter 12, the Tanners of Shelburn, Vermont are introduced. For them, living without the medium of television ensures a connection with a fuller and richer life—something they refer to as "real life" or one that is not interrupted by or co-opted by a mediated reality. Because they perceive television as distancing them from real life, in rejecting it, they perceive themselves as living life more fully. Again, from a family systems perspective, the importance of this belief in shaping their day-to-day life is considered.

Section three, on television as an industry, includes two chapters that define television as an agent of culture. In chapter 13, "Choosing to be Different," I discuss television, and the industry itself, as something that symbolizes cultural homogeneity. For some, not having television allows them to exist, or to believe they are existing outside of the mainstream culture that is television. In the belief system constructed by Sam Steinberg and his family, living without television is not only a means of achieving what they refer to as the "good life," but is a means of constructing a life uninfluenced by popular culture. Because they believe that television represents a homogenizing influence, they have eliminated it as a means of distinguishing themselves from the culture. Drawing on work by Theodore Adorno (1991) and his use of the term "culture industry," and by George Gerbner (1976) and his concept of "mainstreaming," we examine television, or personal beliefs about television, as an agent of mass culture.

In chapter 14, I discuss the idea of battling the industry for control of the home. Unlike those who screen out sex or violence, for some viewers, eliminating television is a means of gaining control over what comes into their home, even if their decisions differ markedly from what many other viewers would or would not accept for their families. Anika Bradinski and her family, and others like them, pit themselves against "Hollywood" and "the media" in a battle over social control of their homes. They avoid television because they feel the media industry has too much power in deciding what constitutes entertainment and for whom. Drawing from Theodore Adorno's work on the culture industry (1991), I discuss Anika's family in terms of their desire to choose what they will watch and what their children will consume. Unlike those who screen out content, these individuals object to what they perceive to be the industry's ability to control viewers' choices. For them, rejecting television in general, while selecting programs they perceive as revolutionary is a means of regaining control from that industry.

Finally, in chapter 15, I review the concepts of uses and gratifications and family systems theory as they apply to nonviewing homes. I also draw several conclusions about families who live without television. In addition to the themes discussed throughout the book, such as time use or rejecting consumerism, I draw out some of the broader similarities that can be seen among nonviewing families. I discuss four characteristics of nonviewing families. First, nonviewers, as compared to viewers, are generally more zealous and idealistic. Second, nonviewers are more protective, or what I refer to as *directive*, parents. Third, they feel strongly about being *engaged* in their lives, and their home lives reflect this. Fourth, they believe themselves and their families to be iconoclastic. In this final chapter I discuss how these characteristics are related to the other ideas discussed throughout the book. Finally, I discuss the idea of television as a choice and consider how this choice might work, or not work, for a given family.

Goals of the Book

So once again, why write a book about people who live without television? They are small in number, although it is not clear exactly how many homes are TV-free. Nonviewers are not a powerful voting block and, surely, they are not corporate America's dream. They do not seem to have made a mark on our culture, because few popular articles and few academic studies have been conducted with them as a focus. Perhaps the best reason to study families who live without television is so that we might question our assumptions about television and the family in general. By looking at those who do not watch it, by looking at those who are outliers in the normal distribution of television audiences, we might gain a better understanding of the role of television in the lives of families.

The first goal of this book is to describe how and why those who live without television have given it up. Because television is such a ubiquitous part of our life experience, it may be interesting to examine the choices of those who are not the norm. These everyday critics may have something to say about television that has not been previously explored. Therefore, if we examine their attitudes and beliefs about politics, religion, and consumerism, connecting these factors to their decision to live without television, we may come to a better understanding of all of these elements.

A second goal of this book is to explore what happens when families do live without television. Whereas much research has examined the influences of television on family life and perhaps even more research has examined the negative effects of violent television or sexual media, relatively little research has asked what happens when we do not watch. Therefore, a second goal is to describe the families who live without television and to explore how they use their time and what they believe about family life.

Chapter 2

Sample and Method

In order to understand the present study, this chapter discusses the participants in the study and the methods that were used to obtain the data. In total, there were 120 nonviewers and 83 television viewers who participated. The sample was made up of children and adults who participated in in-depth interviews, completed surveys and kept time-use diaries; although not all participants were involved in all three of the data collection strategies. In order to make the book easier to follow I also provide a brief sketch of those participants who are mentioned repeatedly throughout chapters.

Overview

Three different strategies of data collection were used in this study and both nonviewers and television viewers participated in each. First, in-depth interviews and in-home observations were conducted. Second, questionnaires were completed and third, time-use diaries were filled out. A majority of the nonviewers participated in all three portions of the study; however, the television viewers who participated in the in-depth interviews were not the same as those who filled out the questionnaire and time-use diaries.

Participants

Nonviewers

One hundred twenty nonviewers participated in the in-depth interview portion of the study, representing 62 different families. Of these individuals, 72 were adults. Most (n=99) of these individuals also completed the surveys and time-use diaries; the remaining 21 decided not to participate in the remainder of the study because of the additional time commitment involved. These 120 participants are in every way a convenience sample and cannot be thought of as representative of all nonviewing individuals. Of the 62 different families, two were single adults living alone and three were single adults who had one or more adult roommates. The remainder were either single or married adults living with children. The size of the households interviewed ranged from 1 to 11. The oldest adult was age 66, and modally, the adults were in their 30s.

The education level in the nonviewing adults was diverse, ranging from some high school to those with graduate degrees. Two participants had some high school education, 18 completed high school, 13 had some college, 19 had a college degree, and 20 had either some graduate work or held a graduate degree. Although the sample is too small to claim that it is representative, at the very least it is clear that nonviewing families range widely in the level of education of the parents.

Similarly, the employment of the participants varied considerably. Represented in the nonviewing adult sample were several stay-at-home mothers, a piano tuner, a deck washer, three librarians, two school teachers, two individuals who were or had been in the military, a stone mason, a photographer, an artist, a social worker, a plumber, three college professors, and one unemployed individual. Although this list does not include all of the jobs reported by participants, it does suggest that nonviewing adults include blue collar and white collar workers in a wide range of professions.

Although I did not ask for religious affiliation, it did arise spontaneously in 27 of the interviews with the 72 nonviewing adults. Religion arose in five of the interviews with 48 nonviewing children. Of the adults, 23 mentioned their Christianity, and of those 20 called themselves born-again Christians, fundamental Christians or Bible-believing Christians. In other words, 20 might be referred to as members of the religious right. Three simply mentioned that they were Christians, without elaborating further and 4 interviewees spontaneously mentioned that they were not religious or were agnostic. None of the 20 viewers mentioned religion. Therefore, it appears that for some nonviewers, living without television is in part related to religious beliefs.

Lastly, I asked the 72 adults to provide a self-ascribed ethnic identification. A vast majority (n=64) referred to themselves as white or Caucasian. Some indicated that they were of Italian, Irish or Lithuanian descent. Two interviewees were Latino. One was an American Indian, two were Asian and three were Asian American.

Among the nonviewing children, there were 22 boys and 26 girls who participated in the interview portion of this study. The youngest was a 6-year-old girl and the oldest was an 18-year-old boy. In many cases, when the children were either too young or simply not available or willing to be interviewed, parents provided information about their children that I report in the book; however, these children are not counted in the sample size of children mentioned above.

Although I attempted to post on Web sites that I thought might attract a variety of participants (e.g., home school Web sites, religious Web sites, a Web site targeting parents who discuss issues such as vegetarianism for their children or the value of cloth diapers), I did wonder who I might be missing. Why, for example, were there no African American respondents? On average, African Americans watch more television than the overall American average. Is it, then, that they are less likely to live without television or was I simply missing this group by virtue of my method of contact? The method of sampling leaves no way of knowing. In addition, although a broad range of education and professions are represented, because I posted on the Internet and used newsletters in schools that were in non-urban communities, I did not reach the urban poor. Once again, is this group made up only of television watchers or are there nonviewing families from among the urban poor who I did not reach? Again, it is unclear from my sampling method. Overall, the sample was diverse in terms of level of education, types of job held by the adults and family composition. However, the sample was somewhat homogenous in terms of ethnicity.

Television Viewers

In addition to the nonviewers who participated in the in-depth interviews and surveys, the second and third groups were the viewers. The first group of participants were viewers who completed the questionnaire and time-use diary portion of the study (n=63). They were selected for participation by a nonviewing family who had been asked to identify and select their own "family match." I simply asked nonviewers to find a person or family who they felt was like them in terms of self-ascribed demographics, including approximate age, ethnicity, socio-economic status, religiosity, and whether or not they had children. The only difference was supposed to be their television viewing status. Nonviewers eagerly sought viewers, often asking an adult sibling and her family or a friend and family, to participate as their "match." They became quite specific about the match, citing to me similarities such as, "our husbands are both in Iraq," or "we attend the same church," or "he's my brother and our families are a lot alike."

Viewers in this portion of the study represented various levels of education from some high school to a graduate degree. Modally, they had earned a Bachelor's degree. The sample was predominantly white with one individual identifying herself as Latina and one identifying himself as African American. Like the nonviewers, a wide range of professions was represented, including both blue- and white-collar professionals. They were also similar to the nonviewers in that they were modally in their 30s. Family size ranged from one to seven. Approximately half identified themselves as having a religious affiliation.

The second sample of viewers (different from those viewers who had participated in the questionnaire and time-use diary) was a convenience sample of 20 television viewers. These viewers participated in in-depth interviews so that I could pursue some of the same issues as had been discussed with the nonviewers. Among the 20 adult viewers included in the in-depth interview portion of the study, two were high school graduates, four had some college, six had a Bachelor's degree, three had some graduate school, and three had a graduate degree. Included in the sample were 15 women and five men who practiced a range of professions. The 20 adult viewers also included five business professionals, four stay-at-home mothers, three teachers, two mechanics, one landscaper, two students, and three people who worked more than one job.

Among the 20 viewers, Christianity in particular was mentioned by two of them and religion in general was mentioned by an additional five. Religion was not mentioned by the remaining viewers. There was no systematic difference in spontaneous mention of religion during the interview among viewers and nonviewers. The 20 viewers who participated in the in-depth interviews came from the Northeast (n=4), the Southeast (n=12), and the Midwest (n=4). The 15 adult viewers included 12 individuals who identified themselves as white or Caucasian, one who identified herself as African American, and two who identified themselves as Latino. Once again, because the sample is small and non-random, these basic demographics should not be taken as necessarily representative of viewing families in general.

Individual Participants

Mark Armstrong is an architect who lives in New Bern, North Carolina. He is in his forties and is a single father of a 13-year-old boy and 4-year-old girl. He has lived without television for most of his adult life.

Sam and Estania are unmarried partners in their early 30s. Sam is in school and Estania works at the local grocery co-op. They live in a medium-sized town in southern New England with their infant daughter and one additional roommate. They have lived without television for approximately 2 years.

Deborah Hansen is a single mother with twin 11-year-old boys. She works as a librarian and lives in Boston. She has lived without television for approximately 3 years.

Nick Fulvio is 14. He grew up without television and lives with his parents and older brother in Connecticut.

Annie McAdams and Arthur Randle are both in their 30s, live in Connecticut with their 8-year-old son, Alex, and 5-year-old daughter, Leah. Arthur is a professor and Annie teaches high school history. They have lived without television for 10 years.

Charlotte and Thomas Ford live in the Midwest. They have 10 children and one grandchild. They identify themselves as conservative Christians and have not owned a television at any time during their adult lives. Charlotte is a stay-at-home wife and Thomas is a minister.

Lynne and Jonathan Selridge both come from military families and Jonathan currently serves in the military. During the latter portion of this research, he was deployed to Iraq. They have one young son and Lynne was pregnant with their second child.

Natalie and Mike Carlson live in southern New England with their two children, Rachel and Levi. They are in their late 30s and have lived without television for a majority of their married life, although both grew up watching television. Natalie is a lactation consultant and Mike is a media specialist for the local school system.

Eric and Rebecca Tanner live in Vermont. They have 3 children. Rebecca was a Montessori teacher, although she now home-schools her own children and does not work outside of the home. Eric works for a natural toy company, where all toys are made of wood and other non-plastics. They gave up television approximately 2 years ago when one bet the other that they could not live without television for a month.

Sam Steinberg and Mary Peters live with their young son Jeremy in a small town in Connecticut. Mary is a school psychologist and Sam is a journalist. They are vocally politically liberal and have been living without television for approximately 7 years.

Anika Bradinski lives with her husband Kevin, and their two children, 19 year old Milan and eight year old Danielka. Anika is a Polish immigrant who still holds strong ties to her Polish identity. She and her family live in southern New England in a small, college town. They have lived without a television for more than a dozen years.

Method

In-depth interviews

Nonviewers were contacted for in-depth interviews in one of several ways. Some (n=5) responded to a small blurb that appeared in the newsletters of three local (i.e., Storrs, Connecticut) schools. Two participants responded to a flyer posted at a local food co-op. From those initial contacts, I was given the e-mail addresses of an additional four families. I also posted on five Web sites, simply asking if any TV-free families wanted to be interviewed. I provided my e-mail address and potential respondents contacted me. It is from these Internet postings that I received the largest number and the most diverse participants (n=43).[1] Online, I was contacted by those with no high school diploma and those with a graduate degree. Household income ranged from those who were unemployed and whose earnings were $5,000 per year to those exceeding $100,000 per year. In addition, these initial postings resulted in nonviewers providing the e-mail addresses, and in some cases phone numbers, of additional potential interviewees. Whenever possible, I provided my e-mail address and asked people to contact me. In three cases, friends gave out the phone numbers of friends without television. These I contacted by phone only after hearing from the initial participants that their friends had given permission for me to call. In other words, only those who actively sought an interview participated in this study.

Throughout this process, I conducted in-depth interviews with 120 nonviewing individuals and 20 viewers. Television viewers were included in the sample of interviewees to achieve a balance in terms of responses to specific questions that I asked the nonviewers; however, when comparing the nonviewing families to viewing families, I also draw on the extensive literature that exists about television watching and its effects. Ultimately, it was important to gain some understanding of viewing families' attitudes, beliefs, and use of time and I used a variety of primary and secondary sources to do this.

Of the 120 individuals interviewed, most were interviewed on one occasion for over an hour. Twenty were interviewed and visited on more than one occasion. I also used home visits as an ethnographic platform. Visiting families allowed me to make first-hand observations about participants and about their surroundings. In some cases, I interviewed entire families; in others, I interviewed husbands and wives. In a few cases, I interviewed only a father or a mother in a family. When possible, I interviewed children (age 18 and younger), and all of those had a parent or parents who also participated in the interview.

Time-use diaries and questionnaires

In addition to the in-depth interviews, 63 of the adult nonviewers and 29 of the child nonviewers (age 6–17) filled out questionnaires. A matched sample of 62 adult viewers and 30 child viewers (age 6–17) filled out questionnaires

---

1   Because I interviewed multiple individuals in some households, there were fewer total responses to my inquiries and postings than there were in the final sample.

that were identical to those filled out by the nonviewers. Because the time diaries involved a greater commitment, 50 of the adult nonviewers and 25 of the nonviewing children ultimately also completed a two-day diary; 50 of the adult viewers and 20 of the child viewers filled out diaries.

Items on the questionnaire assessed the extent to which individuals felt they were up to date on local, national, international news and popular culture. I also asked about their degree of involvement in their communities, the importance of various issues (e.g., wealth, religion) in their lives, and their time use and satisfaction with it. For the adult surveys, Likert-type items were used with a seven-point response option, ranging from 1 (*strongly disagree*) to 7 (*strongly agree*). For the child survey, Likert-type items were also used; however responses ranged from 1 to 5. These quantitative data resulted in 184 questionnaires reported from 63 adult viewers, 62 adult nonviewers, 30 nonviewing children and 29 viewing children. In the questionnaires, I also asked parents about their children. For adults with children younger than 6 years old, I have some parent-report data but no corresponding child interviews. These children were not included in the sample of children (n=69) reported earlier. Throughout the book, I have identified when the data comes from the children themselves and when it comes from their parents about the children.

The time-use diaries were kept by each person for one weekend day and one week day that had been randomly chosen by me in advance. Participants were provided with a time diary, with all possible times listed in half-hour blocks. For each block, participants identified their primary and, if relevant, their secondary activity. Later, these data were used to determine how much time individuals spent in various activities such as reading, chores, sleeping, hobbies, etc. Because the sample is somewhat small, I used the diaries to assess only differences between viewers and nonviewers in amount of time spent in reading, chores, and also in hobbies/ activities. Less common activities, such as participation in volunteer work, did not occur frequently enough to make comparisons between groups. Instead, fairly broad categories were formed. For example, in the present analysis, chores and childcare were averaged for each individual in the sample. A diary entry was identified as either a chore or childcare if it was clearly identifiable as cooking (e.g., making lunches), cleaning (e.g., doing laundry), outdoor work (e.g., mowing yard) or childcare (e.g., bathing a toddler). In terms of childcare, disputes exist in the literature (Mattingly & Bianchi, 2003). For example, some scholars argue that spending time with children (e.g., taking a baby on a walk) may constitute a chore or may be coded as entertainment/free time. Ultimately, I decided to count only childcare (e.g., feeding, bathing) as a chore. Furthermore, an activity was counted as a hobby if there was no immediate need involved (e.g., going on a run was counted as a hobby/sport; going to the grocery store was not). This method is consistent with the operationalizations used by scholars who study time use (Mattingly & Bianchi, 2003).

A Vocal Minority?

In conducting this research, two issues struck me regarding the data collection process. This project was different from the many others I have been involved in over the years and it is this difference that is perhaps telling. In 1991, I collected my first data set for a conference paper. Since then, I have conducted dozens of studies that involved literally thousands of children, adolescents and adults. Many of these studies involved writing letters to parents, asking permission to allow their children to participate in research that had been deemed safe and non-intrusive by fairly restrictive institutional review boards. I estimate that I have received about three times the number of rejections as I have consents. Like almost all social scientists, I have been hung up on, had nasty notes jotted on consent forms, and been stood up even after a particular time had been scheduled for one participant or another. In short, it is hard to find people who are willing to participate. Until now.

Consider the following story: Allison Wersch responded to a posting I had on a Web site. This was quite common. I would post and wait for the e-mails to roll in. And roll in they did. I was shocked at the number of voluntary respondents who took the time to jot down my e-mail address and contact me. Allison was one such respondent. Typically, respondents would e-mail me and we would have a brief exchange. I would hear about soccer practices and dentist appointments and sick spouses that made some evenings or mornings better than others. In Allison's case we finally settled on a date and time. But some issue in her carpool caused her to miss my call. She e-mailed me an apology and asked if we could reschedule. We did, but then an emergency in my family caused me to miss our appointment, and I was not able to let her know in advance. Again, we exchanged e-mails. Finally, almost two months after our initial contact, we had our interview.

Allison may have been an excessively patient person; however, so many of the respondents were flexible in their scheduling and seemed willing, even eager to participate. What this suggested to me is that this issue is important to the people who participated. They wanted to talk about it, seemed pleased with their decisions to live without television and felt it important that they get their message out. These were the most eager, willing, open participants I have ever worked with. I was amazed. I felt, even before the interviews themselves began to unfold, that I was on to something by mere virtue of the fact that people were active and vocal about their lives without television. For some it was a small decision, but for most, it had become a passionate one.

Chapter 3

How Nonviewers
Gave Up Television

In this chapter I discuss the various ways that nonviewers gave up television. Based on the in-depth interviews and the many stories told by the nonviewers, three different themes emerged. Individuals, couples and sometimes entire families gave up television through attrition, or a gradual decline in interest in television; they give it up by kicking the habit because television itself had started to interfere with aspects of their lives, or they gave it up for structural and environmental reasons. In this last situation, people stopped watching because some event forced television out of their lives and once they could get it back again, they had grown accustomed to living without it. In addition to exploring the reasons that people have for giving up television, I also introduce several theoretical approaches that support the colloquial explanations provided by the participants. Family systems theory examines how television, or lack of it, becomes part of the system of the family—part of its social environment. Displacement theory introduces the notion that television viewing interferes with other activities that fulfill the same functional role as television viewing. Lastly, the uses and gratifications approach examines individuals' motives for using various media. From this perspective, we consider that viewers watch television to be entertained, to facilitate social interaction and to gain information.

There was a time I naively imagined that those who gave up television had wonderful stories about doing so. Perhaps they got fed up with biased news and threw the set in the trash that night. Maybe the children's programming had gotten so violent that they dramatically carted the set off to the dump. Although there were a few participants' tales approaching those of my imagination, most were mundane. Of the 120 interviews I conducted with over 60 families, only seven stories culminated in dramatic events. The rest were rather boring as stories go; however, they did offer insight into the processes by which viewers give up television. By examining the process across various individuals and families, three methods of giving up television emerged. In some cases, which I have called *attrition*, individuals gave up television with no initial intent to do so. Rather, it faded from their lives. In other cases, individuals and families intended to give up television. The process was effortful and motivated by specific reasons, such as a belief that television was interfering with a couple's relationship or that the content of television was perceived as inappropriate for themselves or their children. I have called this *kicking the habit*. Lastly, in the case of *environmental reasons*, some event, such as a set breaking, caused the home to become television free; however, the set was not replaced because those involved decided that being without it was preferable. Next, we'll look at each of these three processes in greater detail.

Attrition

For approximately one-third of the families who gave up television, the process by which they gave it up might generously be called vague. When asked how they came to live without television, they'd crinkle a brow and think a bit, as if trying to recall what they'd had for dinner two Saturdays ago. These people came to live without television by *attrition*. By this I mean that television faded away from their lives gradually. Over the course of months or even a few years, they watched less and less until they found themselves watching none. How did this occur?

When asked, often husbands and wives would look at each other, as if for clues of some vague event in their mutual history. They would try to trace it back by where they had lived at the time. Sam and Estania, who had been roommates before they became partners and started a family, recalled the event jointly. First, Estania said, "Remember, we lived with that guy and he had that big console? And then we always tried to put a shroud over the TV because we didn't want it to be the center of attention?"

"Right," Sam recalled. "Then he moved out, right? And he took it with him?"

"Yes, and then didn't we have another person, that woman with the TV? Wasn't that after him?"

Sam again: "But maybe that didn't count because she kept it in her bedroom and we never watched it. Then we never got one."

So how did Sam and Estania give up television? I'm not sure I know from their interchange and certainly it does not seem like they did either. Television did not leave their lives because of some dramatic event. Rather, television left because their interest was, or had become, so low that they decided it would be easier and more pleasant, or perhaps just less hassle, to give it up altogether. In this way, for some people, giving up television arose from sheer lack of interest. They would recall a program or two with fondness, but certainly not with passion. For many of these people, they revealed that their reasons for living without television arose, in part, after they gave it up. One participant summed it up this way: "My reasons for not having it now are not different from when I first gave it up, but they have been cemented." Another said, "If anything, I have become more of a zealot." For those who give up television by attrition, they often have reasons for not watching it, but those reasons become stronger once they become truly TV-free and television has fully faded from their lives.

Kicking the Habit

The stories that could be called dramatic all fall into the category I refer to as *kicking the habit*. For many individuals and for parents specifically, they arrive at a point where television has become a problem. Faced with the problem, they decide that rather than extensive measures of regulating, mediating, and controlling television, the easiest action to take is to get rid of it. For some, it is a decision made by a parent in response to the behavior of the children. Or, a spouse talks, teases or bargains the other into giving up television. For almost all of these individuals, there is a strong belief at the onset that television causes trouble. They believe it increases aggression, they worry it eats up too much of their time, or they feel that it causes too much conflict with other family members.

Deborah Hansen, a single mother with 11-year-old twin boys, worried that television had become a problem in her family. She and her two young sons had lived with it when the boys were babies. When she separated from their father, the television stayed with him. The boys came with her. Then, she recalls, "When they were six, they asked for one. I didn't want it to become a forbidden fruit so I did get one. We used it for DVDs and then when they were ten they started asking for shows. That lasted about nine months. I wasn't angry or anything when I did it. It had just become a problem." So, Deborah carried the television out to the trash when it was in perfectly good working order, mechanically speaking. Her sons accused her of being crazy as they watched her trudge down the stairs and put the television on the curb. She responded, "Yes, I am crazy. Deal with it." For Deborah, television caused conflict in her family. Her sons would beg to watch more or ask for certain shows that she had forbidden. Because she perceived the conflict as a negative consequence resulting from television, she opted to get rid of it.

Another adult participant recalled that, as a child of about seven, she and her siblings were watching television after school one day. Her father walked in the front door and found them watching an episode of *My Three Sons*, a show that they were permitted to watch. When one of the sons on the program started "mouthing off to the father," her own father quietly stood up, walked over to the set, turned it off and said, "We won't be watching that anymore." Apparently he did not mean that show or even that day. The next day, the television was gone. In this case, the content of television, the negative modeling of parent–child interactions, was seen by her father as cause for getting rid of television. The family never did get television again and, interestingly, this woman went on to marry a man who also lived without television when she met him so the idea of getting one never came up. When I asked this couple how they gave up television they responded, "We didn't."

In both the case of Deborah Hansen and the father who quietly ushered the family television out the door after the *My Three Sons* incident, what was interesting, as both reported spontaneously, was that there was no anger in the decision. It seemed, both to Deborah and to the father, the solution was so obvious that it did not require any great emotional show to carry it out. For these individuals, getting rid of television was indeed kicking a bad habit, but not one with which they had much emotional involvement.

However, it is not only that parents are worried about the consequences of television watching for their children. Adults without children also worry about "kicking the habit." Perhaps the story that captures how we all imagine people get rid of television occurred to a young couple from Vermont who were childless at the time. Rebecca Tanner is a school teacher. She told her husband, Eric, that she could tell which kids in her class watched a lot of television and which did not. As the discussion went on, and her husband teased her about her criticism of television, she claimed she could go one month without it. He was doubtful, so they made a bet. He kept watching, but she gave it up for a month. After the month went by, they both decided to give it a month, a first for him, a second for her. And by the time that was up, they just never turned it on again. They actually decided they liked living without it. Again, it was Rebecca's conviction that the children in her class who were more focused, read more, and were more creative watched less television that resulted in their bet. Rebecca began with a belief that television had negative consequences for children. Eventually, that resulted in their rejection of television for their own family.

All of the anecdotes above are about individuals who are in some way frustrated with television, either its content or the effects they assume it to have on viewers. However, some individuals who drop television do so not because they do not like it but because they are concerned that they do. As a direct result, they get rid of it. These participants often referred to their viewing as an addiction or at the very least, brought up the issue of control. For example, for Dan Schmidt, a single man living in Boston and for Mark Armstrong, a single father of two living in New

Bern, North Carolina, television had become an intruder into their lives. Dan felt it was a "really bad habit"; Mark felt he has an "addiction to moving images" and both got rid of it to regain control.

Dan tells the story this way:

> I had developed a really bad habit of getting home from work late and turning on the news then vegging out in front of sitcoms until 12:30. And then I became very sleep deprived. And it became clear to me that something had to give until finally I just kicked the TV out. It wasn't mine so I told the owner to come and get it. I had to get it out because I knew I'd keep watching it.

The owner came, retrieved the television set and Dan became TV free. For him, having it there but not watching it, unlike Estania and her shroud, was not an option.

Mark's story is somewhat different from Dan's. He said he recalled having a TV once, when he lived in Boston. Someone had given it to him and Mark said, "basically, it held up a big fern...if you want TV in Boston, you just look out your window." So he was not addicted to it entirely, because he clearly had gone without it, even when it sat in his living room. In this way, Mark was similar to Sam and Estania, the couple who could not quite recall how or when they'd given it up. Yet in other ways, he mirrored Dan. For example, when talking about his relationship with television, he says he could spend all night in front of the screen because he is "enamored of images." He says living without television has relieved him of "that addict feeling," and he says about programs that are out now, those he wants to avoid to keep his TV-free lifestyle: "I had a near miss one time with *The Sopranos*." He had started watching it at a friend's house, then had the friend tape it for him so he could watch it on his VCR and then, he recalls, "it got its hooks into me." Although Mark became TV free much like those in the attrition group, his relationship with it is similar to those who kick the habit. He feels television, "sucks you in and then three hours are gone." Like an addict, he worries about the consequences of watching just a little bit. He admits his fascination and ultimately feels safer without it.

Others who gave up television because they wanted to regain control of their time mentioned similar feelings. They described how, after getting rid of television, they "jonesed" for it or "missed it pretty bad." But in the end, most forgot about it. They described how it was hard at first, got easier and ultimately they didn't even think about it. For them, they became TV free by kicking the habit.

Interestingly, in each of these cases, the participants or their families believed that television was harming them in some way. Although these stories are few in number, research by Cantor and Wilson (2003) has found that parents who believe that television has negative effects are more likely to restrict it for their children. It is perhaps not surprising then that those who have actively gotten rid of their televisions, sometimes in rather dramatic ways, also believe in the negative effects of television for themselves and for their children. Despite this, exciting stories of parents tossing the television set in the trash or spouses giving up television on a bet were rare. Rather, attrition and one additional method, environmental features, were more common.

Environmental Features

Frequently, some environmental or structural feature would intervene to cause television to leave the home. Steve Sim, a native New Yorker living in Manhattan, reported that he lived in an apartment that was so small that:

> I left the TV under the desk and would drag it out when I wanted to watch something. Then 9/11 happened and my reception was totally shot. Nothing. I didn't watch TV for months. And when the reception finally came back, I had started to get my news other ways and fill my free time in ways that I liked better anyway. So I gave it away.

Like those who came to live without television through attrition, many who got rid of television for structural or environmental reasons had somewhat low interest in it to begin with. But an event occurred that delivered the final blow.

For example, Sam Steinberg and Mary Peters, who will be discussed at length in chapter 13, bought a piece of land and decided to build a house. There was no network reception to speak of and their only option was a cable line; however, the house was being built along side of a large rock face. The cable company informed them that their best bet was to blast through the rock, a rather expensive option. "It was a lot of money," recalled Sam, "But [giving it up] wasn't a big deal, a big decision. It was easy." In other words, for many people—although certainly not all—they did not kick a television habit, as one might break free of cigarettes, but television was taken from them and they didn't care enough to get it back. For some, after they could get it back, like Steve from Manhattan, they did not bother. Unlike families who gave up television through attrition and allowed television to fade out of their lives, eliminating it as an after-thought, families who drop TV due to environmental features have television taken from them. They are still watching television at the time of the intervening event, but they do not make an effort to put television back in their lives. For these families and for those who give up TV through attrition, television leaves their lives due in part to low interest in it. They may believe that television has negative effects, which may be why they do not attempt to get it back when some obstacle enters their paths, but from the interviews conducted, it appears that their strong opposition to television often came *after* the set was gone from their homes.

Ultimately, then, becoming TV free seems to occur in different ways, but not in an infinitely different number of ways. Either it faded from their lives without incident, or there was some conscious decision to get rid of it because it had started to take over too much time or mental space in their lives, or television left due to circumstances but then did not seem worth resurrecting. Although some individuals showed a combination of features in their decision to get rid of television, the most commonly mentioned feature overall was attrition. In other words most, although certainly not all, individuals and families who give up television are not very attached to it to begin with.

Giving Up Television: Theoretical Approaches

Uses and Gratifications

When considering why nonviewers give up television, the uses and gratifications approach offers some insight. By utilizing this framework, it appears that the gratifications that viewers get from television may simply not be the same for nonviewers. In other words, viewers are motivated to watch television to satisfy certain needs. Nonviewers are likely to have similar needs, but are unlikely to find television viewing an adequate way to satisfy those needs.

The earliest research on television grew out of a focus on public opinion, on voting patterns, and on how television affects viewers (Klapper, 1960). After decades of research on the effects of mass media that emphasized how media influences viewers, attention turned to understanding the viewer and how s/he uses television. This approach argued that the motivations for media use vary from person to person and depend on the situation. Furthermore, motivations for media use may mediate effects. Based on these early observations, the uses and gratifications approach emerged. The now classic uses and gratifications précis seeks to understand

> the social and psychological origins of needs which generate expectations of the mass media and other sources which lead to differential patterns of media exposure (or engagement in other activities) resulting in needs' gratifications and other consequences, perhaps mostly unintended ones.
>
> (Katz, Blumler & Gurevitch, 1974, p. 20).

In other words, our predispositions, our previous experiences with media and our interpersonal interactions all shape our expectations for what needs media will fulfill. These expectations in turn shape our patterns of media use.

For example, expectancy–value models of communication predict that individuals seek out various forms of communication due to the expected outcomes of a particular choice (Babrow, 1989). In a television environment, viewers may seek out a television program to fulfill entertainment needs if they expect, quite simply, to be entertained by it. If the program meets this need, it is sought out again. If not, other fare may be explored. It is worth noting, however, that the needs individuals bring to the viewing situation are not always met by the programs they watch. For example, those who watch television because they are lonely often find themselves more lonely after viewing (Perse & Rubin, 1990). Why then might television be used repeatedly as a salve for loneliness? According to the uses and gratifications approach, if one alternative does not work, individuals will seek out other functional alternatives, but only if they exist. Therefore, patterns of television use are shaped by expectations for need fulfillment. Patterns of repeat exposure may be shaped by need gratification or lack of functional alternatives.

The uses and gratifications approach has identified several main needs— or expectations for need fulfillment—that television may meet for adults and children. Individuals use television to pass time, to have companionship, to facilitate social situations, to learn, to escape, to be entertained, to be aroused, and to be relaxed (Rubin, 1981). These dimensions can further be collapsed into three general categories for television viewers: television fulfills entertainment needs (e.g., escapism, arousal), social needs (e.g., companionship, social facilitation), and information needs (e.g., learning). In the case of television viewers, the uses and gratifications approach offers an explanation for audiences' viewing patterns through an examination of their needs and their need gratification. In short, viewers have social, entertainment, and informational needs that they believe television will fulfill. However, this approach may also provide some insight into the behavior of nonviewers.

Nonviewers have given up television for a fairly straightforward reason: the needs that they have are not met by television. Consistent with the uses and gratifications approach, they have found functional alternatives that meet their needs more effectively than television does. Note that in the original conceptualization of uses and gratifications, Katz, Blumler and Gurevitch (1974) suggest that there are indeed functional alternatives to media use (i.e., "engagement in other activities"); however, given the obvious focus of media effects researchers, considerably less research attention has been paid to the functional alternatives than to media itself. For nonviewers, on the other hand, "functional alternatives," or those activities other than television that meet their needs, are the primary focus.

Consider the needs met for viewers by television: entertainment needs, social needs, and informational needs. Although nonviewers did not directly articulate their motives and behavior using this uses and gratifications approach, it is clear from the interviews, their attitudes and their behavior that they believe television does not entertain them in a way that they find satisfying. It interferes with, rather than assists, their social interactions and does not, in their view, provide them with information that they find useful or thorough. Many echoed the feelings of Mark Armstrong, a single father of two children. He said that one of his main objections to television is that it is not worth his time. "Really, the advertising is without cleverness," he said. "The shows are a bit dumb. The canned laughter, the violence...I mean, I hear there are some good shows out there but I'm not convinced. The news is shallow, and frankly, I'd rather play with my children." In one statement, Mark identified the three broad uses of television: entertainment ("the shows are a bit dumb"), social uses ("frankly, I'd rather play with my children"), and information ("the news is shallow"), and claimed that television satisfied none of these.

Entertainment

In the uses and gratifications approach, entertainment is one of the most common uses of television. Individuals are motivated to watch television to fulfill the need to be entertained. Sean Greene, a father of two living in New York City, argued that to him, television is not entertaining or enjoyable. "It's really bad writing. It's formulaic and predictable. I find it boring." Anika Bradinski called it "insulting," and Ted Randolph, who is retired from the military, called it "complete crap," and he was not the only one to do so.

It would be a lengthy exercise to catalogue the disparaging descriptions of television made by nonviewers. A simpler, and more theoretically meaningful explanation may be this: for nonviewers, their entertainment needs are not met by television and, as uses and gratifications would argue, only when expectations are met will individuals return to the same stimulus to meet those needs. Instead, nonviewers find that reading, taking walks, talking to family members, hiking, and playing music and games all fulfill a need for entertainment more effectively than watching television might. What Katz, Blumler and Gurevitch (1974) referred to as *functional alternatives*, those activities that meet the same needs as television (e.g., playing a board game to meet entertainment needs), not only meet their entertainment needs, but do so more effectively. Consequently, as uses and gratifications theory argues, if patterns of use are shaped first by needs and later by fulfilled needs, the fact that nonviewers gradually stopped watching may simply be a case of unmet needs being met by other alternatives.

Related to the entertainment uses of television, television is also used to pass time. Many viewers mentioned this need for themselves and for their children. Adults discussed pastimes such as knitting, or what one nonviewer called "light reading." For their children, they distinguished between entertaining stimuli such as games and those that were less absorbing. One mother said of her two boys, aged 7 and 10, "They need to unwind sometimes and just chill out. Right now, they're in a Calvin and Hobbes stage. Adam will just sit on the green chair and read Calvin and Hobbes." Therefore, the need to pass time, typically fulfilled by television in viewing households, is met by other stimuli in nonviewing ones.

Social Facilitation

A second function of television, social facilitation, is filled for viewers in two ways. First, television can afford companionship to those who have none by filling an empty room with human voices. Second, it can act as a social lubricant. In other words, television either provides an easy topic of conversation with friends or it can act to fill air space when it is on, thus easing the need for conversation. In this way, audiences can sit around a television with family members and spend time together, yet not expend the emotional and psychological energy that may go into talking. Therefore, viewers perceive television as fulfilling a social need. However, nonviewers perceive the social use of television as a drawback, not a benefit. For example, Kyle Neff is a 31-year-old artist living in Boston. He is single and lives with a roommate who spends half her time out of town for her job. However, Kyle perceives television as "killing" social interaction rather than facilitating it. Although this theme was echoed by many respondents, Kyle listed this complaint against television as his strongest. This objection ties neatly to the notion of television as a social facilitator; however, from Kyle's perspective, television fails here.

Kyle argues that without television, "I definitely have better relationships. I'm more sensitive to it and I avoid places with TV because it's a huge conversation killer. I get so much more out of human conversation. Two people or a bunch of people can have a great conversation rather than fall into a catatonic state...I talk to people. Without TV, I'm more inclined to have a conversation." On another occasion, Kyle complained about a bar that he recently had to cross off of his list of favorites. "I have this list of bars," he said, "and it keeps getting smaller—that don't have TV.

Sometimes, like this one that was my favorite, they'll close for renovation and when they reopen they have these huge plasma screens and it's such a disappointment. So now I don't go there. But I like bars without them. They're good for conversation."

Isabel Slanovich, also single and living without television argues that for her, when friends talk about television she feels that it gets in the way of more interesting conversations. She says, "It can be such a wedge. Because you can talk about that stuff and then you never have to talk about the deep or hard stuff." Again, from a uses and gratifications perspective, television can provide topics for conversation that provide common ground for viewers. However, nonviewers perceive this as a detriment, perhaps harming the quality of social interaction.

Married couples also pointed out that they talked more, and sometimes more deeply, without television. Anna and Victor Taylor have been married for 20 years. When I asked Victor what they did with their free time, "talk" was his first answer. "We've been married a long time and we haven't had television at any point in our marriage," he said. "I can honestly say that we just talk a lot. We talk about everything. Of course there are some things we don't talk about in front of the kids but otherwise, we talk about everything. We don't have TV to fall back on so we can do that." So a second use of television, as a social facilitator, is also seen as a need unmet by television for nonviewers. Once again, functional alternatives stepped in to fill the void. If the social need fulfilled by television was companionship for viewers, nonviewers replaced it with human interaction such as talking with family members or chatting on the phone. If the need was social facilitation, nonviewers might mention going out to a bar or taking a walk, because, like television viewing, these activities are opportunities for talk with less pressure. When talk is the accompaniment of another activity, such as television viewing, or walking, people seem to feel less pressure to talk. Talk becomes part of the activity rather than the sole activity. Similar to television viewing, these activities fill the natural quiet spaces during interaction; and for nonviewers, they are not only good functional alternatives, they are actually better ones.

Information

A third use of television according to the uses and gratifications approach is that television can meet informational needs. Television can provide surveillance by simply reporting on events or it can update us when we seek out more information, such as during a natural disaster, a war or an election. Although television is the primary news source for many Americans, news can obviously come from other sources, both mediated and interpersonal. For nonviewers, it is these other sources that fulfill their informational needs either because they perceive television news to be inadequate or because they simply do not have a very strong need for information.

First, as we will discuss in chapter 8, for many viewers, the format of television news does not lend itself to in-depth coverage of political and/or world events. Lynne Selridge considers herself "very politically engaged." But she says

> Television, with all its quick quotes and snappy headlines, can't keep me informed. It's so shallow and you can't really learn anything because just when you get interested in the story it's actually over. Then I have to go online to find out what happened anyway.

Similarly, one mother of two girls states, "Television and news don't mix. You have the 30-second story and just when you think you might want to know more about it, it's over. So then you have to go to the newspaper or the Internet to find anything out."

However, it is not only the lack of depth in television news to which nonviewers object. They object to the format, as well. Kyle Neff argues that, "They combine entertainment with news and it just makes no sense. And all of the slick anchors. It's not about the news at all." As will be covered in detail in chapter 8, the format of television news, its brevity and its focus on the sensational, does not allow for serious attention to social and political issues. Many individuals also discussed the entertaining aspect of news as one of their objections to it. Chapter 8 will focus on television news, both its depth and its format, and therefore will not be covered here.

Overall, nonviewers' informational needs are not met by television, and as a result, they seek out functional alternatives. Functional alternatives include the Internet, newspapers, the radio or other people. The Internet was mentioned by 72% of the 72 nonviewing adults (n= 52), although 15% (n=8) of these only had access at work or the library. National Public Radio (NPR) was mentioned by a full 83% of the respondents (n=60). Interestingly, many noted a bias in NPR reporting (some saying it was too liberal, others that it was too conservative); however, at least, they claimed, it was more in depth. In addition, 48% (n=35) of respondents relied on either a newspaper or news magazine (e.g. *The Economist*, *Time*) to keep them informed. Therefore, many nonviewers turn to these functional alternatives to meet their informational needs primarily because they think that television cannot meet these needs effectively.

And what of the informational needs of the others, those who did not read the news online or listen to the radio? These individuals used interpersonal channels to get their news. And many of these had low informational needs. Mark Armstrong claimed that "If something important happens, someone will tell me." Danielle Long asked, rhetorically, "If I can't do anything about it, do I really need to know?" Still others lamented their situation. Estania said, "I guess I wish I knew more. It would be good to have evidence for my ideas and to know what's going on. We keep talking about getting a paper delivered, but..." Here, she trailed off. Without the need for information, a functional alternative is not necessary.

Overall, nonviewers gave up television in one of several ways and for numerous reasons. But from a macro perspective, the main reason they gave it up is because it did not—and does not—meet their needs. Rather, they have found other ways to meet those needs that do the job more effectively than television. Entertainment needs are met by reading, walking, and hobbies. Social needs are met through human interaction and information needs are met by the Internet and National Public Radio or through personal interaction with people in their community. So for those living without television, the most straightforward explanation for why they do not have it was probably articulated by Arthur Randle. When asked why he and his family did not have television, he responded, "Don't want it and don't need it."

Displacement

The notion that nonviewers eschew television in part to have time for other activities is parallel to a hypothesis often forwarded by mass media theorists: displacement. The displacement hypothesis claims that one effect of television is that it merely displaces or takes the place of other activities. From children's imaginative play (Valkenburg, 2001) to time spent in free reading (Winn, 1985), increases in television time are frequently associated with decreases in time spent with other activities. The mechanism by which television displaces other activities has been explored by several scholars, often utilizing data on children (Mutz, Roberts, & Vuuren, 1993). Although several mechanisms have been proposed (e.g., the marginal activities hypothesis, the engagement hypothesis), two that seem to have the most support are the functional similarity hypothesis and the functional reorganization hypothesis.

The first, the functional similarity hypothesis, suggests that television may act as a displacement for other activities by forcing out activities that are functionally similar (Hornik, 1981). Increases in television time might decrease time spent with reading, radio listening or movie attendance. Like the uses and gratifications approach, the functional similarity hypothesis assumes that activities are pushed out only when television fulfills the same needs as those activities.

However, it is possible that other activities do not simply get pushed out of the way. Rather, television and other activities might coexist if there is a reorganization in the function of various activities. In other words, if I used to read fiction to be entertained but television now serves that purpose for me, I might continue to read as much, but I might develop a preference for nonfiction. Again, the reorganization hypothesis meshes well with uses and gratifications. Television and other activities are pursued not because of their form per se, but to fill some need, be it social, informational or relaxation. Therefore, television may displace other activities in cases of a functional similarity between the two but television may also cause a functional reorganization of other activities.

However, these hypotheses beg the question: Does television displace other activities? The answer, for children and for adults, may seem, on the face of it, rather obvious. After all, if we increase time spent with one activity, we necessarily decrease the time available for other things, such as reading, time spent with family or exercise. Evidence here is mixed (Mutz et al., 1993). The introduction of television does seem to displace some activities when it is newly introduced into a community but once the novelty has worn off, and viewing levels decrease somewhat, people do not automatically go back to their old activities. Therefore, the more important concern is not *if* television has some displacement effect but *what* television is displacing, when, and why.

For example, many nonviewers claim that without television, they spend more time with family, more time reading, more time exercising, more time in hobbies. In short, according to nonviewers, their time seems to be filled with enriching, engaging activities. Perhaps two related issues arise from this discussion of displacement. First, what kinds of activities occur when television is turned off? To answer this question, we may call again on the uses and gratifications approach. In other words, the answer may lie in the needs that are being fulfilled by television or other replacement activities. For example, television may displace reading a novel when someone is merely looking to be entertained. In this case, avoiding television may well result in more reading and vice versa. Certainly, many nonviewers talked about their reading habits. Many noted that they relaxed in the evenings with a book in the same way that viewers relaxed in front of their favorite television program. Therefore, the displacement hypothesis is intimately linked with the uses and gratifications approach in that activities do not appear to be displaced randomly. Entertainment television may displace free reading or playing board games. Watching the news may displace reading the newspaper. While displacement, especially the functional reorganization hypothesis, offers a broad-based explanation for this phenomenon, uses and gratifications, with its focus on motives and need fulfillment, offers a more detailed, yet parsimonious, explanation.

The second issue related to displacement is one of causality. Specifically, we might ask if displacement explanations may mask broader differences between viewers and nonviewers. In other words, the displacement hypothesis may suggest that children in homes without television may read more than children in homes with it. But it is possible that children in nonviewing homes would read more even if a television were present. Differences in family norms, beliefs, values, and attitudes may be at the root of these differing patterns of time use, leaving the presence or absence of television as a mere artifact. To address this issue, we will utilize family systems theory.

Systems theory

Systems theory itself was originally applied to biological systems (Bertalanffy, 1972) to understand how a complex system might adapt to changing environments and to changes within the system. One of the most basic premises of systems theory is that to understand any system, the whole and not the individual parts must be examined. Since its inception, systems theory has been applied to diverse systems, including engineering applications, business organizations, and more recently, families. Gregory Bateson was among the first to apply systems theory in social and psychological realms. His work with people with schizophrenia examined both the schizophrenic individual and his/her environment. Bateson argued that given a dysfunctional family environment, schizophrenic behavior becomes not only more understandable but perhaps adaptive for the individual (Bateson, Jackson & Haley, 1956). Work by later researchers began using systems theory to understand families in general. Given the basic premises of systems theory as it is broadly understood, its application to families is appropriate.

For example, in the broadest sense, systems theory is the study of the abstract organization of phenomena, independent of their substance. The phenomena are related to one another through some regular interaction; they are interdependent and exhibit some coherent behavior as a result. A system is open to and interacts with its environments, including information in the environment, and can acquire qualitatively new properties. In other words, it can evolve. Therefore, to truly understand the system, no one part can be studied independently. Rather, systems theory focuses on the arrangement of and relations between the parts which connect them into a whole. Given these principles, families can readily be thought of as systems. There are familial boundaries to identify those who are in the family and those who are not; there is more or less fluid interaction between family members and the human, material, and informational environment; and there are both short and long-term goals within the family that are achieved through family state variables and family processes.

As social scientists began to explore families as systems, they began to identify components of those systems that might apply more readily to social systems than to mathematical or biological systems (Bochner & Eisenberg, 1987). For example, in systems theory, input from the environment and subsequent adaptation by the system is a major component of the system. Within a family, information (such as "the effects of television") might be one kind of input. When this information is taken into the family, it may become a family belief, assumption or myth. That information is then used by the family to affect rules and norms in the family. In many ways, the relative accuracy of the information is irrelevant in its effect on family functioning.

Take, for example, the myth that sugar makes children hyperactive. In several experiments, the test group of children is given sugary foods and the control group is not. Based on the subsequent behavior of the children, parents and trained observers are unable to accurately identify which children had consumed sugar. Therefore, it is clear that sugar does not affect children's behavior. Certainly those events at which sugar consumption typically occurs—birthday parties, family events, social gatherings—may make children excitable, but sugar itself does not. Yet the myth lives on and may guide decisions and behavior within the family. The belief guides rules about when to have and not have sugar. The belief may also guide parents' expectations for children's behavior when sugar is consumed. Furthermore, these decisions and subsequent behaviors may influence interactions between family members. If I give a child sugar, and the child and I expect hyperactivity as a result, might this expectation not cause specific behavior in both the child and me? In short, family beliefs affect family behavior and become part of the family system.

In the case of the displacement hypothesis, it is possible that children in homes without television read (or play outside, or play board games) more than they do in viewing homes because television is not displacing these activities. But it is also possible that in nonviewing homes, general attitudes and beliefs about *other* engagements (such as the value of playing outside or playing board games) may influence those behaviors. We would expect, then, that children from these nonviewing homes would play more, regardless of the presence of television. Once again, television and its presence would be a mere artifact. The family norms regarding play (for example), the family attitudes about it and their beliefs regarding it would be the main causal agent in the complex behaviors of a given family. In this way, systems theory accounts for the *other* behaviors enacted in nonviewing families but does not offer television (its presence or its absence) as the true mechanism. Rather, systems theory would place the explanatory weight on family attitudes and beliefs, arguing that they, and not television, account for behaviors as far-reaching as television ownership, church attendance, and the power–authority structure in the home. These behaviors might then serve to reinforce individual beliefs or they might cause adaptation in beliefs. Because of the interconnectedness of all aspects of the system, and because of the bi-directional and feedback nature of many of the relationships, systems theory would argue that attitudes can affect behavior but behavior can equally affect attitudes. This approach does not minimize the role of television. Indeed, it does not minimize its stated effect. However, it does place television in the broader context of family life, affording it power as a cause, an effect, and sometimes, a mere artifact.

Certainly, among viewing families, a broad range of viewing behaviors exist that cannot be accounted for by the mere presence of television. This circumstance makes systems theory a particularly appealing and instructive explanation for the behaviors of viewing and nonviewing families alike. In the following chapter, I will introduce these theories and concepts to illustrate and explain various phenomena in viewing and nonviewing households.

Chapter 4

Attitudes Toward Living Without Television

In this chapter, we look at how nonviewers feel about living without television and how they think others perceive them. I report on the attitudes of adults and of children. Adults, because they have typically made the decision to live without television on their own, are quite positive about living without it. In fact, some are down-right zealots. However, children give a more varied picture of their lives without television. The youngest children, those 10 and younger, generally parrot their parents, stating that they like living without television because they have more time to play and because they are unlikely to develop any bad habits that adults often associate with television exposure. During early adolescence, however, children often miss television because they feel socially different from their television-viewing peers. For many children in early adolescence, difference of any kind is a difficult burden to bear. However, during late adolescence, most children again value their lives without television and no longer regard it as a negative aspect of their lives. To understand this pattern of attitudes in children, I utilize information from the literature on children's attitudes towards smoking as it relates to their own parents' smoking attitudes and behaviors.

When I began this research, I naively assumed that families who lived without television would share other similarities as well. I imagined people similar in their ideologies about television. Consequently, they would approach nonviewing in similar ways. I also thought I would find shared attitudes about raising children, with their beliefs neatly coinciding with decisions about how to manage television viewing. Those most vehement in their attitudes about television might avoid television entirely; those less adamant might watch movies occasionally, but not television. In my assumptions about nonviewers, I imagined cognitive and behavioral coherence. Instead, I found nonviewers share the decision to live without television, but they are not unanimous in terms of beliefs, attitudes, and behaviors. There is no prototypical nonviewing family or individual.

Furthermore, beliefs about television and behaviors regarding it do not neatly merge.

Despite their variety in religious, political, and social beliefs, there was one area of commonality across families without television. Nonviewers seemed to feel similarly in the way they *felt* about living without television. In this chapter, I will address nonviewing adults' and children's attitudes towards nonviewing.

Is There a Prototypical Nonviewing Family?

Although some similarities between subgroups of nonviewers emerged (e.g., conservative Christians), their similarities were not related to television viewing, per se. Rather, nonviewing was related to belief systems around which some nonviewing families coalesced. For example, I met quite a few nonviewing families who defined themselves as politically liberal. Of the 72 adults who participated in the interviews, 40% (n=29) identified themselves as liberal or progressive. Some of them owned a television set to watch movies, and others owned no set at all but owned a computer and had Internet access. Still others owned none of these, preferring to live with almost no electronic media.

On the other end of the spectrum, I met quite a few families who identified themselves as conservative. Of the 72 adults, 43% (n=32) called themselves conservative. Many of these combined this with religious terms such as conservative Christian or conservative Bible-believer. Some of these families did not own a television set at all. A few owned a set but used it to watch videos. For example, some home-schoolers who were also conservative Christians were watching language videotapes to learn Spanish. For these conservative Christians, it was their religion, and in some cases their political ideology, that seemed to affect their decision to live without television; it was this religiosity that was the focal point of the family. Overall, their similarity with other families I interviewed stemmed more from religion than from nonviewing.

The remaining participants (n= 11) identified themselves as politically independent. Some were religious; others were not. They did not want to identify themselves as conservative or liberal. For example, I met Ted Randolph, retired from the Coast Guard, who said, "I'm not some elitist. I'm not liberal although I don't care for the guy in the White House right now." He didn't like to be pigeon-holed, he said.

Ultimately, living without television was a symptom of their attitudes and beliefs. In fact, nonviewers could more easily be categorized by their *reasons* for living without television than they could simply by virtue of their nonviewing. Despite the fact that all nonviewers were not alike in, say, their political orientation or religiosity, they did share a more general approach to their behavior that came across during interviews but was difficult to tap in the surveys. Broadly speaking, these families often held very specific ideas about politics, or religion, or child rearing, or, certainly, television. They then tied these attitudes to the types of behaviors that they, and their families, engaged in. Viewing families, on the other hand, often held beliefs that were more ecumenical and somewhat less zealous and their family behaviors seemed to vary accordingly. Nonviewing families projected an idealism in their beliefs and a corresponding gravity in their behavior. Although the television viewers I interviewed were also opinionated, these opinions were often laced with pragmatism. Their beliefs about how to achieve their family goals were not always as zealously held. In the end, the commonality that could be identified in the nonviewers was a certain intensity of beliefs, attitudes, and behaviors about television, but also about the ideas they associated with it, such as consumerism or mainstream culture. There were other broad-based similarities between otherwise dissimilar nonviewing families. These I will discuss later, as the families themselves, their beliefs, and attitudes are introduced.

Despite similarity in what I have called idealism and intensity in nonviewers, they unanimously shared another similarity as well. They unanimously enjoyed living without television. Of course, this characteristic stands to reason. First, they had chosen to live without television and remained nonviewers, and second, they voluntarily participated in a study about living without television. In the next sections, I will explore adults' attitudes about living without television and then discuss the attitudes of nonviewing children.

Adults

"It's a wonderful way to live"

The responses of nonviewers to living without television was so unanimously positive that it is important to keep in mind that this sample of individuals chose to drop television, continue to live without it and then volunteered to participate in a study about those without television. It would perhaps be more surprising if they did not like living without television. Nevertheless, when discussing their attitudes toward living without television, it was nearly impossible not to discuss their dedication to it. This is a zealous lot.

Those who live without television are quick to list the benefits. They mentioned the amount of time that they had because they were not watching television and then usually went on to list the ways that they did fill their time. They talked about the amount of time they had to spend with and talk to family members and how living without television drew them closer together. They talked about the increased peace and quiet in their homes and in their lives; they talked about reading more. They talked about children who could entertain themselves and play outside with stones or twigs or nothing at all. They talked about the importance of boredom because they believed that boredom gives rise to creativity for themselves and for their children. They talked about not being affected by the violence or sex or consumerism on television, or even by the images of those who are slim and young and perfectly beautiful, which might leave them feeling less slim, less young, and less beautiful.

In fact, nonviewers are nearly unanimous in their positive attitudes about living without television. Rick Drabman, a part-time emergency medical technician who owns a small painting company, has lived without a television for 22 years. He describes living without television as "a wonderful way to live," and one that he has no intention of changing. In fact, most nonviewers in the sample had no thought of beginning to watch television again at any point. Although a couple of families with preschoolers mentioned that they might think about getting television if it became an issue as their children grew older, most believed their life was better without it. Sam Steinberg, who will be discussed in chapter 13, said living without television "is part of what we think of as the good life." In other words, for some nonviewers, they are not giving up anything at all. They are merely living without television to improve their lives.

In addition to the perceived benefits of living without television, many nonviewers see their nonviewing as an identity marker. For some, they even claim that living without television is one of the more important aspects of their lives. Although it may not be the single most defining feature, they believe it to be one of the main ones. It shapes, but also reflects, their identity. Lynne Selridge, who will be discussed at length in chapter 8, was raised by her parents without television and now was doing the same with her son. She says, "When I think about the three things that have really formed my personality, it's the fact that I'm an only child, the fact that I grew up without TV, and the fact that I grew up in a pretty religious household. So it's one of the three big things." Similarly, Mara Simpson, who lives in Kentucky with her husband and three children, says, "We don't watch television and in many ways, that is who we are. I think it's a very big thing that defines us."

For others, they do not define nonviewing as a main factor in their lives but they still perceive it as an integral part. Ted Randolph argues that he and his wife raised their children in many "unusual ways," as he called it. Living without television was one of those ways. He argues that "It's hard to separate the television from the other stuff. It's all a parcel." However, enjoyment and approval of living without television goes hand-in-hand with its importance. As Ted says of his now-grown children, "They are beginning to see the benefits of growing up in such richness. I have no regrets." Nonviewers believe that living without television is causally linked to some important outcomes, but they also see it as an important defining feature in their lives.

"It would make social situations easier"

For nonviewing adults who participated in the study, most had very little negative comment about living without television. Perhaps the only common negative attitude is that living without television could be a problem in social situations. After all, for most people, television is a social topic. It comes up at work, with friends and in our daily interactions. Without access to the television lexicon, the vocabulary of programs and characters and plots, some feel left out. Although most adults said that this was not a major problem, the theme emerged in many interviews. Peter Westman, a single man living in Massachusetts, argued that living without television was only occasionally a problem that affected him socially. He said:

> I think because TV is ubiquitous and I'm in the minority…when I am with people who do watch, then I'm completely left out. And that used to bother me. At work most of my colleagues watch television and there have been times when for all of lunch they'd talk about *Survivor* and I would sit there and just listen and occasionally I'd feel frustrated by my inability to participate. But the funny thing was that even not watching it, I'd catch up and I actually started to know what was going on.

Therefore, living without television can create a knowledge gap for nonviewers, but not an insurmountable one. For example, although some nonviewers could not name a single modern program, others could not only name the programs but knew the characters and some of the plots without ever having seen the programs. In other words, if television is a shared vocabulary, it can be learned from others.

In fact, for some nonviewers, learning about television was something they felt that they had to do to interact with their extended family. Rebecca Tanner of Vermont said she and her husband sometimes have trouble interacting with his side of the family. "They spend time recapping programs with us so that when we are together, we can all talk about the programs. And they keep saying: 'Oh, you don't have television.' And I say, 'Nope.'" Daniel Coleman stated that his brother often made television references and then had to back up, explain what he meant, and then the conversation could proceed. "Honestly," Daniel states, "I wish he'd either stop or that I could somehow get it without actually having to watch the stuff. It's not a big deal but it's like stumbling. And it just keeps happening."

"How difficult is it to give up television?"

Approximately one-quarter of the nonviewers claimed that giving up television had posed some challenges to them, either pragmatically, or, in the case of Danielle Long, ethically. Danielle lives with her husband, their preschool-aged daughter, and her husband's business partner. Like many people I interviewed, Danielle had many complaints about television: there was too much sex, and children who watched it had shorter attention spans and were less creative. When they had had television, she and her husband spent less time interacting with one another. However, halfway through the list of complaints, she paused and switched gears. "Maybe," she said, "I'm not being humble here. I'm preaching. TV is not the worst thing. People have a lot of terrible stuff in their lives. We can't assume everyone's lives would be better if they gave up TV." Similarly, several nonviewers commented that living without television might not automatically confer benefits. Many pointed out that when television is removed, the family life that fills the void is not automatically filled with moments of beauty and shared joy. For example, when one nonviewer reflected on her own childhood, one filled with many hours of television, she recalled it this way: "My mother was a single parent. And we watched a lot of television. She suggested it. But then at least she knew where we were. It was the least of her problems." So it is worth recognizing that what stands in the place of television is not necessarily better. And it could certainly be much worse.

Even for those who have given up television willingly, and who see the benefits, and whose lives appear relatively smooth, giving up television does take some adjustment. Rebecca Tanner, who we will discuss at length in chapter 12, says:

> It has taken us a really long time. When I tell people who might give it up, I say: "Give it six years."…Initially, we did wonder what to do. And now we have time so we started to do things that before we only thought about doing. We both knit, we play games. So it is good. It's better, but it takes time. It does take time to get used to.

Television Viewing as a Choice

Among the many nonviewers who enjoyed living without television, many also mentioned their desire for others to try it, or at least consider trying it. Some even offered pointers on how to do so. Therefore, another aspect of nonviewers' attitudes about living without television is that many are advocates. They want other people to give it a try. For parents, the benefits that they perceive and the reason that they encourage others often have to do with parenting. Although most see the temporary benefit of using the television as a babysitter, they also think the long-term benefits outweigh the loss of the immediate babysitter. Parents who live without television preach the benefits. Anne Tyson, a single mother living in North Carolina, eagerly claimed, "If other parents gave it up, I think they'd love it. Not right away but after a while. And then your kids stop asking for everything and for junk food and everything is easier. I really think everyone should at least try it."

Others simply express their desire that viewers approach their decision to view more actively. Lynne Selridge, who we will discuss in chapter 8, is thoughtful and thorough about her beliefs on many topics, including her nonviewing. She expresses frustration over individuals' willingness to live without questioning the news or political figures. About television she has this to say:

> I feel like so many people don't think of it as a choice. I want people, even if they go ahead and get one, I just want them to know it's a choice. A lot of people don't even realize it's a choice. I don't want to be in-your-face about it, but it is a choice.

In other words, for Lynne, she does not necessarily want to encourage people not to watch, but rather to think about watching and to understand that they can choose not to. Mike Carlson, who will be introduced in chapter 9, echoed this notion when he said, "So when you say TV needs to be less violent, what you're really saying is TV is necessary in people's lives and therefore we need to all work together to make sure it meets our needs." Rather, Mike suggested, we could all get rid of it. And then we would not have to worry about how bad the content was.

Children

Single adults are able to make the decision to live without television without consulting anyone. Of the single adults in the sample, it is not surprising that all are happy with the decision and none seemed willing to change their lifestyle. Presumably, if they felt otherwise, they would have a television. For couples without children living in the home, the decision to live without television was always made jointly and all reported that they had agreed to get rid of it. Sometimes one or the other had been more in favor of the decision but the disagreements were mild and in the end, the television was removed. Again, because of the nature of the sample, it stands to reason that any disagreement between the two involved were not vehement, otherwise, they may not have participated in the study. Therefore, it is only children of families living without television that might voice strong disagreements to their parents' decisions. After all, children are likely to disagree with their parents on any number of decisions but continue to live with those decisions anyway. A child might prefer to eat candy for breakfast, but this preference will not necessarily change the outcome of her diet. Therefore, I interviewed children independently, to find out how they felt about living without television and how they dealt with the struggles they might have with their parents. Parents offered insights into these family dynamics as well, but children's opinions tended to be more candid and less wrought with social desirability.

Among parents in viewing households, some wondered how it was possible to eliminate children's television viewing. Still others questioned the wisdom of it at all. For example, one male viewer commented that by denying children television, there may be a boomerang effect. "I just think these kids will go nuts," he said. "You send them off to college and they end up spending 12 hours a day watching television." And there is a certain cultural wisdom in this. If parents restrict something, will children inevitably rebel?

Perhaps the appropriate analogy can be made here between smoking behavior and television viewing. Both have ample evidence of negative effects (Bushman & Anderson, 2001), and both are behaviors that, as I will argue, are affected by parent attitudes and parent behaviors. Like children's attitudes toward smoking, nonviewing children's attitudes toward television follow a fairly regular pattern. Therefore, I will briefly review the literature on children and smoking to understand how children adopt or rebel against their parents' own attitudes and behavior regarding television.

Over the years, many studies have documented the important role of family factors in adolescent smoking behavior. In a recent, large-scale study on children and smoking, family factors were found to predict both the attitudes towards smoking and smoking behavior in preteens and adolescents (Bush, Curry, Hollis & Grothaus, 2005). Overall, the younger the child, the more similar their attitudes were to their parents'. During early adolescence, parent–child attitudes were still related but less strongly than they had been in early childhood. However, ultimately, parental attitudes, and the parents' own smoking decisions, are strong predictors of smoking behavior in adolescents and young adults (Booth-Butterfield & Sidelinger, 1998). Young children initially agree with their parents, adopting many of their beliefs and attitudes. As they grow older and obtain more information from other sources, their ideas may change.

These new ideas may be affected by peers or the mass media and may be bolstered by their own growing need for independence. However, in the case of smoking attitudes and smoking behavior, young adults are likely to mirror their parents' attitudes and behaviors about smoking. Children from smoking homes are more likely to become smokers than those who grow up in nonsmoking homes. Furthermore, parents who actively convey negative attitudes about smoking to their children also have children who are less likely to begin smoking (Bush et al., 2005). The parallels to television viewing become clear in considering children and adolescents' responses to living without television.

Middle and Late Childhood

Although the sample of children interviewed was not large, the parallels between these children's attitudes and the attitudes of those in the smoking literature are apparent. The youngest children interviewed, those in middle and late childhood, seemed unconcerned with the fact that they did not watch television, and some even spoke openly against it. At this stage, their influence seemed to derive mostly from their parents, who obviously liked living without television. Like children in the smoking studies, the younger children and those with parents who spoke openly and negatively about television had attitudes that mirrored their parents'.

The youngest children who were formally interviewed were in kindergarten and first grade. Six-year-old Chelsea Sommers-Grant reported that her best friend had cable but she did not know if he watched it or not. "How do you feel about living without television?" I asked. "It's fine," she responded. "I like it." Sakito Nishiro, who is 7 and has grown up in both Japan and in the United States, reported that his friends did talk about television. "They say like what the characters did and that it was cool and what cool things they see," he said. "How does that make you feel?" I asked. "I don't know," he said, shrugging his small shoulders. "I don't really listen to them." Another child, a 6-year-old girl, when asked about television, reported that, "It's not good for me and I like playing more, anyway." Obviously, these children think little about television, either having it or not having it. To them, it is simply the way they live and to the extent that they do have an opinion, it simply reflects what their parents might say.

From a uses and gratifications perspective, very young children who do watch television tend to do so to be entertained and to learn. For nonviewing children, play and reading have provided readily available and pleasurable functional alternatives; therefore, television is largely unmissed. Recall that uses and gratifications would argue that television is utilized to fulfill needs, which it can do more or less effectively depending on a host of social and psychological variables. Nonviewing children, especially those who have grown up without television, still have the same needs as other children; they have simply learned to turn to functional alternatives to meet those needs. Because those functional alternatives (e.g., free play) seem as normalized for nonviewing children as television does for viewing children, they feel little anxiety living without it.

As children enter middle childhood, they continue to mirror their parents' attitudes. At this stage, their attitudes are similar to their parents' for two reasons. First, similarity arises because children are parroting parents' words, and second, because they truly seem to have adopted the beliefs held by their parents. For example, several children in middle and late childhood expressed positive attitudes about living without television; several children complained that television was violent, still others complained that commercials were simply trying to sell them products. Sometimes it was extremely clear when children were parroting their parents. Consider 11-year-old Nathaniel, who has lived without television his entire life. His family does not own a television set and does not watch videos or DVDs. They do not own a computer or use the Internet. In part due to their conservative religious background, they have shielded Nathaniel from much of popular culture. When I asked Nathaniel what was bad about television, he responded, "The nakedness in the commercials." His father, who was present at the time, quickly stepped in and said, "But he doesn't know. He's never seen it." Similarly, 10-year-old Avery, when asked about the benefits of living without television, responded that without television "Our brains don't get clogged up with all the shows." Later, when I asked what she thought it might be like to live with television, she answered, "I think I'd be very unresponsible, I guess, because as soon as I got home, instead of doing homework or more important things, like, if you had a pet, feeding your pet or doing homework, you would just sit down and watch TV."

In Nathaniel's case, it is clear that he simply repeated his parents' comments and his father seemed to suggest as much when he stated that Nathaniel did not know for himself what appeared in commercials. It also seems likely that Avery had been told that television clogs her brain or promotes irresponsibility. It is understandable, therefore, that not all of these comments by all of these children can be thought of as strictly their own attitudes. In this case, like children with parents who are vocally anti-smoking, children with parents who make negative comments about television are likely to be anti-television, as well. They repeated their parents' comments, even if they did not wholly understand them.

However, not all of the comments seemed to come from parents via the mouths of their children. During late childhood, children also seemed to develop attitudes of their own regarding living without television. But how do we know when an attitude is a simple repetition of a parent's comment and when it belongs more sincerely to the child? What makes some comments, such as, "the nakedness in commercials," less authentic sounding than others? Usually, two factors would suggest that children's attitudes were merely repetitions of things they had heard. First, like Nathaniel, the knowledge that was necessary to arrive at that opinion was not likely to be available to the child himself. Second, when I spoke to the parents, they often made near-identical observations. In these cases, children's attitudes are not to be discounted. After all, many parents consciously attempt to instill their own beliefs in their children. However, in Nathaniel's case, and in similar cases, children's statements cannot be said to be fully their own.

On the other hand, some attitudes expressed by children seem to emerge more from their own experiences. Their comments were connected to particular experiences they'd had, rather than general things told to them by their parents. For example, Avery told me about an experience that happened in school. "One time, one of my classmates, they like referred—they talked about television in one of their answers in math class. And I thought that was weird." Similarly, her sister reported that she liked playing better than watching television because she could express her own creativity. Although 9-year-old Grace did not articulate it this way, her response revealed a connection she had made, rather than an opinion an adult had expressed. When she discussed what she did instead of watching television, Grace reported:

> I like to play with my plastic animals because it's like me making my own show, so I get to choose what happens. Like sometimes, I think I wouldn't like the shows that are on TV. But I can make my own and just sit in my room and decide everything that happens. I think up how my horses should act and then I act everything out my way. I guess it's like it would be watching television but you can...decide what happens.

Therefore, although children may parrot their parents, they also seem to be gradually fashioning their own ideas by drawing on their personal experiences as nonviewers. Perhaps one of the clearest examples of this came from 11-year-old Nathaniel. When asked what was best about living without television, he responded quickly, "More time to play."

Therefore, from a uses and gratifications perspective, very young children are easily able to replace television viewing with play. Because television serves primarily an entertainment function for this age group, and because play is such an integral part of early and middle childhood, functional alternatives are readily available, and even preferable to them.

Young children do not miss television because they have found alternative ways of filling the needs that television might meet.

Emerging Adolescence

As children age, television, and living without it, ceases to be a private issue, dominated by what their parents want for them and how television is dealt with in their homes. Television takes on a social component, which is developmentally predictable given the increased emphasis on social interaction with peers as children move from late childhood into early adolescence (Tarrant, MacKenzie & Hewitt, 2006). Recall that in the smoking literature, in late childhood and early adolescence, parent–child smoking attitudes are less strongly related than they are when children are younger (Booth-Butterfield & Sidelinger, 1998). Perhaps this is due to increased influence from peers, whose own comments may vary from supporting to criticizing smoking behavior. In the case of television viewing, it appears that late childhood and early adolescence are also times when nonviewers are influenced not only by parents but also by peers. Television begins to serve another increasingly important function for them: television provides social facilitation or is a form of social collateral. From a uses and gratifications perspective, one use of television is that viewers can utilize television as a topic of conversation, allowing them greater ease in social situations.

Anna Burns is 11. She admitted that she worries that her friends think it is odd that she does not have television. She feels left out sometimes when they talk about it, although her concern does not seem intense. We talked about television, what her life was like, what her friends thought, and what her own attitudes were towards television and living without it. I asked her at one point if she wanted television, or if she wished she had one. She replied, "Once in a while I do when I hear my friends talking about shows that were on that were cool and sometimes I feel left out." But the regret, at least in Anna, was mild. A 10-year-old girl also mentioned television as potential social glue. When asked if there were any drawbacks to living without television, she did not hesitate: "I feel excluded." "Excluded how?" I asked. "They talk about it and I can't," she said.

Again, uses and gratifications offer a viable explanation for this phenomenon. As children enter adolescence, social contact and social interaction with peers becomes more important. Because social facilitation is one need that television fulfills, it is reasonable to assume that this need—social facilitation—arises more clearly in adolescence. Deprived of television to fulfill this need, emerging adolescents may miss television. However, it does not appear to be particular content that these children miss. Rather, it is the social glue that television provides that they yearn for. However, various activities can fill the very same needs that television does. In late childhood, when the children's needs may be to be entertained and to learn, play and books take the place of television. However, as children approach early adolescence, their interest in peers increases and with it, their distress about missing out on the social collateral of television. In chapter 14, we will meet Milan. Although he is now 19 and no longer interested in television—in fact, he now holds anti-television attitudes—his step-father, Kevin, recalled that this was not always the case.

It was during one of our interviews that Kevin began a story about Milan. Kevin recalled that Milan had been about 13 years old at the time. With obvious relish and amusement Kevin began the story that perhaps perfectly captured the potential strife of raising an adolescent without television. At one point, I asked Milan, "So did you petition for television when you were growing up?" He responded, "Pretty much." "Pretty much?" Kevin burst out, looking at Milan. Then he turned to me. "I think the statement was, 'You are socially deforming me,'" he said. It was obvious that Kevin loved this story. He continued, "One time in middle school, he was petitioning us for TV. And he said, I think it was this exactly, 'You are socially deforming me because I can't watch TV. This family is nuts!' It was quite the outburst." Kevin grinned at the memory.

Milan calmly defended himself. It seemed they'd been over this before. Milan responded in the same calm, almost inaudible voice he used for everything. "I was definitely an outcast and that was just an added thing. In middle school it's so cliquey and so socially stratified. There's the smelly kid and the one with bad hair, the poor kid. It's the most vicious time... Then in sixth grade I moved." Kevin cut in here, "We lived next to Jake, near the river," he said. "Right," continued Milan, "We moved and there were kids, we were the new family." "And," recalled Kevin, "there were families with TV. He would watch TV with them. We weren't against it, we just didn't have it."

For Milan and his family, there was a brief period of struggle over television. Their collective memory was that this strife lasted only a few months at most. And like Avery and Grace, it was not missing television, per se, that seemed to cause the problem. Rather, it was feeling excluded or "socially deformed" that led Milan to petition his family for television. Once again, television for adolescents is a form of social capital and without it, their social value risks decline. However, by Milan's own admission, a year later, he discovered skateboarding and stopped asking for a television. He had found another, perhaps better form of social collateral. A functional alternative—one that fulfilled the need of social facilitation—arrived and easily took television's place. Milan had found a new activity through which he could bond with his friends.

Several adults who grew up without television recalled experiences similar to Milan's, recalling their lack of television as a means of social facilitation. Danielle Long recalls worrying a lot about not having television as an adolescent. Now 25, she lives in Massachusetts with her husband and 1-year-old baby. She recalls her adolescence with some of the same acute concern that Milan expressed. She recounted that it had been difficult for her and that she often hated feeling left out of conversations about television. "I always felt on the outside. Always," she recalled. "I felt ostracized...I felt stupid when everyone else knew a jingle. I really felt horrified when I didn't know what they were talking about."

Despite evidence from teens like Milan, not all of them seemed to rebel regarding television. I also spoke to Nick Fulvio who, at 14, was close to the age that Milan had been when he felt "socially deformed." Nick grew up more or less without television; however, his grandmother, who lived in the apartment below them, had television. He and his brother Chris would occasionally go downstairs to watch cartoons. However, five years ago, Nick's grandmother moved to Florida, taking her television, and Nick's access to it, with her. So although Nick's parents report that he grew up without television, Nick believes he has been truly without television for only five years, or since he was 9. When Nick talks about television, he states that his parents do not forbid it. They just do not have it. And in fact, among the parents I spoke to, many, although not all, had this sentiment. They know that their children watch television at friends' houses, and that is acceptable. They just do not want television in their own homes. Nick himself is somewhat philosophical about his own lack of television:

> I can't say there's nothing worth watching. I miss the Olympics. That was one thing I enjoyed watching. Certain shows, nature shows. And I guess there is a small gap between kids who have a television and kids who don't. You might get left out of a conversation. Things I wanted to keep up on, I can't so instead I talk to people or listen to conversations—like who won *American Idol*. But I don't lie about it. I don't mind it really.

So, like Peter Westman who felt left out of the lunchtime conversations with his colleagues, but eventually learned enough about *Survivor* from those conversations to join in, Nick has learned the vocabulary without actually watching television. Like Milan and Anna, it is the social aspect of television, and not television per se, that is missed.

As children age, the uses of television expand beyond mere entertainment. Young adolescents, more so than their younger counterparts, use television for social facilitation. In fact, the interviews with nonviewers suggest that social facilitation may be television's most important use during this time in their lives. Other uses, such as entertainment, passing time, habit, and learning can all be replaced with functional alternatives such as reading, spending time with friends, or hobbies. However, when friends discuss television as a means of making social connections, young adolescents are left out. Only when they find another form of social facilitation, such as Milan's discovery of skateboarding, do they easily navigate a nonviewing adolescence.

Other than television-as-social-facilitation, older children and adolescents did not seem to miss anything else about television. Nick Fulvio mentioned that, if given the opportunity, he would not want a television and has no intention of getting one later in life:

> There's a couple of times when we're at a friend's house and we watch television and now, it feels so foreign. The images just flash and you almost get dizzy and after an hour or two, I'm completely done and I want to find something else to do. My parents know I see it at friends' houses but they don't mind. I tell them it gets worse each time I watch it. The reality shows, like *Fear Factor*—that's completely disgusting—or the reality shows where people are just making fun of people. It's not real. It's totally fabricated and it's kind of weird watching all of this awful stuff.

Again, for Nick, talking about television with his friends holds much more appeal than actually watching it.

Nine-year-old Grace, who mentioned that she sometimes felt left out when her friends discussed television, was hard-pressed to come up with any other objections to living without it. When I asked if there were any *other* things she did not like about living without television, there was a long pause as Grace searched for an answer. I waited. Then I tried this: "Do you wish you had one?" "Well, maybe," she said. "Maybe? Why maybe?" I asked. Another long pause. "Maybe some of the shows are funny?" but she did not sound very convinced. For Grace and many other children interviewed, only a single use of television—social facilitation—was valuable. For other functions, such as entertainment, learning, arousal, relaxation or passing time, they found functional alternatives to fulfill the need.

Perhaps predictably, older adolescents' attitudes about television become more sophisticated. Although some of these attitudes may also stem from conversations they have with parents, their attitudes again seem to reflect their own experiences. Milan has very strong opinions about television and has obviously spent some time thinking about the issues associated with it. He described television as a "social illness that is so pervasive it's polluting our culture. It's like life support." Like many of the parents I spoke to, Milan is concerned because he feels television, which he sees as unreal, acts as a substitute for real life. In one conversation, he reported that:

> It's strange. Everyone talks about it and lives vicariously through these people. But on a daily basis nothing new will happen…but after three months, [if] I watch it, I'm like whoa!, everything changed. Ads are like four seconds long. Everything seems so fast and frantic.

Again, Milan now relates his own experiences with television to what he observes and experiences daily. His attitudes no longer parrot those of his parents, although they may still reflect them.

For 14-year-old Nick Fulvio, many of his ideas about television are now fully formed and articulated. He even has plans for the future regarding his own use of television. He reported being grateful to his parents for getting rid of television, and all of this despite the fact that in many ways, Nick is a regular 14 year old. He hangs out with his friends, enjoys drawing and sometimes plays Nintendo. Yet he said:

> It's one of the things I thank my parents for the most and I look at the things that play a role in my life now and I think if I had TV they could have been snuffed out. The games we played as a kid. Those are the things I remember. The drawing, the reading. I see kids who do have television, children who are between 6 and even up to older kids. There are TVs in the car, there are TVs everywhere and I think: when do you play? When do you have fun? When people look back, they're not going to say, "I watched some really good shows." They'll remember other things. So when I think about TV, I wish more people did it [lived without it]. When I have kids there probably won't be TV in the house.

Therefore, Nick's attitudes have been shaped by his parents, but they are also affected by his own experience with media, with play, and with others. Again, parallel to the smoking literature on older adolescents (Bush et al., 2005), parents' vocal attitudes and their own behavior, in this case, television viewing behavior, ultimately predict adolescents' own behavior.

"Much to our surprise, they never ask"

If I had only interviewed parents and they stalwartly claimed that their children rarely, if ever, asked for television, it might seem unbelievable.

But at least two factors support this claim. First, children themselves rarely reported asking for it much, and did not seem to care if they had it. Second, there was consistency across different children's responses, despite differences in age, sex of the child and where they grew up. Television simply was not an issue.

For example, Arthur Randle has an 8 year old and a 5 year old. In contemplating his decision to have no television in his house he is vaguely concerned that his children might be left out. But oddly, he says, they do not ask about television. Arthur understands that television might be important to his children so he is surprised that it simply never comes up. He says, "They have to be putting up with it at school. They're being cut out of the biggest syringe of modern culture. They must feel it at school. But they never ask. I keep thinking that they will, but they don't."

Many parents reported similar stories, even those with older children. For example, Elaine Sloan and Anthony Fulvio are the parents of Nick and Chris who were discussed earlier. At one point, Elaine recalled that when the boys were in their early adolescence, she and Anthony had talked about what they would do when the kids asked for a television. "We had anticipated that they'd object at some point," she recalled. "We thought they'd want to save up their money and get one. But much to our surprise, they never asked." In fact, even when a television was offered as a reward of sorts, some parents reported that their children had turned down the offer.

Ted Randolph has two children, both now grown. He recalled that his children liked to play outdoors, run around, and as he said, "get lost in the woods, that kind of thing." But both were good, responsible kids, so at one point, he and his wife decided to reward them. In telling the story, he still seems amused. He recalled:

> When one was a junior, they were doing really well in high school. So we offered them. We said, "You guys can get a television." We even offered them cable. And they said, we were shocked when they said, "We'll think about it." So a couple of weeks went by and we actually had to remind them. And they said, "nah."

Ted still seemed amazed.

It appears, therefore, that especially for children who are raised from birth without television, living without it is simply part of life and they do not pine for it. Even for those who get rid of television when their children are somewhat older, it is possible. Deborah Hansen, a single parent raising 11-year-old twin boys, got rid of their television two years ago. Although her children occasionally ask, she said that they only begged initially, perhaps for the first two months after she threw it, literally, in the trash. "It's an easier thing if you do it from the beginning but you can do it even later. You can do it. I think you can't be a complete purist but you can take it out of your home and your life. You will not be popular but they will get over it. It took them a couple of months to get over it. Now I just hear it [requests for television] on a snowy weekend."

Overall, then, like adults who have replaced many of the uses of television with functional alternatives, children in nonviewing homes have done the same. With the possible exception of one use of television, social facilitation for adolescents, television seems largely unmissed by children. Furthermore, like research on children's and adolescents' attitudes towards smoking, children's and adolescents' attitudes about television in nonviewing households come from their parents' attitudes, their parents' open discussions about television and from their parents' behavior. Keep in mind that these parents have given up television. Because Lin and Atkin (1989) found that parents who had more negative attitudes about television also controlled more of what and how much children watched, it is likely that these nonviewing parents have the strongest opinions about television. After all, they have given it up. They are also vocal about their views both directly to their children and in general, when their children are in earshot. In the literature on smoking, parents who express negative opinions about smoking to their children have children who also express negative opinions and who are less likely to smoke (Bush et al., 2005). For these children, smoking may not be something desirable that is kept away from them. Rather, it is something they either feel negatively about, or simply do not do. In the case of television viewing, children do not ask for television not only because they do not desire it but also because it is not normative. Children become accustomed to the many ways that they are raised.

How Do People Respond to Nonviewers?

Generally, nonviewers reported several kinds of responses from others to their own decision not to watch television. Friends and colleagues expressed surprise coupled with admiration, or they thought it was strange. Still other peers felt uncomfortable and defensive when the topic came up. However, it is possible that this defensiveness, if it in fact existed, came not from others, but from the way nonviewers themselves talked about television.

Terry Howe, a hospital chaplain living in the Midwest, reported that others often thought what he was doing was great. He said, "Some people agree and say it's the best thing because television is so bad. But they don't want to change really. They say, 'Oh, I could never do that.'" Similarly, Yoshimi Nishiro, a mother of two young boys living in New England, said,

"Especially my friends back in Japan, they say it's a really good babysitter. They say, 'Oh, I couldn't do it.' And so sometimes I am tempted to get a television."

"If we were crack dealers, we'd get better treatment"

Despite some mention of the admiration others felt, nonviewers talked more frequently about how strange others thought they were. Some reported that their peers thought them only mildly unusual, whereas others reported that their peers thought them downright bizarre. Take Ryan Jones, for example. Ryan lives in Alabama with his wife and stepdaughter. He talks about living without television and his own Christianity in such an intricately interwoven way that it is clear the two ideas are inseparable. In fact, Ryan said of television that "Everything that the Bible holds up as wrong, television glorifies. Everything that Christianity stands for, television goes against." In other words, he holds strong ideas about television and about Christianity and about how the former interferes with the latter. Given his strong feelings about television, it is perhaps not surprising that Ryan also gets, or feels that he gets, strong reactions from his peers about his nonviewing. At different times he claims that due to his nonviewing, his peers "think we're in a cult." At another point, Ryan claimed dramatically, "If we were crack dealers, we'd get better treatment from society than by not having television!"

In Ryan's case, it is not clear whether others respond so strongly to him because he does not watch television or because he is quite vocal about his beliefs. He himself admits that he does like to discuss his views about television viewing and about other topics as well; however, he has become less vocal as he has gotten older. In talking about television, Ryan said, "Early on, I took a more aggressive approach, but that was short lived. Now I just do what I think is right." It is possible, therefore, that the responses Ryan, and some other nonviewers, feel from peers and colleagues has more to do with their discussion of television than about their decision not to watch it.

Others report similar responses. Andrea Haggerty, who lives with her husband and two sons in Massachusetts, said that generally she tries not to bring up the fact that they do not watch television because it makes people somewhat uneasy. She reported:

> Some people get a little uncomfortable. They think *we* think they are terrible parents. My in-laws think we are kind of bizarre. We asked them to turn it off, if it was on in the background. And that was weird and a bit uncomfortable. We don't even want them [their children] to watch it somewhere else. We don't want them to see it. We have so

few people we know who don't watch TV. And I think that with all of the marketing to babies, it feels like a lot of people don't know. I don't think I'll change anyone's mind, so then we don't even bring it up. I'll just say that I've heard people say it's harder with the second baby. But I don't really believe that.

By her own admission, Andrea has asked others to turn off a television set that is on in their own home. It is possible that when others claim that not watching television is strange, it is something else they are responding to. In Ryan's case, it may be because he confronts those who do watch television. In Andrea Haggerty's case, it may be because she asks others to turn the television off when she is in their homes. It is at least possible that viewers do not object to nonviewers' decisions, but they do object to sanctimoniousness.

"We don't look like people who don't have TV"

In fact, there is additional evidence to support this contention. First, many nonviewers reported that they never brought up the fact that they lived without television. In fact, they would avoid mentioning it if at all possible. For these nonviewers, they reported that others did not think of them as particularly strange, even if they themselves felt unusual or "out of the loop" at times. For example, Mike Carlson, who we will discuss in chapter 9, said that the most common response that he got when people found out he and his wife and their two children lived without television was one of surprise. In discussing whether living without television ever affected his interactions at work or with his peers, Mike reported:

> Maybe when people meet us and they hear we don't have TV, the reason they're surprised is because we don't *look* like people who don't have TV. I feel like people who have TVs might think people who don't, I don't know, drive a horse and buggy or dress all in black.

In other words, for Mike, who said that it simply did not come up very often that he did not watch television, people responded with mild surprise. Similarly, Lance Vincent, a pastor living in Canada, said that when the topic of television came up, he tried to say as little as possible. "I don't want to broadcast it because I don't want to come across that way," he said, "but when it does, I just say I don't want to be pulled away from other things." In other words, for Lance, living without television is neither something to talk about, nor something to proclaim proudly to others.

For Dan Schmidt, a single man living outside of Boston, he also avoided the topic of television. Sure, Dan reported, he had a colleague at work who watched a lot of C-Span and often liked to ask Dan if he had seen something, to which Dan always had to remind him that he did not own a set. But generally, Dan said, "this is in a specific circle," meaning outside of his C-Span-watching colleague, he did not talk about television so others did not know. He said that when people did find out he did not own a set, he would get mixed reactions. But from talking to Dan, the reactions of others did not seem strong—either because they were not or because Dan did not interpret them that way. For mild-mannered Dan, either possibility seemed equally likely. When it did come up occasionally, according to Dan, reactions were both positive and negative. "Some people avert their eyes politely and other people think it's cool. Some are surprised by it," he reported. Certainly, no one treated him worse than a crack dealer.

However, those nonviewers who were more vocal about it tended to report that viewers were defensive. But, as I argued earlier, it is possible that defensiveness stems in part from viewers' guilt about their own time spent viewing, or it may stem from the attitudes of the nonviewers to whom they are speaking. In the case of one nonviewer who claimed, "Us not having television is a rebuke to those who do!" it is hard to imagine a response other than defensiveness from a peer mentioning a favorite program. Despite this, even some nonviewers who approached their nonviewing quite nonchalantly worried that their peers would be defensive. Mary Peters, who we will meet in chapter 13, compared her nonviewing to being a vegetarian. She felt that in both cases the decision was a personal one but that others felt a need to defend themselves. "It's like not eating meat. I don't bring it up because people feel like I'd be judging them for eating meat. And I don't. I don't care but it does get weird. Some people get weird about it," she said.

Other nonviewers reported that when it came up, peers or friends would say, "Well, I only watch the History Channel," or "I only watch the news." So there does seem to be a certain amount of defensiveness on the part of some viewers and, for some nonviewers, a certain amount of hubris. Only when those two collided did a nonviewer get "treated like a crack dealer." Generally, nonviewers seem to be perceived by viewers as only slightly unusual characters, like a vegetarian or a person who owns an electric car—mildly interesting oddities.

Chapter 5

What is Television?

In this chapter, I utilize the results from the in-depth interviews to develop a tripartite definition of television. Through the research, I have come to see that television means different things based on the attitudes of the participant or based on the particular situation. Television is the content that we watch, it is the medium that delivers the content, and it is the industry that creates, supports, and delivers the content. How people approach their viewing and nonviewing is influenced in part by what they perceive television to be.

Two-thirds of people I interviewed, people who responded to a note in a newsletter, or to a posting on a Web site asking for "TV-free homes," actually owned a television set. Most of them used their television occasionally to watch a DVD or videotaped movie, and some even rented programs that originally aired on television. (See chapter 14: Battling the Industry.) Of these 40 nonviewing homes with a television set, 7 reported that two DVDs or videos were watched per week, 11 reported that one was watched per week, 16 reported that one was watched every other week, and the remaining 6 homes reported that they watched less than that, or as little as one per year. As a researcher I decided early on that my criterion for viewing vs. nonviewing would simply be whether or not the person thought of themselves as living without television, so I never asked specifically when they responded to my ad. I did not screen or inspect homes for a television set. But when it came up, I simply asked, "Well, do you think you live without television?"

The data for this chapter come predominantly from those two-thirds who own a television set. The willingness of these individuals to label themselves as nonviewers brings up an interesting question: What exactly is television if not the box itself? For these nonviewers television is presumably not the set; otherwise, they would not have responded to my ad. Rather, living without television means something else. This gets us back to one of the questions posed in the introduction: What does it mean to live without television, or, as some people call it, to be TV-free? The answer may depend in part on first addressing the issue of the *idea* of television. What is television? The answer to this question will serve to structure the remaining chapters of the book into three sections: television as content, medium, or industry.

Annie McAdams and Arthur Randle

Annie stands 5´2˝ but as she jokes, "I don't act short." Her husband, Arthur, is a good head taller than she is, with the persistently rumpled look of someone who is thinking about other things—or simply not thinking about his appearance. Annie teaches high school history and Arthur is a professor at the local university. Both in their 30s, with an 8-year-old son, Alex, and 5-year-old daughter, Leah, they live on a quiet street with a large yard—a peaceful setting that belies the pace of the house inside.

On this particular Saturday morning, Annie is stretching on her yoga mat, Arthur is walking back and forth between the stove, where he is making pancakes, and his laptop, where he is looking up something on the Internet, and Leah is doing her best to make it impossible for Annie to stretch. She lays on top of Annie, then walks in circles around her, zipping dangerously close to Annie's shoulder stand. In frustration, Annie asks Leah several times to leave her alone, starting first with suggestions of other things Leah might do and gradually moving to more and more direct requests. Finally, in frustration, Annie plays briefly with Leah, laying on her back with Leah balanced on her feet in the air above her. The yoga has been abandoned. Their son Alex walks in from the other room, already half-way through some story he is trying to tell, one that he started before there was anyone there to listen. He heads towards the kitchen counter to inspect the pancakes. Although many families I interviewed cited increased peace as a reason for not owning a television, the McAdams-Randles never mentioned it and certainly have not achieved it. Theirs is a house that hums and buzzes at a steady pace.

When I first ask Annie and Arthur why they do not have television, they reply in near-unison. Arthur: "Don't want it." Annie: "Don't need it." Arthur then repeats: "Don't want it *and* don't need it." When I ask when the decision was made, Annie and Arthur both begin to respond but Annie finishes: "There was no decision and no discussion. It takes no willpower to live without television. We didn't even consider it. It's not a principle." Much of their talk is punctuated this way, by talking over each other, at the same time, in agreement or disagreement, recalling something together or correcting the way it was recalled by the other. When they are not talking simultaneously, they are bumping their comments up against each other, trading witty remarks or having some debate or telling a story in unison, both providing a sentence, a phrase, filling in a word.

Listening to them talk, one gets the sense of a household that is one long conversation. When I ask if living without television has affected their family, Arthur responds: "Well, the kids have more time to do other things." Not missing a beat, Annie responds: "Like fighting." Later, when they are talking about the benefits of not having their children exposed to commercials, Annie says, "Our kids don't expect to *have* things and *own* things." Arthur replies: "But they dearly wish for them." Both Annie and Arthur seem to have strong ideologies that guide their decisions, but they are quick to question each other's—and their own—sincerity. They do not want to take themselves too seriously.

It is perhaps no surprise, then, that Annie brings up the idea that they *do* watch television, they just do not call it that. She says:

> You know, I think it's interesting. It would be interesting to log the hours. I know there have been weeks when the kids have watched two or three hours of videos in one week. So to say we don't have television, sure, we have *control* but we *have* television. With videos, it was like when we got the baby swing. We wanted the one that you had to crank up because at least then you had to engage.

Arthur chimes in here. He disagrees: "But it's not television. We have control. It's over at some point. There are no commercials."

Later, Annie counters: "But all of this is laden with hypocrisy. I don't know if all screens are equal, but it's a screen. They have screen time and there's a certain amount of it and so according to the screen time paradigm, we are way over our allotment. We are hypocrites that way."

Again, Arthur responds: "Okay, so according to screen time, what about computers?"

Annie: "Well, the Internet, the computer. That's huge. We have three computers. We are complete hypocrites because we have the Internet so that's everything that television is and that's going to be a big challenge as they get older. The TV will be small potatoes compared to the Internet. It's such a wonderful resource but that will be a big challenge…I mean what if we spent as much time with TV as we do with…"

Arthur: "Well, that's complicated because I spend eight hours a day in front of the computer, so that's different. It's work. Or you can have the illusion that you're getting work done."

Although Annie and Arthur banter about many topics in this way, this conversation is telling. Asking what is meant by "having television" to those who believe that they do not have it may go a long way towards informing us about what television, in particular, and perhaps media more generally, means in the lives of American families. On one hand, if television truly is the box that projects images, regardless of where those images come from, many who participated in this study *do* have television.

But phenomenologically speaking, they live without television because they do not perceive what they occasionally do as watching television. They think of themselves as TV-free. So television must be more than the box. It is more than an appliance. So what is this thing, television, that enters our homes?

American Families "Watching Television"

In the average American home the television is on for seven hours daily. At any given time, one or more family members may be watching. However, ethnographic research suggests that for at least some of the time that television sets are on, no one is in the room (Morley, 1986). Children begin watching television as early as six months of age and gradually increase their time throughout their preschool years. By age five, they watch approximately two and a half hours a day, similar to the amount watched by adults. Once children enter school, their time spent in front of a television decreases somewhat to two hours per day, perhaps due to their decrease in unstructured free time. However, as children progress through middle childhood, their time with television once again increases. At this point, they sleep fewer hours and once again have more free time. By age 12, time spent with television peaks for most children. At this point they watch about four hours per day, dropping off to an average of three hours by age 16. It is at this point that children seem to have established viewing patterns that remain with them into adulthood (Comstock & Sharrer, 2001). It appears, then, that children do in fact learn to watch television. However, "watching television" itself is rife with conceptual problems.

Watching television can mean many things. Many modes of how people watch are encompassed by the term and, as Comstock and Sharrer (1999) point out, watching television can mean to "browse, momentarily ignore, assemble into a mosaic of contrasting bits, passingly follow, attentively consume" (p. 61). In other words, viewers can be very actively engaged, following the plot and attending to little else going on in their environment, or they can have the television on as background noise with little, if any, attention paid to it. Between these two ends of the spectrum are a myriad of activities and levels of attention that may be called "watching television." However, our concern here is not with attention to television, although that issue may be related to our questions. Rather, we are concerned with what television itself is.

Annie and Arthur argued about whether videos (taped material regardless of where it comes from) constitute television. Other families who I interviewed held steadfast to the idea that as long as it was taped, and individuals controlled when they watched it, it was not television. Nor was it television if it was rented material without commercials. Still others never seemed to consider whether what they did was "television watching." They assumed it was not. These questions, however, are structural. They create definitions that are based on criteria such as: When did it initially air? Are there commercials? What kind of device is used to play the stimulus? These questions, to me, are less interesting because they are about technology—and not about what families do with technology. Furthermore, answering the question using structural criteria (e.g., when did the show initially air) does not provide us with any new insights into media and the family. Rather, to understand what television is, especially to those who see themselves as living without it, it may be best to consider not its structural or technological features, but how it is used. It may be more informative to consider individuals' beliefs about television, what it means to watch it, and why they do not. It may also be informative to consider what families think it means to have a "good" family life and whether or not this life should include television viewing. By thinking about television this way, we can gain insight into the ways in which television has been absorbed into family life.

Defining Television: A Family Systems Approach

Few of the families I interviewed consciously struggled with the definition of television quite as much as Annie and Arthur, although other families' underlying struggles were evident in how they used television or how they talked about it, even if it was entirely absent from their homes. Of the 72 adults I interviewed, 10 told me immediately, either via e-mail or in an early phone conversation, that they had a television, but it was not hooked up to anything. These 10 all reported that, yes, they thought of themselves as living without television. After all, they responded to my interview request.

Other participants told me about their TV ownership later, when we met. Somewhere in the first interview usually, one would say, "I should tell you that we actually own a TV." Then there might be a brief discussion about what they used it for, such as family movie night, until we moved on to talking more about living without television. They did not seem to think of this circumstance as a contradiction nor did there appear to be any great definitional struggle for them. Still others never brought it up specifically but mentioned a movie they had rented. I would then ask if they owned a television set and they would say, yes, they did. For this group, owning a set was not even worth mentioning because being "TV-free" and owning a television set posed absolutely no contradiction at all. Therefore, the personal definitions of television seemed to run the gamut. Some "confessed" that they owned a television set early on in our interactions and others steadfastly held that they did not watch television at all, even if they owned the "box," as one respondent referred to it. Ultimately, they were included in the sample.

With these shifting definitions of television, it may be useful to look to family systems theory to understand precisely what television is. Although television is certainly not a human member of the family, it is more than an appliance. After all, it can fulfill a social function in a way that, say, a dishwasher cannot. In his classic article on the social uses of television, James Lull (1980) argues that televisions in the home fulfill two kinds of functions: structural and relational. Structurally, television can affect talk patterns by influencing when talk occurs and how much is said. It can also be used to provide companionship. Television is also used to fulfill relational functions by providing opportunity for family contact; by creating barriers, especially among family members in conflict; and by facilitating communication by providing topics. Television is the family member that can be turned on and off, relied upon to fill uncomfortable silences between a fighting couple, to tune out a family member who is annoying, or to provide an opportunity to share time for two or more members who want to be in the same room. Based on his ethnographic research of families watching television, Lull argued that:

> Television can lessen the demand for the manufacture of talk and the exchange of thought by providing a sustaining focus for attention which can be employed as a kind of social distracter, rendering less intense the communicative formalities which might otherwise be expected. Since television is used by the viewer as a focus for attention, creating parallel rather than interactive viewing patterns, it also becomes a resource for escape—not just from the personal problems or responsibilities of the individual viewer, but from the social environment.

Therefore, it appears that television is perceived, at least by some viewers, to be somewhat of a social figure. Certainly it fulfills some social roles within the family. No one would argue that a dishwasher can do this. Therefore, television is more than an appliance, although less than a family member. It is clearly social, but it is not a social *being*. So how then, does it fit into the family?

Recall, as we discussed at length in chapter 3, that systems theory argues that the family system—the beliefs, norms, attitudes, behaviors, environment, of a given family—operate in complex and complementary ways to influence the family. Norms influence behaviors, which in turn influence beliefs, which in turn may affect environment, and so on. No single relationship within the system is necessarily direct or unidirectional.

In the case of television viewing, beliefs about television—both what it is and what it does—may influence family decisions about whether to have it, what to watch and what counts as television. These decisions, in turn, affect subsequent behaviors both regarding television (Will it be kept on during dinner? What will be watched?) and perhaps even more general behaviors (Will we go to separate rooms after dinner or spend time together?). Therefore, not only can television itself have a social function but *beliefs about* television, in homes where it is and in homes where it is entirely absent, are part of the family system. In this way, television can be present as a social object. However, even in homes where it is absent it is part of the family system because of the beliefs family members hold about it. In fact, I would argue that the concept of television can be a stronger presence in homes where members choose not to have it than in homes where they do.

For many viewing families, television is such a ubiquitous part of life that having one is no decision at all. It is the most common, the most expected thing to do. Having one requires little thought. In an interview with a woman who does watch television, my interview stumbled along for a while. Then, growing somewhat frustrated, she said, "I can't answer these questions. I never think about my TV." In other words, because she did not think about television, there was no real decision about it: whether to have it or what it meant to have it, or how life was like with it.

However, deciding not to have one requires a set of ideologies, a reason or a belief system that can then be taught to one's children. Many families I interviewed reported that the strongest resistance for their decision not to have television came from their parents—not from their children. This finding is corroborated by earlier research on families without television (Zinmeister, 1997) and lends support to the idea that having no television requires an *alternative* belief system that goes against the one that was perhaps taught initially. Therefore, it may be that living without a television, regardless of how television is defined, requires beliefs about television; whereas living with one does not necessarily. Because information and, by extension beliefs, are part of a family system resulting in norms and ultimately guiding patterns of behavior, television can be thought of as part of family systems, not *only* in families without television, but *especially* in families without it.

The Effect of Media: A Family Systems Approach

Other researchers have also used the systems approach to understand how media are incorporated into family life. In her review of the role of the Internet in family life, Amy Jordan (2002) takes a family systems approach. She argues that media, in this case the Internet, can best be considered from a systems perspective. She reviews how this new medium affects a family's use of time and space, the way family members interact, how gender roles are established and adolescent identities constructed. Although many researchers have argued that other media, such as television, can influence use of time and space or gender roles, a systems approach allows us to look not just at the medium and the content but at television as a broader entity. A systems approach allows us to consider not just the medium but the beliefs, behaviors, and norms within a family that become associated with the use of the medium. By looking at media this way, Jordan was able to address questions concerning the Internet and what attitudes and beliefs the family holds about its use. Jordan argues that:

> Family norms, values, and patterns of the system will both reflect and shape the general approach children take to media and the particular role the Internet will have in the individual and collective lives of family members. The home environment provides structural dimensions of space and time—domains of family life that reflect larger social values and orientations to media…Within this domain children learn to think about the nature of time and the value of time. Such learning is subtly woven into the patterns of the family's day but also explicitly expressed through statements about the best ways to spend time and manage time. (p. 243)

Jordan goes on to discuss how particular activities (e.g., reading, chores) have built-in assumptions about how best to use a commodity, such as time, within the larger family system.

However, as I argued earlier in this chapter, as much as television is part of the family system in families with television (because television influences the information that comes into the home, and influences how time is spent and how interactions are conducted), television is also part of the family system in families without it (because the concept of television has a particular meaning to them). Nonviewing families have belief systems about television and its effects and these beliefs fit into their larger system of beliefs about what attitudes and behaviors are undesirable, what stimulus to avoid or how to spend time. Therefore, television exists for them in a very real way, despite, or perhaps because of its absence. Its absence requires them to defend their decision, even if just to themselves, and these beliefs affect norms for behavior. For example, the idea that "we don't have television because it's a waste of time," can have as much of an effect on a family as the idea that "we watch television together because we enjoy sharing space." Both are ideas and beliefs about what television is, what it does, and how it affects behaviors. These behaviors (e.g., avoiding television, watching it together) affect family interactions, which in turn affect family members' beliefs about the kind of family they are.

Therefore, as Annie and Arthur argued, television has several definitions. Furthermore, the concept of television itself can affect family life and family interactions. In the following section I explore the notion of television. I will propose three answers to the question: "What is television?" For each answer, the individual or family that abides by it has adopted a belief system that is consistent with their broader ideas about family or about their own lives. Although the categories are certainly not mutually exclusive, individuals generally believed television meant three different things. Television to them is defined by its *content*, by the *medium* and its potentially continuous output, or by the television *industry*. The definition that they adopt then fits into their beliefs about family life or about their own lives and helps set patterns for their behavior, especially regarding television use. However, because not all families had single, clear explanations for what television is, there did not appear to be an obvious link between definitions of television and family behaviors regarding it. Rather, definitions of television and specific behaviors were somewhat fluid and were only loosely linked.

What Do We Believe Television To Be?

In this section, I offer examples from adults and children that support the distinction between the three definitions of television. Some of the children I interviewed were in the process of growing up and forming strong opinions about television that were often repetitions of thoughts their parents had voiced. However, ideas about television clearly occupied their own thoughts. So the simplest and most straightforward answer to the question, "What is television?" was easy for them to answer. In many ways, it was easier to ask children some of these questions because they were gamely willing to answer even the dumbest sounding, most obvious questions. When asked: "What is television?" they answered. Most adults could barely help but answer with sarcasm. After a few tries with adults and always getting "the idiot box" or "the evil to end all evils" or, sardonically, "the heart of the home," I gave up. However, when I asked children, they answered, perhaps because they are accustomed to answering adults' ridiculous questions. Like The Little Prince in Antoine De Saint-Exupery's classic tale, who remarked, "Grown ups never understand anything by themselves, and it is tiresome for children to be always and forever explaining things to them," the children I asked patiently offered a sincere response.

For example, 7-year-old Sato, a young boy whose parents had been born and raised in Japan and who himself had spent his time back and forth between Japan and rural northeastern Connecticut, answered only after giving a thoughtful pause. First he lifted his eyes to the ceiling, then he leaned carefully toward the tape recorder: "It's like this box, like the size of a trash can and it has a screen and has some buttons, sometimes a remote control and it has like these numbers of these channels and people like to watch it." A slightly older child, a girl of 10, perhaps eager to get the answer right, said, "Television is either non-animated or animated pictures that they, not pictures, but rolling film that they put on TV for adults and children to watch." In general, children could answer a straightforward question in a straightforward way. Although their ideas about what television *is* could also be complex, the relative obviousness of the question did not throw them off. One example of a more complex answer came from an 8-year-old girl. Like many adults, her belief about what television *is* was wrapped up in her ideas about what it means and what it does. She answered: "It's something that is made for entertainment and also it uses, some people use it for advertising, except sometimes there can be bad things on television."

Adults also had many complex ideas about what television *is*. However, they revealed their thoughts indirectly, through our many conversations about living without it. Always, for the many people I interviewed, television is much more, or perhaps more complex, than the box that projects images.

As I sat in the homes of people who lived without television or when I interviewed them, their beliefs about television and their reasons for not watching it could not always be placed into neat categories. And most people had many reasons for avoiding television and even more beliefs about what television itself is. Therefore, it is not accurate to claim that individuals who had one set of beliefs about television treated it one way, and those who had another set of beliefs treated it another. However, answers did emerge, and in some loose sense, those answers were related to beliefs about what television does and to a belief system that ultimately made for a set of norms for how the family operated. In other words, beliefs about television became part of the broader system. For some, television is about *content*; for others, television is a *medium;* and for still others, television is the entire *industry*.

Although most people at least mentioned television in terms of its content and as a medium, there was generally an emphasis on either content or medium. For other respondents, television is a broad landscape, including the content, the medium, and the industry. For those who were concerned about content, such as violence, sex, language, and commercials, they were somewhat less likely to own a set at all. In those cases, objectionable content occurred on television, in rented movies and in the news. Therefore, it was not enough to screen the medium that broadcasts content; the entire apparatus had to go. Those who saw television more as a medium were more likely to have a set but exercise control over video and DVD rentals. Because they did not like the idea of a potential source of continuous stimuli, they removed the continuity, but kept the opportunity to watch a particular movie or even a program. For those who thought of television as an industry, they rejected television by eliminating it entirely or by gaining control through choice. In the remainder of this chapter, I will discuss these categories in greater detail to answer the question: What is television?

Content: Violence, Sex, and Commercials

Lori Glick and her husband Tom of Winona Lake, Indiana, each came to their marriage without a television. Lori grew up without it and Tom gave it up while he was in the military. He had spent years watching, by his own account, "way too much," and he began to see the content as being inconsistent with his religious beliefs. Therefore, when they met and married, living without television was not even discussed. It was assumed. Now, they and their two children are among the one-third in the sample who do not have a set at all. They also avoid the Internet, for many of the same reasons that they avoid television. When asked about her main objections to television, Lori immediately cites issues of content. "I don't know if there's anything good," she said. "There's the language and the sex scenes. There's crime. There are a lot of things not pleasing to the Lord. I often think, and we say, 'if Jesus were in the room, would he be watching that?' I think our decision is a Bible-based, Christian decision." For the Glicks, television is synonymous with television *content*. It does not matter whether it originated on a broadcast channel or a videotape, as a television program or a Hollywood movie. When they say, "We don't watch television," they often mean, we do not watch the screen. What makes it television is the perceived offensiveness of the content; what makes it problematic is the potential for that content to affect behaviors and attitudes such as aggression, consumerism and sexual beliefs and behaviors.

Daniel and Ellen Coleman of Niles, Michigan, like the Glicks, also do not own a television set for themselves and their five children. In expressing his concerns about television, Daniel's reasons spanned a host of concerns having to do with content. He worries about the sex, especially the images of adultery that he associates with television. He also worries about consumerism for his children. He articulates each of these concerns by stressing the content of television, emphasizing that the main problem with television *is* content. "We do not want to be involved in television because it shows premarital sex and things like that and homosexuality. And television ends up glorifying that. There are no standards in television and there are no consequences," he says. Later, Daniel also expresses concern that television might desensitize children by showing violent images. He reasons that these violent images would not be entirely avoided if he got rid of television broadcast but still rented videos. He argues that, "We avoid the negative influences of the agenda of the messages that influence our minds and hearts and relationships…And the children haven't built an immunity to things. There's a tenderness and gentleness and innocence that we see among those children. There are many reasons for that but one is that they are not absorbing the messages and attitudes of TV."

It stands to reason, then, that those who object to the content of television, and who therefore live without it, might also reject movies and not even own a television as a video monitor. Although this was the case for those with the strongest objections to content, such as those who identified themselves as having very conservative religious beliefs, others who objected to very specific content (e.g., commercials) or objected to depictions of sex and violence for their children, might own a television set, keep it in a closet and pull it out to watch a carefully selected movie. Therefore, those who object to content over medium were somewhat more likely to have no television set at all, but the link between content objections and set ownership was by no means one-to-one. For example, Jane Hart, who will be discussed in chapter 14, has very strong content objections, especially to commercials. The family members consider themselves nonreligious, and they own a set to watch movies. The Tanners, who will be discussed in chapter 12, also consider themselves nonreligious but have no television set at all. Therefore, beliefs and behaviors are not directly linked. Rather, individuals have beliefs that they then translate into behaviors that they find acceptable for themselves and their family *given* these beliefs. For those who object to content, having no television set is the most definitive way to avoid that content, but it is not the only way.

A Medium: Continuity, Lack of Predictability, and Gaining Control

Among those who believed television to be something other than mere content, some owned no set at all and others owned one, but kept it hidden from view, pulling it out to watch movies. Those who did own a set, and who responded to my ad asking for families who lived without television, obviously did not think I meant the box that they owned to watch movies on DVD. To them, that type of viewing is not television. Instead, as articulated by some of the individuals I interviewed, television is a medium that connects to broadcast content, and broadcast content is characterized by two things: the potential for continuous output, and the relative lack of predictability of the content. According to these individuals, the continuous nature of the medium and its lack of predictability can result in interruptions to their lives, cause a loss of control over their time, and, importantly, provide television with power in the social ongoing of their home. Ultimately, to regain control, nonviewers get rid of their sets or eliminate broadcast and cable input and place their televisions in inconspicuous, difficult-to-access locations.

Recall the debate that Arthur and Annie had. Although they debated the topic in detail, discussing and arguing over whether what they had was television, Annie more or less held that it was. "We have television. We just don't have *input*," she said. Annie equated television with content; Arthur was more inclined to say that they did not: "With television, you can't turn it off. It doesn't end." In that regard, Arthur equated television with the medium. For him, if it has a logical endpoint, like a video, it's not television. What makes it television is its *continuous nature*.

Similarly, Lily Lindt, living in New Hampshire with her husband and 2½-year-old daughter says that they got rid of television, "because it's there and there and there. It just feels like it's there all the time." For her, television is also the ongoing nature of the stimulus. Although their family still has a set, they do not "have television." One of their reasons for eliminating it is because Lily sees it as something that interrupts the flow of family life. About this she says, "We started to grow apart. We started not even to talk to each other because it was just there all the time. I'd hate coming home and seeing that blue haze coming from the window. When we got rid of it, we got closer. " For Lily, the "it" is the input and living without it has been a way to keep in contact with her family. Although they still own the television set, they no longer have cable or network access and they keep the set out of sight. By Lily's account they do not "have television," suggesting that television for her is the thing that is "there and there and there." Similarly, Tanis McElrone, a college librarian who lives in Indiana with her husband and 2-year-old daughter, clearly states that it is the medium, and not the content that she objects to. She refers to television as "a continual source of noise." Although the family does not own a television set, they do occasionally watch a movie on their laptop computer. When discussing her daughter and the possibility of getting a television in the future, Tanis argues that, "I think I still wouldn't want to watch it and the more I think about it objectively, the more I'm convinced that it's not just the content but sitting still and the nature of the medium...Neither my husband or I are the kind of people who just sit and watch and watch." Therefore, for Tanis and her husband, although they do not own a television set, it is still the continual nature of the stimulus that defines it.

Interestingly, Tanis and her husband have adopted a strategy that several nonviewers did. Those who tended to think of television as a medium, but who still enjoyed movies, watched rented movies on a laptop computer. By all standard accounts, they did not own a television. There was certainly no television apparatus in their home. Yet, they watched movies.

This laptop-as-home-theatre phenomenon underlines the fact that defining television must be about the way we use media, and not the technological features of the media. In fact, I would argue that those who watch a DVD on their television once a month are not different from those who watch one on their laptop but own no TV set. The important distinction here is that, once again, it is more valuable to define media by its use than by its technological characteristics. As media converge, technological characteristics become less important to those interested in television as a social phenomenon and the home as its setting. What remains is the use of a technology in the family. And if what defines television is its continuity, then a television set, devoid of its continuous output, is no more a "television" than a laptop computer is.

In addition to the notion of television as a potential interruption to life, another idea related to continuity is that television is characterized by a relative lack of control over content. More specifically, the viewer cannot predict what will happen next. For some nonviewers, especially parents, it is this *lack of predictability* that defines television. Once again, this lack of predictability is associated with the medium, and not necessarily the content. Alice Sommers-Grant described one of the last times her 7-year-old daughter watched television, before they got rid of it entirely. She recalled: "The only time we would turn it on is when she had been sick and I got what she had and I needed to take a nap. You know, it would get to two in the afternoon and I would have to lay down, but I didn't take my eyes—or, I did take my eyes off her just to close them and lay down. And one time, *Teletubbies* morphed into *Barney* and then it morphed into *Sagway Cat* and so this was about an hour and 10 minutes that I had fallen asleep and she was there watching it and she started screaming because two bats were attacking the cats in this cave and it was too scary." Later, her daughter, who had not been present at the time of my discussion with her mother, recalled: "When I watched it, when I was littler and I watched *Teletubbies*...these wild shows that I did not like pop up. They just pop up and scare you." For both mother and daughter, the problem with television, what in fact characterizes it, is having no control over what "pops up." For other nonviewers, news and commercials were both cited as sources that might surprise you with content that was unsuitable even if you had enjoyed what you were watching a moment earlier. So television is also television because of its lack of predictability.

The notions of continuity and of predictability suggest that many nonviewers desire more control in their relationship with television. In fact, it became somewhat clear that nonviewers, especially those who perceived television as a medium, think of television as a *powerful* medium. These viewers believe that television can steal time against your will. Although this notion is similar to that of interruption, it affords television even greater power. Not only can it interfere with family life but also its continuity can result in lost hours. After all, anything can interrupt family life—a phone call, a neighbor's visit—but only content that is always there can steal countless hours. Those who object to the medium of television often object to the episodes that *must* be followed or the line-up of show after show after show. For example, Mark Armstrong questions the value of television because it wastes time. In his lengthy and sometimes complex responses, he weaves in ideas regarding the objectionable content of television, but his real concern is the time it seems to take away. Not only does television use his time, but he also feels that it steals his time, against his will. Keep in mind that Mark and his children own a set. They just, by his own definition, do not watch television. It's a "video monitor" as he calls it. For him, the main problem with television is its continuous nature. Consider the following response:

> Well, in addition to having lots of other things that interest me more, I think I feel like time, the clock speeds up when you're facing a cathode ray tube not unlike the net. Time zooms ahead and personally if I find myself in front of a screen—and it's hard for me because I am enamored of images—I could spend all night waiting for something to happen and it never does. And then I end up with such an empty feeling because I've wasted a portion of my life and it feels like it happened on someone else's terms, and for some reason I don't feel that way with a book or a good film. It doesn't seem as bad. I dislike the continual bombardment of idiots telling me to buy this or that. I'm sure there is some seed of benefit but my feelings are it's not worth the amount of uninformation. It far outweighs the actual entertainment. It's like some bad drug: fun for a minute but the down side is really bad. I'd rather do something that requires some physical activity rather than stationary, strapped down. There's not enough time in the day.

Given Mark's ideas about television, and his definition of himself as a nonviewer, it seems clear that television for him not only interrupts his time but also garners control of his time due to its continuous nature. It goes on all night, and one could potentially get sucked in to watching too much. Although Mark admits that he loves movies, they are easier for him because they are over at some point. Even a taped series is a problem because you might want to watch the next one. When Mark revealed that he liked *The Sopranos*, he also admitted that he had to stop asking a friend to tape it for him, "I felt too drawn in," he said. Again, the continuity of it all, the need to watch from one episode to the next, felt to him like he no longer had control.

In fact, the idea that television wasted time, or, in some cases, stole time, came up in almost every interview. Although two children, a 6-year-old girl and a 14-year-old girl, did not mention lost time or wasted time as a problem with television, every other nonviewing interviewee did. From the 8-year-old girl who cited "more time to play" as a benefit of not having television, to the many adults who stated that they had better things to do, time and its use was a major theme. Granted, not all families thought that they used their time productively. Some stated that they "hung out," or simply "waste[d] time doing other things." They often stressed that, compared to television viewing, they simply preferred to spend their time doing almost anything else.

The theme of control was repeated again and again among those who equated television with the medium. Individuals lacked control over interruptions and time use and unpredictable content. The theme of lack of control has been noted in other research on people who do not watch television as well. For example, in their study comparing nonviewers to heavy viewers Foss and Alexander (1996) discuss the theme of television addiction. Both heavy viewers and nonviewers worried about the addictive quality of television and the resulting loss of time. In their study, 8 of the 26 nonviewers they interviewed called television a drug. One woman described television "like a drug that modifies your behavior. Rather than turning it off and finding something else to do, it ends up being on all the time." There are perhaps two things that are relevant here, both of which relate to the concepts of power and control.

First, those who consider themselves nonviewers perceive television to be powerful enough to take time away from them, even when they would prefer not to watch. That is, they imbue it with strength and power that light to moderate viewers might not. Videos, played on a screen with their obvious end point, are not television because they are stripped of their power. As Arthur Randle argued, "With television, you can't turn it off. It doesn't end." Therefore, nonviewers generally believe television to be a powerful medium. One way to regain control and diminish the power of television is to remove its continuous nature, thereby regaining control and predictability over content.

A second notion related to power and control has to do with how nonviewers treated their television sets when they did own them. If these individuals define television as a medium that interrupts family life, what becomes important is not whether a television set is present. Rather, what becomes important is how that set is integrated into the family. For example, Mike Carlson, who describes himself and his family as living without television but who owns a set that they keep in a closet, remarked that, for him and his wife, "we never talk about watching more or about expanding our channels. It's more like, the size of the TV or where will it go." In the case of the Carlsons, television is defined by how they use it and how important it is in their day-to-day lives. Similarly, Estania and Sam kept their television under what they referred to as a "shroud." They wanted it covered and kept out of sight to diminish its power and to gain control over it. For those who believe television is a medium, removing the power of continuous input makes television more like an appliance with a restricted, particular purpose (to watch a movie) and less like a family member that enters into family interaction. Without the perceived power that television has due to its continuity and without the power that family members accord it by placing it in the center of the room, television is no longer television.

In the case of television-as-medium, the use of television becomes its defining feature. Recall that Lull (1980) argued that television serves two social functions in the home: structural (e.g., punctuating conversation, structuring time) and relational (e.g., acting as a barrier between family members in conflict). However, what enables television to fulfill these social functions is its easy accessibility when needed and its continuous nature. It is much less likely to perform these functions if a movie must be rented and the set hauled from the closet each time it is used. Therefore, for those who think of television as a medium, what they are avoiding is the very social use of television that Lull described. It is not always the content that they object to. Rather, they object to television as a potentially powerful social force in their home. For these nonviewers, they think of television as a social enabler. However, they do not want it to perform this social function in their family. By removing its function as social enabler, through the removal of its continuity and its importance, nonviewers remove its power and reduce it from social member to mere appliance. Once it is stripped of its social function, it ceases to *be* television.

The Television Industry

In chapter 14 I discuss at length Anika Bradinski and her family of four who rent *South Park* to watch together on their old VCR, but who still think of themselves as living without television. For them, television is not the content. To some extent, it is not even the medium, although they may be likely to agree that the omnipresence of television is one of its defining characteristics. Rather, what television is for Anika and her family is the television *industry*, the media machine that develops, produces and presents programs, then sells commercial air time to pay for the programming. In this section, I will discuss individuals and families who avoid watching television (although some may have a television set) because they object to aspects of the television industry.

Kathleen and James Holt have two children, an 8-year-old girl and a 4-year-old boy. Although they have many reasons for avoiding television, the commercial presence is one of the main factors. On the face of it, commercials or the presence of commercials may seem to exist in the same category as any objectionable content such as violence or sex. However, for some families who talk about commercials, it is not commercials specifically that bother them. They talk about commercials in the abstract, commercials as a tool created by an industry that sells. Both Kathleen and James object to commercials, but they talk about them as a business, not as a series of 30-second spots intended to sell a product. When discussing why they don't watch television, James argues that, "For me, it's not being part of the whole marketing business." Kathleen agrees when she says, "We just don't want them exposed to that, to any of it." Later, she talks about television as being part of commercialism in general. "I haven't been to a mall since last Christmas, and it's amazing how much is tied to the TV and the media. We don't want to do that." So for Kathleen and James, not having television is not simply about rejecting shows or rejecting commercials, but about rejecting "the whole marketing business" as James calls it, which includes television, commercials and the malls that sell the products.

Other families who are nonviewers also seem to view television as something other than the content, something that includes the *business* that is television. Deborah Hansen, a single mother with 11-year-old twin boys, begins talking about television content, but as she discusses her ideas, her language changes to address the television industry. It seems that the latter is more relevant to her in terms of her decision not to have television. As I mentioned in chapter 3, Deborah Hansen had an unusual story. Unlike many people who gradually give up television, Deborah stood up one day, calmly unplugged the television set and carried it out to the trash. Her sons were 9 at the time. Like other parents, she lists many objections to television, from the way television presents males as stupid to her belief that television isolates people from one another. However, it is the industry that she finds most problematic. In fact, it is the industry that she seems to equate with the notion of television itself. About television she says, "Oh, and the commercials! As far as the children go, I resent the way that television creates junior consumers. TV sells ads and then ads try to sell things to my kids. And I just don't think my children ought to be targeted by business." Here, Deborah's language slips from a discussion of the content of ads ("Oh, and the commercials!"), to a broader discussion of television ("I resent the way television creates junior consumers"), to references that indicate that television is synonymous with the television industry ("TV sells ad and then ads try to sell things to my kids. And I just don't think my children ought to be targeted by business"). By avoiding television, Deborah is able to avoid the entire industry so intimately tied to consumption.

Although these individuals do not always talk about the industry per se, their discussions about television are tied to a belief that there is an industry that is intentionally involved in selling products to or shaping the ideas of audiences. Sonia Flores lives in New York City with her husband and her 5-year-old daughter. She and her husband gave away their television five years ago, in part due to the birth of their daughter. Although, according to Sonia, they first decided to limit their own viewing and then later decided to stop watching all together. In talking to Sonia, most of the major themes emerged: violence, biased news coverage, waste of time and commercials. But what is interesting is the way she refers to television. "I got rid of television because I didn't want them to have access to my brain," she said. On another day, Sonia stated, "I worry less because I'm not watching fear TV. I don't like the way they make everything dramatic and scary. And it's not just the news."

In this case, television becomes something much larger than content. For Sonia, she does not want *them* to have access to her brain, the way they "make everything dramatic and scary." In other words, television is not content or the medium. After all, Sonia does not argue that she wants to avoid a particular frightening program or sensational news story. Rather, she does not want "them," presumably the machine behind the content, to gain access to her.

Perhaps one of the clearest examples of an individual who does not watch television because she objects to the industry is Charlotte Ford, who will be introduced in chapter 6 on sex and violence in the media. Charlotte lives in the Midwest with her husband and ten children. She refers to herself as a born-again Christian. In my conversations with her, she talks at length about the problems of sex in the media. But her beliefs about television fall squarely in the category of *television as an industry*. Charlotte objects to the content of television, surely. But when we begin to talk about what television is, or when she brings it up indirectly, she says, "When I think about television I ask, 'Who are these actors? What are their lives like otherwise?'" Later, she asks, "I wonder how God thinks of it? How is he viewing it?" For her, she has rejected television, the content, the medium and the entire industry. It is not the box that she objects to, although they do not own a set. She objects to the industry and the content is simply the inevitable artifact of that. By accepting the content, she would be accepting the industry whose actions she opposes.

As Charlotte expressed her concern about the sexual lives of the actors in the programs and the agenda of the producers, I am reminded of Kyle Neff. In many ways, the two are remarkably different. Charlotte is a conservative Christian, Midwestern female and mother of 10; Kyle is a male artist living in Boston, who claims to be nonreligious. But about television, they have remarkably similar views in some ways. Charlotte's beliefs about television go beyond the content or even the commercials. When she rhetorically asks, "Who are these actors? What are their lives otherwise? Even if they are playing a good character, what are their real lives?" she expresses a belief that by watching television, she might somehow condone the industry that produces it. She sees content and industry as intimately tied. In one conversation, she recalled, "I knew of one situation where a sodomite was playing someone good. But that's not good. The actors themselves must be good. So I ask myself: 'Who made these programs? What is their agenda?'" Similarly, when I asked Kyle Neff about television, he had this to say: "Television has such a corporate financial backbone that they control everything from education to entertainment. And you have to ask yourself what their purpose is, what their goals are."

Both Kyle and Charlotte see television as more than an apparatus or medium that delivers programming. Both see it as a larger system and both seem to believe that by consuming the content, they buy into the agenda of the industry, although they are likely to disagree about what that agenda is. Nevertheless, Charlotte and Kyle might agree that television is more than content. It also represents the system of financial backing, production, directors and actors that work together to create that content. For those who live without television, television itself may take on an identity that seems to go beyond a medium of entertainment and information. It is an industry, but perhaps even more than that, it becomes part of a personal belief system that ultimately informs personal decisions, parenting decisions, political decisions and lifestyle choices.

Belief Systems, Family Systems, and Thoughts About Television

Overall, there seem to be three categories of beliefs about television and what it means to own one. Television can be content that might include any audiovisual stimulus that can be watched on a screen. Annie McAdams supported this belief when she said, "I don't know if all screens are equal, but it's a screen. They have screen time and there's a certain amount of it and so according to the screen time paradigm, we are way over our allotment." Television can be the medium that is continuously available, replete with commercials and any other content that a station chooses to show. Annie's husband Arthur supports this perspective. Recall that he disagreed with Annie when she said that watching videos was the same as television. Instead, he said, "But it's not television. We have control. It's over at some point. There are no commercials." The continuity of the stimulus made it television according to him. Therefore, he saw television as a medium. When the continuity was removed, so was the power. What is left in its place is a mere appliance and its effect on the family system is minimized. Finally, television can be conceived of as the entire industry. Kyle Neff, supports this point when he says, "Television has such a corporate financial backbone... you have to ask yourself...what their goals are." Most people believe some combination of these, or at least discuss television as if they do. Although very few people discussed their specific ideas about what it means to "live without television" directly, it is clear that these varying perspectives affect their decisions about television. Their beliefs about television affect if they have a set, how they use it, even where they put it. These perspectives are sometimes adopted by their children, and are certainly used in governing norms about television or lack of it in the home. However, these beliefs and behaviors are not clearly and causally linked in a single direction. Rather, for many individuals and families without television, television (or the concept of television) is part of a belief system that informs what they think family life, or life in general, should be like.

Ultimately, what are people doing when they do not watch television? Certainly, they avoid content, medium, and industry. However, when people choose to live without television, they see themselves as making a decision that is about more than just television. Sam Steinberg, who we will meet in chapter 13, says that, "It's a moral decision. I try not to bring it up but it is a decision about what we consider to be the good life." In other words, nonviewers perceive the decision to have no television to be a decision about life, not about television. In this way, television or lack of it is clearly a part of the family system, and avoiding it, too, becomes an important family norm within the system. Avoiding television is what these families do.

However, rejecting television is also part of the family system because it becomes part of who the family *is*. Other individuals, when talking about living without television, would mention that they just weren't those kinds of people, saying, "Neither of us are the *kind* of people who watch TV or eat dinner in front of the TV. We're not that way." So, as part of the family system, television viewing is not merely a behavior but a set of beliefs about how to live well, however that is defined. It can become part of the family identity or part of an individual identity. For example, Kyle Neff says that without television "I definitely have better relationships…I read, I make art, I talk to people. Without TV, I'm more inclined to have a conversation or read or learn something…Without television I have to be more creative with my use of time. Without it, we'd actually have to find out who we are." Clearly, this is more than a decision about watching content on a screen. For Kyle, living without television carries meaning that is tied to his identity as a person.

Similarly, when Ted Randolph, who retired from the Coast Guard several years ago and raised both of his children without television, talks about TV, he, too, sees it as a decision that fits into his worldview. He says, "It's hard to separate the TV stuff from our lifestyle. They [his children] are adept socially. They are comfortable around different people. They couldn't isolate themselves behind the TV so they had to be outside interacting." For him, living without television does not inform his beliefs or affect his family. Rather, it is part of a set of beliefs, part of the whole.

Systems theory argues that because families operate as systems, the beliefs that they hold, the norms that are related to those beliefs and the behaviors that emerge can be seen as rational (L'Abate & Colondier, 1987). In this way, for each family and for each individual, living without television is simply a rational decision that makes sense given their beliefs. As Annie says, "It takes no willpower to live without television. We didn't even consider it." Although not all families claimed that it was as easy as Annie and Arthur report, most argue that after a while, living without television is simply a way to live, not an option whose temptation they are constantly trying to resist. In most cases, it is simply the most logical outcome, given their beliefs. As I discussed in chapter 4 on children's and adolescents' attitudes, children who live without television do not seem to pine for it. They do not often petition their parents to get it and the adults rarely even think about it. Living without television is a rational decision based on a set of beliefs that results in a logical behavior. From this system, individuals construct an identity that may include nonviewer, regardless of how nonviewer is defined. In this way, living without television and the attitudes associated with it is part of the balance that makes up a given individual's or family's life.

Part II
Television as Content

In Part II of the book, I cover those issues that are associated with television as content. Chapters 6, 7, and 8 address sex and violence on television, advertising on television and political issues as they are covered by the news. The people who voice their complaints about television and these issues generally see television as being synonymous with the content that is delivered by it. Part II also addresses various theoretical issues that can be associated with television content, such as desensitization to sex and violence and the social learning of new behaviors.

Chapter 6

Keeping Out Televised Sex and Violence

In this chapter, I cover the issues of sex and violence on television. I review the research that reveals how much sex and violence there is on television and I consider the literature that examines the effects of this content. Through the voices of the participants who have rejected television because of the way that sex and violence are portrayed, I discuss the effects of television on children. Overall, in the present sample, those who consider themselves politically conservative were more likely to mention their objection to sex; whereas those who consider themselves politically moderate or liberal were more likely to voice their objection to violence.

Sex and violence, almost always mentioned in tandem, dominate discussions on the content of television. Nonviewers mentioned them 96% of the time in the first interview. Viewers trailed behind at 80%. This circumstance indicates that most people recognize that there is a thing called content. In fact, among some nonviewers, television itself is synonymous with its content. For them, objections to television *are* objections to content. For example, Charlotte and Thomas Ford reject television almost solely on the grounds of what it shows. Were television shows different, perhaps with no sex and no violence, they might opt to have one. However, the objectionable nature of television content has led the Fords to own no television at all, no family computer and no video games.

In the following chapters, we will cover issues of content. What is it that nonviewers believe they are screening out when they live without television? As we will discuss in this and the next two chapters, concerns over content include objections to sex and violence, objections to commercials and marketing on television, and concern over the ability of television to be an effective tool for keeping up with news and politics. In this chapter, I will discuss the Fords' and other families' concerns about television sex and violence.

The Fords

The Fords are not your average family. If nothing else, the sheer size of the family makes them "above average." They have ten children, aged 8 months to 21 years old, and when I first talked to Thomas, the father, it crossed my mind that perhaps they did not have television because they did not need it. I imagine life in a household with ten children is more entertainment—and work—than most people can handle. Who needs television when so much drama, comedy and news happen daily inside the walls of your home? When I asked Charlotte my standard question about what she did with her time, she merely laughed. Compared to the average American who watches three hours of television per day, she *does* have an extra three hours, but, of course it was a ridiculous question. She wondered aloud how anyone had the time to watch television at all, "With all the cleaning, the wash, the gardening, the projects." She also home-schools all of the children.

Thomas says there is never a dull moment at their house. "Not boisterous—just lots going on," he says. When I ask, he catalogues their activities in a dizzying list: the children share in the home responsibilities like caring for the younger ones, doing laundry, preparing meals, washing dishes, and cleaning. The older children also help their younger siblings with their academic work. The family breeds golden retrievers and they keep chickens for eggs. Six girls play the violin and one boy practices the trumpet. They sing together, they read together, and, sometimes, Thomas and Charlotte go out to dinner, just the two of them. The Fords even share a resemblance. Charlotte and her seven daughters all wear their dark hair long and pulled back neatly from their faces. They favor dresses, jumpers and skirts. Thomas and his three sons wear their brown hair short. He is a pastor at Believers Baptist Church, and Charlotte, with a BA in education, describes herself, not surprisingly, as a homemaker. Along with two of the older girls, she teaches Sunday school classes, and the musicians in the family play in the church orchestra.

The Fords' religious beliefs and convictions are integrated with many decisions they make and certainly, the decision not to watch television is one of them. Religion also comes up casually in conversation quite frequently with all of the family members. It is referred to spontaneously as they describe their days and in a more deliberate way as they discuss their decision making, their beliefs and personal choices. The children and adolescents in the family spontaneously talk about morality, virtue, Christianity, and Jesus Christ.

For example, when I spoke with Thomas, in my second question to him, he mentioned that television would "hurt him spiritually with [his] relationship with the Lord." Likewise, Charlotte brought up spirituality in response to the very first question I posed to her. When I asked Stephanie, their 21-year-old married daughter, how her life differed because she lived without television, she mentioned that first and foremost she had "more time for devotions." Overall, the lives of the Fords are steeped in religion, leading them to interpret many aspects of their lives, including television, through that lens.

Stephanie is married with a young baby of her own and lives with her own family. The other nine children live with their parents, and seven of them are formally home-schooled by Charlotte. The two youngest, a 4-year-old son and an 8-month-old son, are not yet formally schooled. As in most large families, the older children help out with the younger ones, giving Charlotte time to educate some of them while the others watch the preschoolers.

Interestingly, neither Thomas nor Charlotte grew up with television. Thomas's family eliminated it when he was 8, although he could not precisely recall how or why it happened. As he reports about his own father, "one day he just got rid of it." Charlotte, on the other hand, lived with television a bit longer than her husband. Her parents were also Christians, but they did not necessarily share her strong beliefs. She sees the loss of television in her childhood home more of a fortuitous accident than a conscious decision:

> When I was a junior [in high school], I started going to a Christian school and at the same time our TV broke at home. And for my parents, it wasn't a conviction. But for me, I disagreed with it in principle. And I prayed about it and then it broke.

Charlotte is quick to mention that she did not pray that the television would break, only that it did and this was fine with her. As she says, "I watched it, but it took up time. There are so many more beneficial things that I could have been doing. I also had younger siblings and I was worried about the direction they were going." Her conviction led her to petition her parents to keep television out of their home, but as she recalls, the real reason it was not replaced was because no one had the time. She lived on a farm as a child. Her parents worked long hours and she and her younger siblings typically had four or more hours of farm chores after school each day. This left little time for anyone to watch television, let alone worry about replacing the broken one. "In the end," she recalls, "It wasn't really a conviction for anyone but me."

Sex in the Media

As I talked to the Fords, and spoke to other families who had given up television to adhere to their moral and religious beliefs, the idea of sex in the media came up often. Certainly sex is a common theme on television. For example, Kunkel et al. (1999), in research conducted for the Kaiser Family Foundation, found that 70% of all shows include some sexual content, and that these shows average 5 sexual scenes per hour. This finding indicates that the amount of sex on television has increased dramatically since 1998. At that time, 56% of programs contained sex, at a rate of 3.2 scenes per hour and in 2002, 64% of the programs contained sex at a rate of 4.4 scenes per hour (Kunkel et al., 2005). Charlotte Ford is therefore not incorrect when she says, "I tell my kids they can't comprehend the difference on TV from the 1970s to now."

Although Charlotte and her husband Thomas are concerned about many aspects of television, one theme that recurs is sex in the media and how it might impact their children. This is consistent with their religious background given that, historically, the religious right has been involved in cultural issues relating to sex and the way it is publicly perceived and, in some cases, taught. The religious right has long been on the forefront of the debate over sex education in the schools. As early as 1981 Phyllis Schlafly, founder of the conservative political organization The Eagle Forum, which bills itself as the leader of the pro-family movement, wrote that the "major goal of nearly all sex education curricula being taught in the schools is to teach teenagers" to engage in sex.

These early concerns continue to echo today through the push, both at the federal and state levels, for abstinence-only sex education programs in schools. Abstinence-only programs are designed to teach the biology of sex while providing students with encouragement to abstain until marriage. In an abstinence-only program, information about birth control, sexually transmitted diseases (STDs) and HIV/AIDS is either limited or omitted. More recently, with the support and praise of leaders from the religious right, such as James Dobson from the Focus on the Family Foundation, President Bush has increased federal funding for abstinence-only programs. Not surprisingly, many states with education budget problems have welcomed the increase, making abstinence-only programs a source of contention between constituents in school districts across the nation. In this way, sex education has left homes and schools and become a topic for national debate.

That sex has become not only a source of public debate but of television entertainment concerns the Ford family, both the adults and the children. In addition, other families who live without television and who identify themselves as conservative Christians or born-again Christians expressed concern over sex on television more than they expressed concern over other issues, such as commercialism or violence. In addition, those who spontaneously mentioned that they were conservative Christians or "born-again" Christians made negative references to sex on television four times more frequently in the first interview, averaging 4.2 times, compared to those who did not mention their religion or claimed they were nonreligious. These nonreligious individuals mentioned sex on television only once during the first interview.

In fact, survey data on the relationship between religious and political ideology and concern over indecency in the media support this observation. A recent survey conducted by the Pew Research Center (2005) reported that of the 1,505 American adults surveyed, 51% of white evangelical Protestants say offensive entertainment presents a greater danger than government restriction of media content, though only 27% of secular individuals agree. Similarly, a majority of conservative Republicans (57%) believe that indecent entertainment is the bigger threat. In contrast, those who identify themselves as liberal Democrats overwhelmingly believe excessive government restrictions are the larger concern (72%).

However, conservative Christians are not alone in their belief that television shows too much sex. A survey of 1,001 parents of children aged 2–17, conducted by the Kaiser Family Foundation (Kunkel et al., 1999) found that 60% of all parents are very concerned about the amount of sex on television. A full 83% believe either strongly (53%) or somewhat that sex in the media may cause children to become involved in sexual situations before they are ready. Therefore, on average, Americans are troubled about sex in the media, although this concern is voiced more by conservative Christians.

Previous research on families without television also found that these families were worried, among other things, that exposure to television would cause an overemphasis on sexual matters (Zinmeister, 1997). The solution, as many reported, was simply to get rid of television entirely. Like Thomas and Charlotte Ford, whose concern is acute, these families simply did away with television and thus removed what they saw as a threat. When asked what her major objections to television were, Charlotte starts with a biblical quote. "The Bible says, 'set no wicked thing before [my] eyes.' And we try to put only consistent things before us. We can't keep our children in a box but why feed them with those things?" She also expresses concern over the "immodest dress" on television, a concern that was later echoed by her teenage daughters. For example, her 15-year-old daughter, Joy, talked about her cousins who had previously lived without television but had, about two years earlier, decided to get a television for their home. Joy and her older sister both mentioned this and expressed regret that they are now not as close to those cousins. Joy remarked that after the cousins began watching television, "they all dropped their instruments, their standards of dress have changed...We used to be really close but we have drifted apart."

Like her mother, Joy believes that television affects these standards of dress. Similarly, Thomas is worried about the way actors dress on television. He argued that "We...don't like the way it teaches our daughters to dress." Like Charlotte, he is concerned about what messages television might teach his children concerning sex. For the Fords, the very notion of what they referred to as "family values" was intimately tied to ideas about sex. Thomas stated:

> There is so much on television that goes against family values and there's a negative impact. There's the violence and there's the moral issue. I'm trying to teach my children to be morally upright and with the bed scenes on TV...We want them to wait until marriage and on TV that just doesn't happen.

Similarly, Daniel Coleman, a father of three, states: "We object to premarital sex and it seems like TV just glorifies it...We want them [his children] to have good values, family values."

Does Sex in the Media Have an Effect?

Although the intent of this chapter is not to comprehensively review the effects of sex in the media on adolescents and adults (other authors have done so more thoroughly; see Malamuth & Impett, 2001 for a review), it is worth noting that research evidence, both cross-sectional survey data and experimental research, suggests that representations of sex on television and in the movies can influence the attitudes and reported behaviors of adolescents. For example, Brown and Newcomer (1991) examined the relationship between the amount of exposure to television and satisfaction with virginity among adolescents. They found that, overall, those who watched more television reported that they were less satisfied with not having had sex than those who watched less television. Faced with depictions of sexual encounters that are excessive in quantity and quality, especially those depictions that feature adolescent or young adult characters, it may be that teens engage in social comparison. The result may be that their own youthful sexual inexperience is perceived as unusual, and wanting.

Similar results were found more recently by Dale Kunkel and his colleagues, who found a link between dissatisfaction with virginity and exposure to television in a sample of teenagers (Kunkel et al., 1999). Brown and Newcomer (1991) also found that adolescents who think television portrays sex in an accurate way are more likely to be dissatisfied with their own first sexual experience, pointing perhaps to a lack of realism in portrayal of sex on television. Experimental designs have also shown that television exposure is related to attitudes about sex. For example, Bryant and Rockwell (1994) exposed teens to a highly sexual TV drama. The control group saw a neutral clip. Those exposed to the sexual drama later rated descriptions of casual sexual encounters less negatively than those in the control group. Research on sexually explicit media, such as pornography, has also shown that watching it does have a negative effect. In a meta-analysis of 30 studies, Allen, D'Alessio and Brezgel (1995) found that there was an effect of sexually explicit media on behavior such that exposure led to increases in aggression. A similar meta-analysis, examining the effect of sexually explicit media on attitudes, perceptions of norms, and behavior, found that across the 48 studies, there was a significant effect of pornography exposure on sexual deviancy and acceptance of rape-myth ideologies. Overall, then, for both mainstream sexual material and for pornography, a compilation of evidence suggests that those exposed to sexual media experience less satisfaction with their own sexual experiences, and for pornography, viewers exhibit greater sexual deviance, greater aggression, and greater acceptance of rape-myth ideologies.

Violence in the Media

Unlike the topic of sex, which came up more often and with more importance for those who spontaneously identified themselves as politically conservative or born-again Christians, the issue of violence was more likely to arise among those who either identified themselves as politically liberal, identified themselves as nonreligious, or did not mention religion. For example, Mark Armstrong is the father of a 13-year-old boy and 4-year-old girl and describes himself as politically liberal. Although I did not ask participants to decide whether sex or violence on television was more offensive to them, some offered the comparison themselves. Mark claimed that, given the choice of his children seeing violence on television or sex, he was more concerned with violence, including fictional and real violence. He stated, "The violence—you're better off with *Robocop* than the news...The violence on television is totally out of hand. Given the choice of having my children watch two people in bed or two blowing each other up, I'd choose the boudoir. I just plain don't want someone else's violence in my house." For Mark, it is not imitation per se that he was worried about; rather, he expressed concern that, in showing the violence, he was somehow condoning it.

Deborah Hansen, a mother of 11 year-old twin boys, also mentioned violence on television before she mentioned sex. In fact, she mentioned sex on television in passing but then returned several times to the issue of violence on television. She was more concerned with the way that violence was portrayed than she was about violence in and of itself. "Some [shows] are so ridiculously violent. Violence is not for me. Violence [on television] has no victims and for me it's important they learn that violence is not funny, it's not cool. It's bad." Like Mark, Deborah worried that, by showing violence, she would appear to be condoning it. She worried that humorous violence might teach her sons that violence was funny. And she argued that as a society, we have a responsibility to "teach kids the best of what we have to offer. Not glorify the worst."

Both Mark Armstrong and Deborah Hansen are correct about television violence. Certainly, research shows that exposure to media violence does have an effect on aggression, serving in most cases to increase it (see Paik & Comstock, 1994 for a meta-analysis, and Comstock & Sharrer, 2001 for a narrative review). However, is the relationship causal? Although many surveys have shown a correlation between exposure to violence and aggression (e.g., see Smith & Donnerstein, 1998 for a review), the major flaw of survey design is that causality cannot be demonstrated. Because it uses cross-sectional data, it is unclear whether viewing causes aggression or if more aggressive viewers seek out violent programming. However, more sophisticated survey designs, specifically those that use longitudinal data, surmount this problem by looking at the relationship between early violence viewing and later aggression as compared to early aggression and later violence viewing. Research by Huesmann (1986), utilizing longitudinal data that spanned more than two decades, found that although both relationships are significant, the magnitude of effect size is larger for the correlation between early viewing and later aggression, thus lending support to the notion that exposure to violence increases aggression more than early aggression leads to increased viewing of televised violence.

Experiments are also able to contend with problems that surveys cannot. In an experiment, the causal factor (i.e., exposure to violence) is manipulated and an increase in aggression among those who saw a violent stimulus can be attributed to the exposure. Literally hundreds of experiments have been conducted showing an increase in aggression after exposure to violence (e.g., Zillmann & Weaver, 1999). Despite the many experiments that have demonstrated an effect of exposure to violent television, at least one is worth noting in particular because of its external validity. In a now-classic natural experiment, researchers were able to examine the effect of television on aggression in a Canadian town that initially had no TV access and that gradually, over a few years, gained access (Williams, 1985). The study, like many of those conducted in a lab, suggested that television viewing is causally related to aggression. Although laboratory experiments often show this result, they are frequently criticized for being sterile, unrealistic, and lacking in external validity. Because Williams' results converged with the findings of the laboratory experiments and because it was seen as more externally valid, the results are excellent evidence for the negative effects of television exposure on aggression.

However, as Deborah Hansen pointed out, it is not simply a concern about violence, but the way that it is portrayed. Once again, naïve wisdom is supported by theoretical and research evidence. According to Bandura's social cognitive theory of learning, when an event is modeled, four sub-functions govern observational learning; that is, whether or not the modeled behavior is imitated by the observer (Bandura, 1986, 2002). Both internal and external functions govern attentional processes, retention processes, production processes, and motivational processes that may result in imitation. One crucial aspect related to the sub-function of motivation is that of vicarious incentive. Motivation to imitate the modeled behavior increases if the model himself is rewarded for the behavior. Alternately, if the model is punished, the motivation to imitate the modeled action decreases. Research evidence has consistently offered support to the concept of vicarious incentive. When audiences witness an aggressive act being rewarded, they are more likely to imitate that act (e.g., Rosenthal & Zimmermann, 1978).

Deborah Hansen is right, then, in arguing that rewarded violence— when violence is laughed at or shown as cool—is more problematic than violence portrayed with negative consequences for the perpetrator and the victim. She is also correct when she argues that violence on television has no real victims, at least not the kind that might exhibit real pain after being injured. In an extensive content analysis that examined not only the occurrence of violence on television, but also emphasized and studied the contextual cues surrounding that violence, it was found that violence on television goes unpunished (73% of the time); is executed by models who have positive qualities with which a child might identify (37% of the time); shows unrealistic consequences (58% of the time); and is portrayed as justified (44% of the time) (Wilson et al., 1997). So when Deborah Hansen complains that television violence "has no victims... and [real] violence is not funny, it's not cool," content analyses support her. Television violence has no victims; rather, it is often shown as cool and funny.

Another aspect of television violence raised by many participants is its desensitizing effect. Specifically, desensitization refers to the process by which viewers' responses to real violence become weaker through repeated exposure to mediated violence. In essence, the natural disgust or anxiety that individuals feel when they witness real violence is diminished for two possible reasons. First, responsive anxiety is lessened because viewers see televised violence without consequence and, thus, stop associating negative outcomes with violence. Second, repeated exposure to any witnessed event tends to lessen physiological and psychological response to it because initial shock wears off (Dexter, Penrod, Linz & Saunders, 1997; Sparks & Sparks, 2002). Certainly, medical interns in an emergency room are used to this process where desensitization to blood, for example, is a valuable outcome. With decreased anxiety and aversion, the medical professional is better able to cope with the problem at hand. However, decreased psychological (Krafka, Linz, Donnerstein & Penrod, 1997) and physiological desensitization (Linz, Donnerstein & Adams, 1989) to aggression, filmed and real, may not be a beneficial outcome for the rest of us. Researchers have long argued that one way that television violence may increase real-life aggression is by way of this emotional desensitization. For example, Thomas, Horton, Lippincott and Drabman (1977) found that children exposed to a violent media clip in an experimental setting were less responsive to peers they thought were in distress than children who had not been previously exposed to the violent clip. Furthermore, desensitization can also occur in studies that use sexually violent material (Krafka et al., 1997).

If exposure to violent or sexually explicit material can cause desensitization, then it is possible that lack of exposure to this television content can increase sensitization to it. Many who live without television strongly believe that as a result of living without television, they and their children are more sensitized to media violence that they do see. For example, Tanis McElrone, introduced in an earlier chapter, lives with her husband in Indiana and is the mother of a 2-year-old girl. It was only somewhat recently that she and her husband stopped watching television. Like many families, the birth of their daughter was the impetus for getting rid of television entirely, although it was something they had talked about doing throughout their relationship. But, like some young couples I interviewed, especially those without children, watching television was something they did together. They saw their viewing time as an opportunity to bond. Only gradually, after they had been married for several years, did they begin to perceive the time they spent in front of the television as time that did not bring them closer together. This realization led to an agreement, made between the two of them, that they would watch television only on certain evenings. Gradually, they watched less and less and eventually, when their daughter was born, they agreed to give it up entirely.

Tanis talked about this gradual shift, emphasizing that only after they had quit watching television completely did they begin to perceive their favorite program as violent, "The first year we were married, the main thing we watched was every episode of 24 and that was the one time we always watched. But since then, after we gave it up, someone gave us some tapes of the second season, and we were really affected by the violence so even that show became less appealing." In other words, a show they had always watched, one that Tanis labeled a "favorite" was perceived differently after the television had been off for some time. Tanis noted that "maybe the second season *was* more violent but part of it was that we hadn't been watching so we *saw* the violence more." In other words, by removing television exposure, they became *re*sensitized.

Families without television expressed surprise that their children were so sensitive to television content. For example, Daniel Coleman, who is the father of five children, recalled an instance when his sons were young. He and his wife decided to let them watch *The Wizard of Oz* as a special treat. Granted, this movie is a classic not only in terms of cinematography but also in its ability to create fright in generations of young children (Cantor, 2002) but their point was similar to that of other parents: their children were more susceptible to media images than they imagined other children were. In retelling the story, he seemed to recall vividly how frightened the boys were by the movie. Like many parents of nonviewing children, he also expressed concern that his children had not built up any defenses against television. He recalled, "Our boys were terrified because they hadn't been brought up with it and they were so sensitive to it. The horror. They had a tremendous sensitivity because they hadn't built up this immunity...I think there is a [desensitizing] effect and I have to believe it is a tremendous effect."

Similarly, Annie McAdams, the teacher and mother of two young children discussed in chapter 5, recalled an incident where she and her husband rented the movie *Two Brothers* for the children. In it, an adult tiger is killed by hunters, leaving two tiger cubs behind. Annie recalled that she fast-forwarded through the part with the hunters since her children were upset. Another upsetting scene arrived, and again, she had to fast-forward. By the third instance of fast-forwarding, she began to think that the process was ridiculous. "I kept saying, 'Okay, we won't watch this part but the mom goes away and...' I had to fill in so much because of what we weren't watching that it seemed crazy. We weren't even really watching it." She recalled that they watched very little of the actual movie and spent more time discussing the scary parts or fast-forwarding through the upsetting scenes. In the end, she reported that she and her husband worried that their children were *not* desensitized: "What if Alex were to go to a birthday party and accidentally see something? He'd have no defenses." But then, Annie continued, "How crazy is that? We have to toughen him up so he won't be bothered by violence and suffering? Shouldn't we be bothered by violence and suffering?"

Many individuals also reported that the longer they had gone without television exposure, the more sensitized they became. Rebecca Tanner, a mother of three living in Vermont, recalled that she had been visiting her aunt and sat in a room, reading to her 3 year old while her aunt watched television. "I flipped because they were showing burn victims on TV and I flipped. And my aunt was like: 'It was only on for a second.' And I think the longer we don't have television, the more fanatical I get about it and the more I notice it." For Rebecca Tanner, Annie McAdams, and Daniel Coleman, the problem seemed two-fold. First, they wanted to keep their children away from the violence on television. But there is a second related problem. Without television exposure and the desensitization that results, they believed that their children were more susceptible to images that they might be exposed to, perhaps unintentionally, at some later time.

Adapting to a Television World

Because of the potential for sensitization to television images due to their nonviewing, even families without television struggle with it. Most expressed a desire to keep these images away from their children. However, these same nonviewers often believed that in a culture where television is so common, some desensitization might be necessary to avoid having their children become emotionally distressed when they experience some exposure. Here, the consternation of these nonviewing parents reminded me of Sam Steinberg and Mary Peters, a family who rejected the popular culture of television by living in what they perceived as relative cultural isolation. Even as they lived without television, they wondered if they might need it on the job or to fit in with friends. They wondered if their son might need it to be part of his peer group. The larger question seems to be: How do individuals reject a single common aspect of culture, be it television, a car, western dress and yet operate smoothly in that culture?

Perhaps the best answer comes by drawing again on family systems theory. Although avoiding a common element of popular culture such as television may cause some problems, the problems are dealt with in the moment. The beliefs about television that a family holds become as important as the behavior of a particular member (e.g., talking to peers about a recently aired program). The belief becomes important enough to the identity of the family that inconveniences due to lack of television are dealt with in the moment. For example, a child who is frightened by a program at a relative's house may be soothed and the program removed. The immediate problem is solved while in the wider context of the family, the importance of the family belief system (e.g., "television violence is not for us") is maintained. In the case of the Fords, rejecting sex and violence not only keeps the problematic content out but also allows the family to maintain its image of itself as a family who "remains pure," as Charlotte Ford says. For the Hansens, it allows them to maintain the image of themselves as a family who believes that violence "is not cool. It's bad." Therefore, consistency between beliefs about television and beliefs about how best to deal with it allows for coherence in the family system. To families without television, this perceived consistency is more important than the potential inconveniences posed by living without it.

Certainly inconsistencies abound. People insist they do not watch television, but they do watch *South Park*. Families worry about the effect of television content but they use the Internet for entertainment. When these inconsistencies occur, nonviewing families—perhaps all families—have beliefs and myths and cognitive sleights-of-hand that allow them to maintain their beliefs about their family: we're moral, or we're different from other families, or we abhor violence, or we eat at the dinner table. We're *that* kind of family. And for families attempting to keep media sex and media violence out of their homes, they believe they have solved this problem by getting rid of television itself.

Chapter 7

Minimizing Consumerism

In this chapter, I review the literature on advertising, that which targets adults and that which targets children. Utilizing both the survey research and the results of the in-depth interviews, I discuss how nonviewers feel about advertising and by extension, how they feel about consumerism. Parents of children who are not exposed to commercials generally believe that their children are less materialistic than children who do watch television. I examine their responses from a family systems approach.

Concern over commercials, or more broadly, marketing targeted at children, was mentioned spontaneously by approximately 80% of the adult nonviewing respondents during the first interview. After concern over sex and violence, marketing was the most frequently mentioned content issue. Although many individuals mentioned the potential influence of commercials on children, even adults without children mentioned that living without commercials made them "think about buying stuff less often." Interestingly, of the 20 interviews with viewers, all of them parents, 100% spontaneously mentioned that commercials were a problem. They complained about trips to the grocery store where children asked for junk food that they had seen in a particular commercial. They also mentioned that their children asked for toys seen on television. Nonviewers, on the other hand, talked about their own and their children's *lack* of desire for things. Among these nonviewers and their objection to commercials, television is clearly synonymous with content, and removing that content is ultimately what removing television is all about.

In the survey portion of this study, several questions targeted the notion of consumerism. Using Likert items and a 7-point scale ranging from 1 (*strongly disagree*) to 7 (*strongly agree*), adults responded to items about how much they valued certain qualities or possessions. Among adults, nonviewers were significantly less likely to agree that wealth was important to them ($M=3.19, SD=1.25$)[1] than viewers ($M=4.14, SD=1.35$, $t=4.09$, $p<0.05$). However, there was no significant difference between nonviewers ($M=4.67$, $SD=1.50$) and viewers ($M=5.10$, $SD=1.56$) in their belief that professional success was important to them. Therefore, it appears that to some extent, nonviewers do value consumerism less than their viewing counterparts; however, they value their professional success equally. As we will discuss in this chapter, nonviewers generally believed excessive consumption was something they wanted to avoid for themselves and for their children. Among viewers, consumption itself was generally not disparaged. Whereas parents in nonviewing households complained about *consumerism* itself, parents in viewing households were more likely to complain about the *arguments* that television commercials caused between themselves and their children. The family conflict, not any underlying objection to consumption itself, seemed to drive their beliefs about commercials. Parents in viewing households wanted to eliminate the arguments with their children; they did not seem to want to eliminate their children's desire for consumer goods.

Among children, only one question addressed an aspect of consumerism. Children were asked to respond to the statement: "Having the toys that other kids have is important to me." Using a 5-point Likert scale, nonviewing children were somewhat less likely to agree ($M=2.48$, $SD=1.09$) with this statement than were viewers ($M=3.17$, $SD=1.05$; $t=2.45$, $p <0.05$), suggesting that at least for a specific issue, such as desire for toys, nonviewing might be associated with lower consumerism.

Parents of nonviewing children often commented that their children rarely asked for toys, even when circumstances required that they do. For example, one mother recalled that when her daughter Rachel was 4, she asked for only one gift for Christmas: chattering teeth, which, as far as she could tell, was not actually a toy at all. Anne, a mother of two boys ages 7 and 11, said that her relatives often asked the boys what they wanted for birthdays or Christmas. The relatives grew frustrated when her sons never seemed to come up with an answer. In sum, parents who participated in this study reported that their children did not ask for things. They claimed that their children did not ask for particular toys by name or by brand, although they might occasionally ask for a general kind of toy (e.g., a dump truck, a stuffed giraffe). Nonviewing parents also reported that their children did not ask for junk food. Although one might suspect a certain amount of social desirability in parents' responses, the responses

---

1 M (mean) represents the average score of the participants. SD (standard deviation) represents the average distance of the scores away from the mean. In other words, mean and standard deviation give us some sense of where the participants' attitudes fall in general and what the range is of those attitudes. The larger the standard deviation, the more diversity there is in their attitudes.

and even the stories themselves were very similar from parent to parent, suggesting validity.

Children as Consumers

In the United States, $2 billion are spent annually on marketing and advertising to children. Despite the enormity of that sum, it is apparently money well spent. Children's direct influence on parental purchases are estimated to be about $188 billion, with children between the ages of 4–12 spending an additional $30 billion of their own money each year (Shah, 2003). Today's marketers are interested in advertising to children for at least three reasons. First, children have their own spending money. More than ever before, children are given money to spend on toys, clothes, entertainment, meals, electronics, movies, videos, and music. Many of these decisions are made independently of an adult's input. In other words, it makes sense from a marketing perspective to advertise directly to children, tapping into, or perhaps creating, wants and desires. Second, children influence the way adults spend money. They influence household spending on food and products but they also influence decisions like choice of restaurants and even the purchase of the family car (Gunter & Furnham, 1998). Third, by reaching or creating a child customer, advertisers are potentially creating a life-long devotee (McNeal, 1992).

In other words, advertisers love children and "over the past two decades, marketers and advertisers of children's products have developed a massive and diverse spectrum of strategies to reach the child consumer" (Valkenburg & Cantor, 2002, p. 61). Although not all consumerism can be attributed to television, many parents interviewed believed strongly that their children wanted less because they did not watch television. Lynne Selridge, who will be discussed in greater detail in chapter 8, mentioned that her son rarely asked for things. She said:

> We were on the road a while ago and we never do this but we stopped at McDonald's. And we decided to get him a happy meal. And he got the little toy inside and held it up and said, "Look, Mom. Look at this little blue man." And it was Batman but he didn't know that. So that kind of innocence for consumerism is wonderful. Now he has this man he can play with and it's any man, not Batman, so it can do anything. He didn't know to ask for it but now that he has it, that toy can be anything. And I love to see him outside stacking rocks. That's what he needs, not new toys or more toys or more things.

To Lynne, without television her son was able to experience things in a less defined, more creative way. He was able to play with toys without having his play defined by the toy and he was able to play with objects, like rocks, that were not defined as toys at all. To her, lack of consumerism allowed for more creative play in general.

For others, such as Rebecca Tanner, who will be discussed in depth in chapter 12, consumerism is linked to self expression. She believes that by avoiding consumerism, she and her children are able to express themselves and be independent of what marketers tell them to be. In fact, Rebecca argues that in the US, we are in danger of having purchasing become our greatest form of self expression. As she put it, "I don't want to be what I buy." She also describes how her ideas and her attitudes emerged gradually after she stopped watching television. Her family got rid of their set seven years ago. Currently, without television and exposure to commercials, Rebecca says, "I've changed a lot of the views I hold. There's been an excavation process where I slowly realized which ideas were mine and which ones have been planted. I know more about what I like because I haven't been told and I know more about who I am because I'm not just a market niche. And now I feel like I can take responsibility for my own thoughts."

Although others who lived without television echoed Rebecca's concerns, they are certainly not the only ones to have decried the link between consumption and identity. Cook (2001) argues that as a nation, what *defines* us now is consumption—what we buy, what we wear, what car we drive. Like Rebecca's belief that she had to excavate her own ideas and extract them from the marketplace that is television, Cook argues that as a culture, we now "confuse personal autonomy with consumer behavior." In a consumer culture, the greatest freedom of choice we can imagine is the freedom to choose what to buy. He suggests that:

> The children's market works because it lives off of deeply-held beliefs about self-expression and freedom of choice—originally applied to the political sphere, and now almost inseparable from the culture of consumption. Children's commercial culture has quite successfully usurped kids' boundless creativity and personal agency, selling these back to them—and us—as "empowerment," a term that appeases parents while shielding marketers. Linking one's sense of self to the choices offered by the marketplace confuses personal autonomy with consumer behavior.

While Cook goes on to argue that selling to children and confusing self-expression with consumer behavior dates back further than the invention of television, the power of television comes from both its ubiquity and its constancy. In homes with television, advertisers can reach us at any moment.

Although the critique that modern culture rests almost solely on consumer culture is not a new one (Spring, 2003) and certainly advertisers have sought to reach adults and children long before every home was equipped with a television set, the idea that ridding yourself of television works to essentially solve, or at least minimize, that problem is a belief strongly held by those without television. They repeatedly cite their own lack of consumerism and their children's lack of desire for things. For example, Kathleen Holt has two children, Lucy who is 8 and Brad who is 4. Kathleen is mild-mannered but when she starts talking about consumerism, her normally moderate language takes a hyperbolic turn. About commercials, she says:

> I just hate them. They all try to tell me that I should buy this or buy that to have a better life. But why should I spend extra money and why would my life be better? Things are sold so easily and the stupid little things that media show to be so important, they are so unimportant. Sometimes, I get so mad because I'm not going to buy their stupid product.

Kathleen also believes that her children are less acquisitive because they do not have access to television. Kathleen argues that "Lucy almost never asks for anything. She isn't warped by the whole marketing scheme. It doesn't come up and it's nice not to be having that argument."

Is it true that advertising to children "causes arguments"? In a large scale study of 360 parent–child dyads, exposure to advertising was found to be related to family conflict. Specifically, the more exposure to advertising children had, the more purchase requests they made and the more materialistic they were. In addition, these purchase requests led to family conflict, disappointment and family dissatisfaction. Overall, families who watched more television reported having more frequent arguments about consumption, spending and purchasing. In other words, exposure to advertising is indirectly responsible for strife in the family and for unhappiness (Buijzen & Valkenburg, 2003). Perhaps, then, families without television are on to something. If exposure to advertising increases purchase requests and conflict in families with television, then are not families without it likely to have fewer conflicts about purchases? Certainly nonviewers believe this is the case. To them, their nonviewing is responsible for minimizing conflicts in the home. However, consistent with family systems theory, *beliefs* about the family and its functioning also influence actual behavior (Bochner & Eisenberg, 1987). In other words, families without television have decreased their children's and their own exposure to commercials, but they also *believe* that doing so is a worthwhile endeavor.

Recall that from a systems theory perspective, when a family operates as a system, each part of the system, including the cognitive aspects such as information from the environment and beliefs held by the family, affect its functioning. In the case of television viewing, factors external and internal to the system may influence children's consumerism. First, in a family without television, children's access to *external* information about products is limited, in some cases drastically, by their lack of access to television. Given that the average child is exposed to approximately 40,000 television advertisements per year (Kunkel & Ganz, 1992) or put another way, 110 commercials per day, it is understandable that children who are unexposed to these ads ask for the advertised products less frequently. But according to many parents interviewed, their nonviewing children often do not know what the products are. Therefore, one explanation for their relatively low consumerism is simply their low exposure to advertisements and to external information about products. As they age, children may become more exposed to products through trips to the grocery store or by information provided through friendship networks, but the direct influence of commercials is largely absent.

But *external* information is just one element in the system of the family. *Internal* factors, including parents' beliefs and their behaviors, might also affect television ownership and consumerism. In terms of beliefs, many nonviewing families believe that television causes materialism. They disapprove of materialism for themselves and for their children. They talk about the desire to curb consumption and to own fewer things. As Rebecca Tanner said, "I think people have too many clothes and I have asked people to stop giving them [her children] clothes because I think we all have enough." Therefore, *parental beliefs*, in this case anti-materialism, are likely to have a direct influence on family spending. Furthermore, systems theory argues that parent beliefs are passed down to the child and influence child behavior. Not surprisingly, then, if nonviewers avoid television specifically to minimize their own consumerism, they pass this belief on to their children in any number of ways, only one of which is eliminating television. Nonviewers may also make statements, such as Rebecca's cited above, that criticize consumption. At the time of this exchange, Rebecca's children were playing on the floor within earshot. It is possible that these remarks, as well as others made by Rebecca on separate occasions, influence her children despite the fact that the statements are not made directly to them. Therefore, family beliefs may well affect consumption but may simultaneously affect the decision to live without television.

A second internal factor related to both consumerism and television ownership is that of parent behavior. Many people whom I interviewed talked about the fact that they simply avoided shopping. One mother stated that she had "not been in a mall for more than a year." Another stated, "Sure, I go to the grocery store and [I go to the store] when the kids outgrow their sneakers, but we don't shop for fun." This, too, contributes to children's lower level of consumerism. Parents who do not take their children shopping often may indeed note that their children do not ask for things at the store. Their children simply have fewer opportunities to make purchase requests.

Overall, then, from a systems perspective, no single external feature (e.g., children's lack of exposure to commercials) can be said to affect low consumerism. Rather, low consumerism may be related to external information *and* internal family features such as parental anti-materialism, parental disapproval of shopping and parents' negative comments about consumerism. In sum, low consumerism, negative comments about consumerism, elimination of television and less time spent shopping are all part of the family system, each factor recursively influencing the others.

Ultimately, living without television is part of a coherent system that includes family beliefs and family behaviors. One outcome of this entire system is few purchase requests by the children and fewer arguments about consumption between parents and children. It is the *coherence* between beliefs and behaviors that seems to contribute to family harmony. Similarly, it is possible that in families where parents value consumption for themselves and consciously encourage it in their children, and where money is in steady supply, there are few conflicts about consumption either. Again, the coherence between family beliefs and behaviors may contribute to harmony.

As Cook (2001) points out, "Kids are keen to...adult hypocrisy, especially when they are told to hold their desires in check by a parent who is blind to her or his own materialistic impulses." In the end, it is likely that conflict results not only from children's desire to consume but also from the inconsistency between what the children want and what the adults want for them. In general, then, low consumerism in children who live without television may be only partly due to their lack of exposure to commercials. Instead, family belief systems about consumerism, family buying behaviors, and a family's decision to live without television are all likely to influence children's desire for things.

Chapter 8

Politics and Civic Engagement

This chapter discusses television news, particularly as it relates to individuals' involvement in political issues. From both the surveys and from the in-depth interviews, I argue that viewers and nonviewers have somewhat different attitudes towards politics and civic engagement. Because television news, with its expensive air time, can provide less-detailed news coverage, those who get their news from television may be less well informed than those who get their news from newspaper, radio or the Internet. To support this, I introduce Bourdieu's (1996) concept of the reality effect, which is television's ability to convince people that it is objective and true via its vivid images. I draw parallels between this and George Gerbner's theory of cultivation, which argues that the more television people watch the more their own view of reality is similar to that presented on television. Lastly, I review the findings from the survey portion of my study that suggests that viewers are more likely to keep up to date with local and national news than nonviewers, but not necessarily with national and international politics. Nonviewers are more likely to be involved in their communities by voting and volunteering their time. I discuss this final finding in terms of displacement and in terms of systems theory.

The third most frequently mentioned content issue among nonviewers was the lack of depth in news coverage about politics. News and politics came up spontaneously in 60% of the interviews with nonviewing adults but arose spontaneously in only 10% of the interviews with viewers. From these data, it appears that, whereas both viewers and nonviewers perceive sex, violence, and commercials as content problems, generally only nonviewers perceive television news to be problematic. Viewers rarely made negative comments about the content of television news. If television news did come up among viewers, it was only to mention that they watched it. Therefore, nonviewers are generally dissatisfied with the depth and quality of television news that they have seen. This objection to television assumes that the defining feature of television is its content. In this chapter, I discuss nonviewers' perceptions of television news and consider whether or not television can adequately provide for viewers' information needs.

From the survey portion of the study, it appears that viewers and nonviewers are keeping up with politics and news in somewhat different arenas and these differences may reflect differences in where they get their news. Viewers feel more informed about local news and politics and about popular culture than nonviewers but there are no differences in how well-informed viewers and nonviewers feel about international news and politics. Furthermore, nonviewers report voting in elections more than viewers and volunteer their time in their communities to a greater degree. Overall, then, nonviewers are getting their news from different places than viewers and are perhaps more engaged in the political process. Therefore, in the latter portion of this chapter, I draw on work by Putnum (2000) and others to make links between media use, political knowledge and civic engagement.

Lynne and Jonathan Selridge

Lynne and Jonathan Selridge both come from military families. Jonathan's father is a retired Army nurse, and Lynne's father is an Air Force chaplain who is still on active duty. One of Jonathan's brothers is an Army scout with the 101st Airborne Division and currently serving his second tour in Iraq. Jonathan's other brother is also in the military, serving as an Air Force mechanic stationed in South Korea. So it is perhaps no coincidence that Lynne and Jonathan found each other. They share not only similar backgrounds but a similar tendency to question things: ideas, principles, authority. Lynne admits that she's struggling with her religious beliefs because she questions some of the assumptions, the rules and the doctrines. Similarly, Jonathan himself works in one of the few places in the military where questioning authority, rather than following it, is encouraged. He is a sergeant in the Air Force, but more specifically, he is an Explosive Ordnance Disposal Technician. In other words, he is sent places to identify and defuse bombs, and, as he pointed out, the technicians often call the shots in these situations.

When we talk about what Jonathan does, Lynne is quick to make the connection between what Jonathan does and how he thinks—how both of them think. She says, "In any other military career, that sort of thing [questioning authority] is unacceptable and the lower-ranking men just blindly follow orders, especially orders from an officer. In what Jonathan does, it's very different. The techs are taught to be inventive, assertive and encouraged to think for themselves. It's those qualities that keep them from getting killed on the job." Because of this shared tendency, they talk about many issues as well. Lynne muses about the discussions they have. "We talk a lot about what we read," she says. "I'll read something during the day and we'll e-mail each other back and forth about it. Or we'll talk about it in the evening. We'll really analyze things and I feel like we're really weird to have those conversations. I don't know if other people converse like that." This tendency to question and analyze things ultimately contributed to their decision to give up television.

Giving it up happened gradually but arose in part from their shared objection to, as Lynne calls it, "blindly following what we hear." Jonathan recalls that, although they had considered television a problem for nearly a decade, their ideas solidified several years ago. In discussing it, he says that, "I was in this used book store and I found this copy of this book: *Amusing Ourselves to Death*. By then we'd pretty much given it [television] up. But I read the book and then I gave it to Lynne and she read it. And it really hit some of the ideas we'd been talking about." They object to several aspects of television, including the time it takes. However, their strongest shared objection is the belief that television takes complex political ideas and frames them simply, avoiding complexity and grey areas. As Lynne says of herself and her political opinions, "people line up on one side or the other and I see more tangents. I feel like there's so much grey."

The stories Lynne and Jonathan tell often contrast what others tell them is right with their own beliefs. Lynne recalled disagreeing with her physician on a few occasions about his recommendations for her and, later, for her young son. She also recounts another story, originally told to her by Jonathan. In it, she herself makes the connection between their jobs, their beliefs, their politics and, ultimately, their decision to reject television. "Several years ago, Jonathan had an incident where he was in a bomb suit defusing something and looked up to see a one-star general standing there watching him. He said, 'Sir, look at how I'm dressed, and then look at how you're dressed. One of us is very wrong.' The general immediately backed off." And to Lynne, it is all connected. She went on to say:

> It does relate to politics. Just as Jonathan is not awed by someone's military rank, he is similarly not awed by those in political power. If they don't back their words and reputation with solid actions, he has very little respect for them. He has even less respect for the television commentators who feed on the political world. At the 2000 Republican National Convention, Jonathan was assigned to do hand-searches of the various camera and equipment bags that the broadcast journalists were bringing into the arena. He was disgusted by the rude and arrogant behavior of the various famous talking heads and was

appalled that people around the nation would be glued to their TVs that very night soaking up the words of those commentators, as if they were some sort of intellectual gods.

For Lynne and Jonathan, what they perceive as their difference from others does not spread across their entire lives. They live in an unassuming, yellow one-story house that looks nearly identical to the two houses on either side, in a neighborhood of similar homes. As she says, they would rather put their money into their retirement plan than into their home-decorating projects. They are not trying to be different. They are not trying to be unique or counter-cultural. Their difference, muses Lynne, comes from some internal struggle and not for some need to mark themselves as exclusive. As Lynne describes herself, it is her inner life that feels different, and not all of the trappings that go with it. She said, "When I'm out in the world, I interact just fine, but when I think of how we are at home privately, or how I think on the inside, I think our attitudes are so different."

In various conversations and interactions with Lynne and Jonathan, the connection between who they are and what they do becomes clear. For both, it is the critical eye toward authority and information that motivates many of their decisions, choices and behaviors. For Jonathan, it comes out in his approach to his job. For Lynne, it comes out in her current struggle with her religion. For both of them, it is intimately related to politics and ultimately led them to give up television. For them, television, and the way that it provides a false sense of authority and knowledge, goes against their beliefs and their understanding of how political thought is best approached. As Jonathan argued, "Television speaks to the worst in us. It hits us at an emotional level and the whole format doesn't encourage the rational mind."

Television as Authority

For a majority of Americans, their primary contact with news and politics is via television (Pew Research Center, 2005). Although the Internet is achieving growing importance and newspapers, while usage is down, still provide access to political information, it is television that puts a living, moving face on the news. However, as McLeod, Kosicki and McLeod (2002) argue, politicians "learn to speak in brief sound bites, and advertisements are increasingly limited in length. Neither affords the opportunity for any sustained political reasoning, even if the candidates were inclined to reason" (p. 221). In other words, television, by virtue of its brief sound bites and reliance on images, is not a medium that lends itself easily or willingly to sustained political discourse on complex and nuanced issues. Therefore, one problem with television as a source of political information is that, as a medium, it may be ill-suited to conveying multiple points of view or the finer details and minor distinctions that are so important in political and social issues.

In addition to the images themselves, the viewers' own processing strategies may affect how television news becomes an individual's political reality. Again, critical scholars and social scientists offer support for the role of television in influencing our social realities. Consider Bourdieu (1996) who argues, "The political dangers inherent in the ordinary use of television have to do with the fact that images have the peculiar capacity to produce what literary critics call a reality effect. They show things and make people believe in what they show" (p. 21). According to Bourdieu, television's ability to convince us that what is shown and what is said is somehow a direct and unadulterated version of truth creates a situation in which viewers accept messages without the critical stance that is necessary to make decisions about complex issues. Television, or more specifically television news relating to politics, does not present us with news that is framed as a version of what happened. Rather, television news is framed as fact. Bourdieu further argues that "one thing leads to another and ultimately, television, which claims to record reality, creates it instead. We are getting closer and closer to the point where the social world is primarily described—and in a sense prescribed—by television" (p. 22). In other words, if television presents a *version* of reality, but calls it reality, it has, in an instant, taken a bias and given it roots.

Although Bourdieu's (1996) argument is incendiary, quantitative research has supported his theoretical positions. Take, for example, cultivation theory (Gerbner, 1969). Cultivation theory is one of the most frequently cited theories in the media effects literature. Its straightforward premise argues that the more television we watch, the more our view of reality begins to match the one presented on television. Although cultivation initially focused on television violence, suggesting that the excess of violence on television contributed to viewers' belief that the world was a mean and frightening place, more recent research has examined many aspects of television reality (Gerbner, Gross, Morgan, Signorielli & Shanahan, 2002). Empirical research on the cultivation effect generally finds support for a correlation between television exposure and perceptions of the real world. Whereas the effect of fictional programming on social reality perceptions may not directly relate to news exposure—because even the greatest cynic would hold that news conforms to at least some conventions of nonfiction—cultivation theory is relevant in attempting to understand how all television informs our political reality.

For example, crime stories that appear in local news may report real events; however, the frequency with which they appear on the news may result in viewers' over-estimations of crime frequency in their community. This in turn may influence behavior, such as whether audiences vote for a candidate with a platform based on curbing crime or improving education. In fact, social reality perceptions that have been cultivated by television have been shown to influence actual behavior related to those perceptions (Nabi & Sullivan, 2001). Therefore, quantitative data lends support to what Bordieu (1996) referred to as a "reality effect."

How does this effect occur? Shrum (2001) has argued for a heuristic processing model of television effects. This model suggests that television exposure can affect the cognitive accessibility of a construct (e.g., frequency of crime in a community) and that individuals tend to process information heuristically. That is, when heavy viewers are attempting to retrieve social information from memory, information about that topic may have come from television. The ease of accessibility of television information is greater among heavy viewers. Furthermore, information is retrieved in this way because we tend to process and retrieve information heuristically, making it likely that we use television exemplars, even fictional ones, unless motivated to engage in a more systematic memory search. Both heuristic processing and the accessibility of information in memory make it likely that heavy viewers, as compared to their lighter viewing counterparts, experience the cultivation effect. Overall then, television might hinder our understanding of complex political issues due to both characteristics of the medium and characteristics of the viewers' cognitive processing. The medium is responsible for its preference for short sound bites—a preference that encourages politicians to use them in the first place. The human processing mechanism is responsible for its own preference—that of heuristic processing. When combined, complexity stands a slim chance of making it through the political sphere, over the airwaves and into the thinking, assessing, judging mechanism of the American voter. The simple "truths" of television stand a much better chance.

In the end, the problem is not only that television portrays a specific version of reality, one that is guided by commercial interests rather than a true desire to inform the public, or that humans tend to process in heuristic ways that result in a social reality cultivated by television exposure. Rather, the problem exists in the interplay between television and the viewer. "Public opinion, argued Lippmann (1922), responds not to the environment but to the psuedoenvironment constructed by the news media" (McCombs & Reynolds, 2002, p. 2). For public opinion to be shifted, to move, or to even *exist* in response to an event, a public must first be informed. That information, even in cases where it is discovered through interpersonal channels, is initially rooted in some mediated channel. What started as a real event becomes a pseudoevent when it is reported on by the news media. Even when bias is kept to a minimum, it still exists to some extent.

But the next step is perhaps even more important. The event must go from a pseudoevent back to a real event when it is taken in by audiences. Certainly they do not approach it blindly or without question. But some of the general textures of the pseudoevent may remain and live on as the event. From event to pseudoevent, back to event, we "know" our politics and our news because, as Bourdieu (1996) argued:

> Every word the television news people use, often without thinking and with no idea of the difficulty and the seriousness of the subjects they are talking about or the responsibilities they assume by talking about them in front of the thousands of people who watch the news without understanding what they see and without understanding that they don't understand. Because these words do things. They make things. (p. 20)

Bourdieu's perspective of viewers is pessimistic. He believed that they do not understand what they see, and worse, do not understand that they do not understand. However, many nonviewers feel that they are not a part of Bourdieu's non-understanding masses. They point out that they are particularly critical of news and often question it as a valid and unbiased way of getting political information. Kyle Neff, the 31-year-old artist living in Boston, worries about the "corporate financial backbone" of television and what effect that has on the news. He would prefer it if television were a "public forum. Then I'd feel like I was getting a slice of real political information rather than what someone has spoon-fed me for their own purposes," he says. Kyle also argues that news and entertainment are combined in such a way that it is unclear if news is meant to inform or entertain. He argues, "If it is supposed to entertain, how can I trust that its other goal, to inform me, isn't being overshadowed?" This is, according to Kyle, one of the reasons he does not watch television. Not only does he not enjoy it, he does not trust it.

Television News, Depth, and Lulling Ourselves into Apathy

So what is the objection to mediated news, especially when it comes from television? Perhaps the biggest criticism, shared by many nonviewers, is that television news simply lacks depth. Jonathan Selridge says he does not watch television news despite his avid and personal interest in politics because in the 30 minutes it might take him to watch a television newscast, he can become more fully informed about more topics by getting news from a newspaper or the Internet. Conversely, he can get the coverage of television news in much less time. "All those hours in front of the TV, those are wasted hours. People say 'where do you get your news?' I go to the Internet and I get 30 minutes worth of TV news in two minutes," he says.

Lynne is also frustrated with television news, but for her, the problem is with the quality of coverage. So instead, she surfs the Internet to find full transcripts on the Library of Congress Web site; she actively hunts down conflicting stories so that the opinions she arrives at are, as she calls them, "[her] own and not formed by some commentator." "She is a wonderful researcher," says Jonathan. It is all of the additional research that allows Lynne to feel comfortable in her own positions, even if they are inconsistent with one political "side" or the other, or sometimes both. The news, which to her provides only one side of the issue, is not capable of really informing viewers about what they need to know. She says, "The shortness of a news story is terrible. On TV you cannot capture anything in depth. I'll read a headline and if I'm interested, I'll go to the Library of Congress and read the transcript and on TV you can't get that depth and really the depth makes all the difference."

So why does television news seem to lack depth of coverage? Why is it that many nonviewers believe that it can't possibly keep them politically informed? Although the answers to that question are complex, McLeod et al. (2002) explain that the reasons stem predominantly from economic pressures. Prior to the advent of cable, television news was piped into living rooms across America on just a few network stations. There were newspapers to be read as well, but for those who enjoyed a dose of television news, they were forced to select from just those three broadcast networks (with FOX arriving on the scene somewhat later). Audiences were plentiful. With the expansion of cable, and then of the Internet, fewer people are left relying on network news which translates into massive loss in revenues for those networks. With operating budgets down and fewer resources available for news production, how can news still be efficiently produced? Simply this: news comes less and less from costly reliance on in-depth reporting and instead comes more and more from cheaper sources such as press releases and press conferences. It is cheaper to send one reporter to one press conference than it is to have a news team spending days hunting down various sources to put together an in-depth, well-researched report. Cheap news is single-source news. McLeod et al. (2002) further argue that:

> Although concentration of media ownership has been seen as a problem for more than half a century, recent corporate takeovers have added to the problem. News has increasingly come under the control of executives whose values are shaped by their experiences in financial or entertainment circles. This leads to attempts to make

the news more appealing to broader audiences, prompting stronger demands for entertainment values in story selection and structure. (p. 222)

So, as Kyle Neff pointed out earlier, news is becoming entertainment, or as he succinctly put it, "They combine entertainment with news and it drives me mad."

So the most obvious problem with combining news and entertainment, or even replacing news with entertaining tidbits that have elements of news, is that the public is less informed. Neil Postman (1985) argued more than 20 years ago in *Amusing Ourselves to Death*, that the nature of television makes it practically impossible to convey news with any in-depth coverage and that at any rate, we desire entertainment so much that we do not want in-depth coverage, anyway. He argues that, first, a news show is a:

> ...stylized dramatic performance whose content has been staged largely to entertain. [This is] reinforced by several other features, including the fact that the average length of any story is forty-five seconds. While brevity does not necessarily convey triviality, in this case it clearly does. It is simply not possible to convey a sense of seriousness about any event if its implications are exhausted in less than one minute's time. In fact, it is quite obvious that TV news has no intention of suggesting that any story has any implications, for that would require viewers to continue to think about it when it is done and therefore obstruct their attending to the next story that waits panting in the wings. (p. 103)

Therefore, according to Postman, one problem with news is that, as a medium, it is incapable of providing in-depth coverage because of its financial obligation to keep us watching. It is therefore necessary to keep it short and move on to the next item. However, Postman argues that this is not the only issue. The second one is even more problematic.

Not only do financial constraints turn news into entertainment, but, according to Postman (1985), we actually prefer it that way. Simple information is lighter and more pleasant than the complexities of politics. It is easier to digest and it does not overwhelm us. Postman concludes by arguing

> there are two ways by which the spirit of a culture may be shriveled. In the first—the Orwellian—culture becomes a prison. In the second— the Huxleyan—culture becomes a burlesque...In the Huxleyan

prophecy, Big Brother does not watch us by choice. We watch him, by ours. (p. 155)

In other words, we are lulled into *not* wanting to know more. We have been amused into apathy. So this two-fold problem points us in a particular direction: once we have been lulled into apathy, and entertainment gets better ratings than real, in-depth coverage, and once we believe the news because of the reality effect that is before us, then our decisions and our political beliefs are shaped, of all things, by a very real war indeed. The political beliefs of the majority are shaped by television ratings wars.

And who relies more on what the majority of people believe than politicians? Their very livelihood, their election to and tenure in office rests on agreeing with what most Americans believe. Therefore, what ultimately guides policy decisions? Jonathan Selridge believes it is television. He strongly believes that his life is dictated by television news. It is not, he says, that well-reasoned politicians are making policy decisions that are good for the country, or the economy or for him. Rather, policy, he believes, is influenced by television ratings.

Perhaps because of the inherently dangerous nature of what he does and because he works for the US military, it is interesting to hear Jonathan critique it and to critique the media that is our conduit to the government. After all, policy decisions regarding war, for example, affect him in ways that find him flying off to Rome, or Botswana, or currently, Iraq. For him, media act as the intermediary between his employer, who makes decisions about his life, and the constituents who vote in or out various potential employers. And he feels strongly about this. He explains: "I'm in the military. I'm on the bomb squad. It's my ass on the line when a policy decision is made." But Jonathan goes on to critique not just the policy but what goes into the making of those decisions. He says:

> When those national decisions, that discourse is made via TV—think about it—people get their information from the TV and then they don't think as much about what is really going on in the world. Instead, they get it from TV and they don't even have time to think about it because it's just continually blasting messages...people don't question enough the motivation of speakers. And the motive of everyone on TV, the producers and directors and commentators, is to get the ratings. And then politicians have to go off of what polls say so they're making decisions based on decisions that are made by people who are deciding based on ratings.

Here, Jonathan becomes frustrated, not just by the line of reasoning, but by what he sees as the inevitable conclusion. "So I get to go out there.

I'm out there based on ratings and what can you do?" he says. "We're a democracy but really when everyone gets everything from television, you have to wonder who is really in charge."

Jonathan's thread is a complex one, but not unreasonable. Ultimately, he argues, some combination of information and entertainment directs the course of his world. In a better world, full of our better selves, politicians would have beliefs that, in their view, would best guide the social, political and economic forces of the world around us. News would really report national and world events of importance, including the opinions of and decisions made by international leaders. Citizens would vote based on this information. Instead, we watch what entertains us, resulting in higher ratings for infotainment. Entertaining news informs our decisions, resulting in what is known as "public opinion," and politicians listen to public opinion. Is Jonathan's belief that his work on the bomb squad is influenced by television ratings really such a stretch? Although it may be a simplification, it has, like many straightforward explanations, the beauty of parsimony.

Overall, many nonviewers, like Jonathan and Lynne, indicated that before they gave up television entirely, they faced a growing frustration with the quality of television news. This led them not only to give up television but in some cases to seek out news from other sources. As a result, they state that they are less up to date on local issues, national news and popular culture. However, they do seem to keep up to date with national politics and international news. In the next section, I discuss viewers' and nonviewers' reported *knowledge* of politics and news, their civic *involvement* and the connection between the two.

Exposure to News and Civic Engagement

In the surveys, I asked viewers and nonviewers to report how much they knew about and kept up to date with local news and local politics, national news and national politics, and international news and politics. I also asked if they voted in political elections, volunteered time in their community and felt community involvement was important to them. Across most measures, there were differences between viewers and nonviewers on these items. Overall, nonviewers report being less informed than viewers about local news and politics, national news and popular culture. They do not report being less informed than viewers about politics at the national and international level, however (see Figure 8.1). Furthermore, nonviewers are somewhat more involved in their communities, one indicator of overall civic involvement, and they are somewhat more likely to vote in political elections than viewers. Specifically, nonviewers were significantly more likely to report that involvement in the community was important

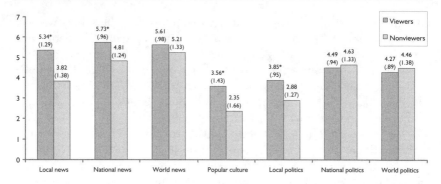

Figure 8.1 Means and standard deviations for viewers and nonviewers on exposure to news and political information

Note: (*) indicates that means are significantly different at $p < 0.05$ for viewers vs. nonviewers

to them ($M=5.03$, $SD=0.95$) than viewers ($M=4.11$, $SD=1.02$; $t=5.19$, $p < 0.05$); nonviewers were more likely to agree that politics were important to them ($M=4.41$, $SD=1.46$) than viewers ($M=3.76$, $SD=1.33$; $t=2.55$, $p < 0.05$); and nonviewers were more likely to agree that they voted in political elections ($M=5.01$, $SD=1.66$) than viewers ($M=4.09$, $SD=1.33$; $t=1.75$, $p < 0.05$). Therefore, the pattern of differences seems to suggest that viewers are more likely to keep up to date with local and national news than nonviewers, but not necessarily with national and international politics. Furthermore, nonviewers are more likely to be involved in their communities by voting and volunteering their time.

Jonathan's and Lynne's attitudes may offer insight into the survey results. If nonviewers are frustrated with the depth of television news, they may seek out sources such as the Internet or NPR because they believe these sources offer better news coverage. However, as a consequence of avoiding television *news*, in particular local television news, nonviewers reported they were less informed about *local* politics. Therefore, as I will discuss shortly in greater detail, nonviewers' preference for particular news sources may lead them to report being more informed about national and international news, but may simultaneously leave them less informed about local issues that are not covered by these sources.

What do these differences suggest? The first findings, concerning individuals' patterns of knowledge, are related to the fact that many nonviewers gain access to information from the radio (NPR was the only source mentioned by name), newspapers, news magazines, or the Internet. Viewers, on the other hand, mention television news, often as their primary source, although they mention other media as well. The differences in knowledge, therefore, derive from the different foci of these media. NPR, the Internet, and some newspapers are likely to focus on national politics or international events, offering the nonviewers who use them a supply of information about national and international politics. Viewers, however, receive a proportion of their news from television and therefore receive different content. Although television news provides information about national and international politics, local news stations obviously carry more local information or give their national stories a local bent (Brosius & Kepplinger, 1990). Therefore, nonviewers may be more apt to miss coverage of local issues because they are not watching local television news. As for differences in knowledge of popular culture, even national television news, such as the CBS nightly news, mentioned the wedding of celebrity couple Tom Cruise and Katie Holmes, something that was not covered by NPR. Therefore, knowledge obtained about issues—local, international and Hollywood—is at least partly determined by where one gets information.

However, the survey results also suggest that viewers and nonviewers are somewhat different in other ways. If voting and volunteering are indicators of civic involvement, then how is it that nonviewers, who report knowing *less* about local issues than viewers, are actually more involved? Perhaps news and political knowledge are distinct from engagement. Perhaps the former are useful only to the extent that they inform the latter. Perhaps individuals can be exposed to news but remain unconnected to it.

Several scholars (e.g., McLeod et al., 1996; Putnum, 2000; Shah, 1998) have examined the relationship between television exposure, knowledge and civic engagement. Whereas knowledge of news and politics was initially seen as an indicator of engagement, many scholars have begun to distinguish between political information consumed by the public, and political and civic *engagement* by that public. In fact, some researchers have argued that indeed, television—even television news—has served to erode civic engagement (Putnum, 2000). Unlike Postman (1985), who argues that the negative effects of television stem predominantly from its inability to adequately provide detailed information which would ultimately generate rational discourse, Putnum argues instead that simple lack of time for civic involvement among viewers—and not lack of knowledge—is to blame. He suggests that people spend too much time watching television, leaving them socially isolated and without time for real civic involvement. From this perspective, the television world is not the Huxleyan burlesque, luring potentially informed voters with its inane appeal. Instead, television is a simple habit, consuming viewers' time and luring them away from real connections with real people in real communities. Even time spent learning about the goings-on of the world does not automatically connect viewers to that world. We can watch, unmoved.

In fact, it is possible that the sheer volume of information available on television news makes viewers feel less powerful. So much is going on that one viewer could not possibly affect change. Unlike the somewhat more selective search of the Internet reader or the newspaper peruser, like Lynne Selridge, the television news viewer is bombarded by information. In this case, less information, or at least purposefully sought information, may be more. That targeted, though limited, information may ultimately empower the audience, while the television news viewer may simply drown in disconnected bits of information. In fact, empirical research does suggest a link between exposure to specific media content and civic engagement. Therefore, more of everything does not make a fully informed person.

Several empirical studies have tested the link between television exposure, content type, political knowledge, and civic engagement. Whereas some authors have found support for Putnum's (2000) contention, arguing that television news decreases viewers' understanding of the political process (Bok, 2001), others have found that exposure to television news is *positively* correlated with knowledge (e.g., McLeod et al., 1996) and with political interest (Shah, 1998). Therefore, it is somewhat unclear whether exposure to television news causes engagement, knowledge, or interest. How then do we make sense of these seemingly contradictory pieces of information? To do so, two issues must be kept in mind. First, media scholars have long recognized that in measuring television exposure, content matters, and not all content is created equal, not even all news content. Second, political knowledge and political engagement are distinct constructs. While political knowledge is an important component of engagement, it is ultimately not a sufficient condition to achieve it. Therefore, we must turn to research that has considered these issues.

Hooghe (2003) examined both the amount of television viewers consumed and the type of programming watched. He also simultaneously looked at political attitudes and time spent in civic activities. He found that while moderate amounts of viewing did not seem to erode time spent in community activities, spending more than 20 hours a week in front of a television did seem to have a corrosive effect. This suggests that Putnum's (2000) argument that television has destroyed civic engagement may be an overstatement. Only when television significantly cuts into free time does it also detract from community involvement. However, Hooghe also found that exposure to entertainment television seemed to contribute to viewers' feeling of political disengagement and powerlessness; whereas exposure to news contributed to political empowerment. Overall, then, an active political citizen might spend some time with television, perhaps on news and current affairs programming, but then spend additional time involved in community activities.

Ultimately, it may be that nonviewers stress the importance of politics and community involvement in their lives yet live without television because, like the viewers in Hooghe's (2003) study, many access news and political information from sources other than television. Although some nonviewers were Luddites, opposing technology and technological change based on reason or gut, and some were happy to reject knowledge of the world beyond their own street, many more simply turned to other media to keep politically informed. In fact, some were news junkies, like James Stein, a high school teacher who, by his own admission, was something of an Internet addict, reading at least two or three newspapers online every day. Lynne Selridge reads transcripts that she gets online from the Library of Congress. Many reported getting their news from NPR at least twice a day and still others read newspapers. In other words, for many, the objection was not to news, just the way that it is portrayed on television. Many are attempting to take Lynne's approach when she says, "Now, I finally think that my opinions about politics have not been formed by a commentator."

In the end, civic engagement seems to come from at least two sources. As Hooghe (2003) and others (e.g., Cappella & Jamieson, 1997) have argued, a sense of political empowerment is necessary to engage in the political process and in civic activities. In addition, time to be involved, or at least the perception that one has time, is needed. Many of the nonviewers felt that by giving up television, and getting their news from other sources, they have gained both. In charge of their political educations, they felt empowered to seek out the information they wanted. Of course the greater amount of free time provided them with a sense of freedom to pursue community involvement.

Although those who have argued in favor of media literacy have done so convincingly (e.g., Potter, 2005), giving up television as a means of becoming more politically and civically engaged is not an absurd solution to be undertaken only by a handful of eccentrics. Consider the following arguments: television news is driven by the desire to increase market share; therefore, it must often fall back on simple strategies to grab and hold the audience's attention. Like tabloid news, television news must focus on things that can incite enough curiosity to keep us watching, but not so much analysis that it might either be costly to produce or worse— turn off the viewers who disagree. Television news, to keep us watching, must bathe us in benign curiosities. Furthermore, exposure to fictional programming does take time. Although Putnum's (2000) argument that television has destroyed civic involvement may be excessive, the finding that exposure to television entertainment contributes to feelings of political powerlessness is not. Therefore, civic engagement can best come from in-depth news coverage and less from entertainment programming of the kind that is currently being aired. How can this be achieved? Postman (1985) argued that

> We must, as a start, not delude ourselves with preposterous notions such as the straight Luddite position as outlined, for example, in Jerry Mander's *Four Arguments for the Elimination of Television*. Americans will not shut down any part of their technological apparatus, and to suggest that they do so is to make no suggestion at all. (p. 158)

However, for some Americans, most notably those interviewed here as well as those interviewed in previous research on this topic (e.g., Brock, 2001; Foss & Alexander, 1996; Zinmeister, 1997), getting rid of television *is* a solution and one that they have voluntarily undertaken. For some, getting rid of the "apparatus" is not in the least preposterous. Instead, it is the most reasonable solution of all.

Part III
Television as Medium

In Part III of the book, I include the chapters that present television as a medium—one that potentially interferes with our use of time, interferes with our social interactions and may cause children, by its very presence, to develop less creative imaginations. The participants seem to believe, and the survey research cited in this section seems to concur, that television is not necessarily its content, but its mere presence, potentially on-going. It is this presence that nonviewers object to and it is this intruder that they believe they have eliminated from their lives. In this section, I introduce the concept of autonomous children, who, according to their parents, have developed this autonomy because they do not have television to fall back on. The following chapters present time use as it relates to viewers and nonviewers and I discuss the concept of creativity, which parents believe develops more fully in children who are raised without the medium of television. Lastly, I discuss those nonviewers who believe that television interferes with what they refer to as "real life."

Chapter 9

Autonomous Children

In this chapter, I use the words of the participants to introduce the concept of autonomous children. Parents often referred to their nonviewing children as "easy," or "independent," or "autonomous." In recalling their experiences as parents, they report that without television as an easy source of entertainment, their children have become very good at entertaining themselves. They also report, that as parents, they have not been able to rely on television as a babysitter and have, therefore, become better able to steer their children towards other, more independent activities. To frame these responses, I consider the research on children, television exposure and attention span. I also review recent findings on a possible link between television exposure and Attention Deficit Disorder. Lastly, I discuss family systems theory which predicts that parents' expectations for their children's behavior can affect children's actual behavior. Using systems theory, then, it is possible that children's behavior is affected by the expectations of their nonvieweing parents, and not by nonviewing per se.

Many nonviewing parents expressed that raising their children without television has benefited them in the long run. Without television as a constant and easy entertainer, their children have learned to entertain themselves, showing greater independence and autonomy. For these parents, content is less the issue than television's potentially continuous, ever-available nature. As a medium, they believe television hinders children's ability to become independent. Although many parents of viewing preschoolers see the immediate benefit of television as a babysitter (Kunkel et al., 1999), nonviewing parents believe that with easy access to television and its potentially constant stream of images, children's attention spans may be shortened. Of the 72 nonviewing adults interviewed, 63 were parents with children living at home. Of these 63, 50 of them (79%) mentioned that without television their children were what might broadly be called more autonomous. They used words like "easier," "easily entertained," or "more independent." Parents mentioned longer attention spans that resulted in less need for parents to intervene. Among the parents whose children did watch television, half mentioned that television made their children "irritable," "difficult," or shortened their attention spans. However, all of the viewing parents mentioned that television was or had been an invaluable babysitter. In this chapter, we explore the concept of "easier children" and its possible relationship to television exposure. In this chapter, and in the following three chapters, television is defined as a medium.

Natalie, Mike, Rachel, and Levi

Natalie Carlson pulls up in her blue Subaru wagon with its local food co-op stickers on the bumper and spill of boxes in the back. She tells me that her husband Mike and children Rachel and Levi are at a school function and, opening her front gate, informs me that they should be home any minute. As we make our way into the house, Natalie offers me tea and a biscotti. "I made them" she says, and adds "but not just for this." I wonder if this is to help me feel welcome or assure me that she is not overly concerned about this visit—perhaps a bit of both.

Natalie is 38, tall, lean and dressed in jeans, a sweater and a pair of clogs. Her brown hair is pulled back in a braid. The kitchen in which we sit has broad, exposed beams in the ceiling, a woodstove in the corner and a round, wooden table. She has a calm air and moves at an unhurried, even pace. Just as the water starts to boil, her husband Mike comes in with Rachel and Levi trailing behind. Everyone struggles out of their coats and boots. More tea is made. Natalie asks about the outing and Rachel, Levi and Mike begin to answer at once. Rachel and Levi trail off and Mike gives a brief accounting.

Finally, we all settle down at the kitchen table. The family assembled, I notice how similar they all look—not just Rachel and her brother but the entire family. Thirteen, with long brown hair and blue eyes, Rachel is a carbon copy of her mother down to the long silver beaded earrings. She has the same self-contained calmness, sitting at the edge of her chair throughout most of our first 90-minute interview. Levi, 8, also sits quietly through the interview. He gets up a few times to pour himself more tea, but always returns and settles down once again.

Natalie has lived without television for 20 years, Mike for somewhat less, although both agree that they have lived without television for most of their marriage. What they are not sure of is how, exactly, the decision was made. For Natalie, she thinks it may have been when she moved out of her mother's house and went away to college at 18, well before she met Mike. Because she was "poor and busy," as she puts it, she just did not think about TV—she did not bother to get one. Recalling her college years, she thinks most people in her dorm did not have TV.

She also recalls, as some people in this study reported, watching so much TV as a child that it caused somewhat of a boomerang effect. Having grown up with a single parent who was stressed for time, her mother may have needed TV as a babysitter at times, or simply felt too tired at the end of the day to do much else. "I remember once saying to my mom," recalls Natalie, "'We don't do anything together.' And she said, 'Well, we watch TV together.' And I said, 'Huh? Are you kidding me!?' Maybe," Natalie muses, "that is what changed my mind about TV."

Mike also grew up in a house where the TV was often on. "Yeah," he recalls, "I watched it a lot." He also thinks this may be part of the reason why TV is something he does not want in his life, especially for his children. But how they came to agree on this point, whether it was a conscious decision, or not, neither seems to recall clearly. When I ask them if they agreed about not having TV in their house, a conversation erupts, one that I heard over and over again in kitchens, living rooms, and across phone lines. Natalie clarifies for me that they *do* have a television, kept in their bedroom, not hooked up to anything, and used to watch an occasional movie.

Mike and Natalie spend some time discussing exactly when they made the decision not to have a television. They walked through their dating years, various apartments they had rented, noting in each if they had a small set, where it was kept ("in a closet in one apartment, but then that one broke and we didn't replace it for a while"). Finally, Mike starts talking not about the instrument called television, but the concept of television—living in a home where people "watch television." He says that although they have had a small TV (usually kept in a closet) and also *not* had a TV, what became important to them was not the television set but how they approached it, treated it, and what they wanted to do with it. The focus of the discussions he and Natalie had was the role TV would play in their lives. Like many nonviewers, they do not perceive television to be the set; rather, they define it in accord with the tripartite model. In Mike and Natalie's case, they see it as a medium.

To them, television's main characteristic is its ability to interfere with family life. By leaving the set in a closet, and not using it for broadcast or cable programs, they perceive that television loses its power to disrupt their lives, and in fact, ceases to *be* television. After all, they identify themselves as living without television despite the set that sits in their bedroom. To families like the Carlsons, when someone must haul the television out to watch a video and put it back afterwards, the perceived power no longer belongs to the television, but to the user.

For many nonviewers who do own a television set, where that set is kept becomes very important. Estania and Sam kept their set under what they called a shroud; many families kept the set in a closet. Natalie and

Mike keep it in their bedroom, because, they say, "It shouldn't be where everyone is all the time." Because televisions can define family space (Silverstone, 1994) by drawing members to it, it is often placed in central location in viewing homes, with couches and chairs turned towards it. In fact, in each viewing home I visited, the seating arrangement in the living room was set up for optimal viewing. Of the nonviewing families who owned sets, especially those who thought of television as a medium, all of them kept their televisions hidden, making it difficult to access them. By removing television from the center of the room, they not only minimized its importance, but also, in their eyes, removed its very status as a television. Keeping a television set peripherally located in the home may also help retain a family's perception of itself as nonviewing, while it helps redefine important family activities.

Many nonviewing families referred to the importance of their living room or kitchen table as the place they talked, read or played games. "We always play Scrabble at the kitchen table," one father of three remarked. "It's funny," stated a mother of two toddlers, "People walk into the living room and they look around. I can tell they know something is missing. Maybe they don't know what it is. But for us, that room is for talking and reading, not for staring at a TV." Therefore, activities define family space and to the extent that a television set is the center of focus in a room, it also identifies that activity as primary. In families without television, chairs and couches most often faced each other.

Perceived Convenience

When Natalie and Mike discuss television, many of their conversations are about their family or about the children. Natalie remarks that if they were going to get access to broadcast or cable television, it would have been when the kids were younger, when television could have been an easy babysitter. Now that the kids are no longer preschoolers, it seems unlikely that they will start watching TV. Like many parents, Natalie noted that when Rachel and Levi were younger, having a television might have been a convenience. Similarly, Lily Dawson, a parent with a 2-year-old girl, described it this way: "It's not always easy. I think to myself 'half an hour is not going to kill her and then I can go take a shower.' But really, then I think it's such a short, slippery slope. So it's easier just not to have one."

However, in discussing the convenience of television, Natalie and Mike agree that living without it has benefited them, although it is Natalie who talks more about it. She talks about how her decisions as a parent mesh in very clear ways with her profession. A lactation consultant at two local hospitals, she helps new mothers cope with the physical and emotional struggles of nursing a newborn. As Natalie explains (and as the data support), babies who are breast fed have fewer ear infections, fewer respiratory problems, and fewer visits to the pediatrician than babies who are fed formula (Gdalevich, Mimouni & Mimouni, 2001). For this reason, many hospitals and insurance companies have seen the benefits of encouraging new mothers to nurse. However, Natalie is not concerned much with saving the insurance companies money on pediatrician visits. In the long run, she notes, having a new mother learn how to breast feed requires little more than a healthy mother, which is much easier than sanitizing bottles and bottle nipples and mixing formula. Although it may be hard to learn to nurse initially, Natalie argues that it is much easier for mothers in the long run. As Natalie talks, I wonder how this conversation is related to television viewing. It is an interesting story, and clearly she is committed to what she does, but how did this affect her decision to live without television?

"I think of it this way," offers Natalie. "I talk to my clients about *perceived convenience*—how something that seems easier immediately may not be easier in the long run." She goes on to say that some women find it difficult to learn to nurse, to get the baby and the mother coordinated, and that a bottle, which is readily available and initially easier for the baby, seems like the simplest solution. However, Natalie goes on to argue that after the initial learning is over, nursing is actually easier. The baby is more easily soothed and feeding the baby is a simple process, without many steps or much equipment.

Without television, Natalie continues, it was sometimes harder when her children were younger. Television seemed like a simple solution that was readily available, but in the end, Natalie thinks her children can entertain themselves more easily, have long attention spans and are rarely bored because they know how to find or create activities for themselves. Natalie believes that living without television has not only made her a more vigilant parent, but also the decision has actually made parenting easier in the long run, as her children got older (now ages 8 and 13). She says:

> Especially when they were younger or preschoolers, it forced me to do a better job, to be a better parent. If they were bouncing off the walls, let's go outside for a walk instead of clicking on the TV. And that's not to say that I never let them watch a video, *ever*, but not that often. So I always had a craft set up while I cooked dinner, or some crayons. So it forced me to do that because if I had a TV, it would be an out...And my friends would say, "Oh, I got an hour of quiet." But the costs afterwards. I just don't know if the benefits outweigh the risks, when they are bouncing off the ceilings.

Natalie argues that after watching television her children would be less calm. After "zoning out in front of the television," as she calls it, "they would have all this energy." Therefore, she thinks that the costs of using television as a babysitter would be children who are harder to keep entertained in the long run.

Like her professional life, where she coaches parents to take the hard route initially, she believes that her decisions, especially about television, have paid off in making things easier. And what does it mean to have "easier" children? Natalie believes that her children are easier because they have not experienced fast-paced programs that are available simply by turning on the television. She says, "I think it has come back to us in a good way because they aren't bored so easily. They get bored and then they go off and find something to do. And it can be a calm something, not a mile a minute...They can be very thoughtful about what they want to do." They are easier, she suggests, because "they don't expect someone else to entertain them."

Another way that living without television actually makes family life easier is that many parents noted that there were no fights and arguments about television itself. As one parent who has no television says, "I tell people I don't have TV because I'm a lazy parent. I just don't want to have all the arguments. So we don't have TV and we don't have to argue about it." In fact, studies of parent–child disagreements suggest that parents and children do argue about how much and what type of television children should watch, with more arguments occurring about this topic the younger the child (Reisch et al., 2000).

Independent Children

One of the characteristics I notice about Rachel and Levi, and about most of the children whom I either interviewed or met when interviewing their parents, is that they did not need much entertaining. If there were younger children in the house, they played quietly while the interview went on, in the room where we were talking, in their own rooms or in the adjoining kitchen or den. Older children, like Rachel and Levi, sat and listened, sometimes offering their thoughts, sometimes just absorbing the conversation and sometimes, staring blankly off in space, looking as if they were paying no attention at all. What they did not do was fidget or interrupt with questions unrelated to the topic. They did not claim boredom or ask for suggestions of things to do. Although in any given sample of children, some will be focused and calm, what struck me was that many of these children were. Perhaps what their parents meant when calling them "easier" children is that they are more autonomous children. They required less adult attention because they seemed to make their own way through the day.

This autonomy, as some parents called it, or this calmness, as others noted, may be related to television in two ways. First, the notion of autonomy may be part of the relationship between television exposure and children's attention spans. When parents argue that television's fast pace harms children's ability to play on their own and to entertain themselves, what they seem to be arguing is that sustained attention to independent play is the first step towards autonomy and independence in other realms. Second, the notion of autonomy may be related to parents' expectations for how television would affect their children's behavior and to their beliefs about how their children *should* behave. These expectations and beliefs may in turn affect the actual behavior of their children.

Television and Children's Attention Span

Many parents believe that television affects children's attention spans. Among both nonviewers and viewers alike, they believe that the fast cuts, the colors and the music can hinder children's natural drive to explore in an ongoing, sustained way. Lily Dawson, for example, worries that television would harm her daughter's long-term ability to sustain attention. "I think she has a growing brain and TV would make it too cluttered in her mind. Her mind needs to grow and she needs to be busy doing other things for that to happen," she said.

Linda Hoffman, a 44-year-old mother with a 10-year-old boy and 7-year-old twins, was among the viewing families who also expressed concern over the effects of television on her children's attention span. She stated that there was "tons" of research on the effects of television on children's ability to sustain attention. She worried about it and reported that she had recently heard a motivational speaker talking about precisely this topic. The speaker's own research had found a link between television and children's ability to attend, although his research was limited, consisting mainly of his observations of his own children. Linda agreed with the speaker because, as she noted, after her own children watch television, it is hard for her to get their attention. Several other parents in viewing households also talked about children's inability to pay attention to anything other than television or a video game. One father said this of his 10-year-old daughter, "She can sit still for three hours in front of the TV...but with homework, she can barely manage two minutes without saying it's boring."

In addition to the fast pace of television, the medium is something children *receive* with relatively little effort on their part. The excitement, the stories, the action is taken in by them. Contrast that experience with the play experience, or the experience of homework, as noted by the father above, which children must *create*. It is possible that prepackaged entertainment affects children's desire and ability to construct their own experiences. This desire and ability to create is yet another component of autonomy and may well be related to the notion of attention span.

Concern over the effects of television on children's attention span dates back at least to the early 1970s when programs such as *Sesame Street* were criticized for their short segments and quick pacing. Whereas some saw *Sesame Street*'s design as appropriate for the naturally short attention span of the preschoolers who were the audience for the program, others saw it, and perhaps television in general, as limiting the development of longer attention spans. After all, the argument went, if children are fed a diet of short segments and editing that favored several cuts per minute, how could they develop an attention span that was appropriate for, say, school, with its slower pacing? Weren't programs like *Sesame Street* creating a generation of children who could not pay attention?

Although parents of nonviewing children seem to think so, the earliest evidence was mixed. The 1970s saw perhaps the first wave of criticism leveled at television's potential impact on the attention span of young children. Although much had been made in earlier research of other effects, such as aggression, less concern was expressed about children's cognitive development. However, by the 1970s, critics such as Marie Winn (1985), with her incendiary book, *The Plug-In Drug*, brought renewed attention to the issue of television and children's attention span. No quiet critic of television, Winn argued that television was destroying the minds of children, creating non-thinking zombies whose attention spans had been ruined by the ever-moving images of television. Despite the attention paid to Winn's diatribe, the earliest scientific research did not directly support her contentions.

Dan Anderson, a pioneer in research on young children and television, together with his colleagues at the University of Massachusetts, conducted a study examining the contention that television shortened children's attention. In this experiment, children were randomly assigned to watch either a fast- or a slow-paced version of *Sesame Street*, while children in a control group listened to a story read by a parent. Afterwards, 13 different measures of attention span were used, including time spent on an activity, number of toys used during a play period and reaction time to a developmental task. No significant differences were found between any of the three groups that would indicate lowered attention span resulting from television (Anderson, Levin & Lorch, 1977). Reviews of the available (although limited) literature claimed that the balance of findings suggested that television, especially when watched with an adult who could help mediate content, was beneficial to children's cognitive development and attention span (Quisenberry & Klasek, 1977). Other researchers, perhaps piggy-backing on this early debate, claimed that television, with its use of both linguistic and iconic forms that mirrored those used in everyday life, could actually benefit children's cognitive growth (Shannon & Fernie, 1985). By presenting children with language and visual stimulation that was both similar to and more varied than what they might see in everyday life, television could help children develop cognitively. Although no empirical literature supported this claim, it was appealing because adults were anxious to have children expand their contact with iconic forms.

Although the concern over the effects of television on attention span seemed to abate somewhat during the 1980s, at least two events served to bring it back into the forefront in the early 1990s. Although the two events were not linked, they shared a topic that once again captured the interest and attention of parents and researchers. First, a book decrying the effect of television on children, especially on their attention span, was published and widely read. Second, Attention Deficit Disorder (ADD) garnered press attention as more and more children were diagnosed with this affliction.

In 1990, Jane Healey's book, *Endangered Minds: Why Children Don't Think and What We Can Do About It*, vehemently criticized television and once again, cited it for destroying the attention span and concentration of American children. It took a flamboyant look at the role of television in the cognitive and social development of children. In that same year, the number of children in the United States who were diagnosed with ADD or Attention Deficit-Hyperactivity Disorder (ADHD) rose to over 1 million for the first time.

ADHD is a syndrome characterized by inattention, impulsivity and hyperactivity. When hyperactivity is not a significant factor for a given individual, the condition is sometimes referred to as Attention Deficit Disorder. These symptoms are associated with learning, behavioral, and emotional problems and are thought to have both neurological and environmental causes. The syndrome affects approximately 5–7% of American children (National Institute of Mental Health, 2008), although these numbers represent only diagnosed cases, causing some experts to argue that the number is much higher. Nevertheless, concern about the syndrome has increased in recent years due in part to increased incidence of diagnoses.

As a result of this increase, the very concept of attention span is once more at the forefront of public debate concerning children. Whereas some argue for a strictly neurological explanation for ADD and ADHD, others argue that environmental factors such as parenting and, yes, television, are partly to blame for the rise. Are the broad spectrum of behaviors associated with ADD and ADHD related to television exposure?

Recently, Geist and Gibson (2000) conducted a partial replication and extension of Anderson's early research on television and children's attention span. These researchers compared preschoolers' ability to attend to an educational task after watching either an educational program on PBS, a children's cartoon on network television or listening to a parent read a story. Children who saw the network television children's program made more changes in activities during a subsequent free play situation and spent less time engaged in a single activity than children who were read a story. This study suggests that some children's programming may in fact have a negative effect on children's attention spans.

At least two issues may account for the conflicting findings of the two studies. First, the stimulus materials in the two studies were different. Whereas Anderson and his colleagues used only clips from *Sesame Street*, a program designed for the express purpose of teaching children, the Geist and Gibson (2000) study used a network cartoon. It seems likely that because the latter is meant solely to entertain, it may contain more elements, such as quick pacing, zooms, and cuts that may have more of a negative effect on cognitive factors such as attention span. Second, in testing an outcome such as attention span—a variable that is developed and established over time—a single program may have somewhat of a sporadic effect on children. If this is the case, experimental studies of television and children's attention span may well have different outcomes at different times. Results from Anderson's early study (Anderson et al., 1977) and Geist and Gibson's (2000) later one may suggest only that effects on children's attention span may be intermittent.

It was not until recently that longitudinal data became available, allowing researchers to look at causal links between television exposure and attention (something that cross-sectional data is unable to do) and also to consider long-term impacts, an effect that a single experiment may be unable to consistently detect. Research conducted by Christakis, Zimmerman, DiGiuseppe and McCarty (2004) looked at children at age 1, 3 and again at 7. Among the many variables measured were television exposure, measures of attention, and a diagnosis of ADHD. Even controlling for early attention differences, the authors found a relationship between television exposure and later ADHD. The study included more than 2000 children and found that for every hour of television watched at age 1 and age 3, there was a 10% increased likelihood of the children developing ADHD by age 7. The authors argue that because television depicts images and events at a pace much faster than real life, television exposure may be causally linked to the development of ADHD. Like the parents who live without television, Christakis and colleagues also argued that the speed of television, its pacing and fast cuts, may over-stimulate the brain. Unlike real life that proceeds at a rate that is slower and less dramatic, allowing a youngster to explore his or her immediate environment, television presents images at a speed that is rarely replicated by children's actual day-to-day experiences.

Although more research is needed, this latest study seems to offer some support to the contention made by parents in nonviewing households that living without television has made their children "easier." As I argued earlier, if easier means more autonomous, with an ability to entertain themselves, what are the interconnections among autonomy, attention span, ADHD, and television exposure? First, children's television is fast-paced, with singing, cuts, zooms, and action. Second, television is readily available. To watch television, children do not necessarily need to create anything or generate a stimulus in need of their attention (like they might with an imaginary game). They need only sit and consume. Because of these characteristics, watching television may ultimately dampen children's ability to create and sustain focus on more internally inspired stimuli. They may become accustomed to externally generated, fast-paced images. Being accustomed to this stimuli may, in some cases, create a need for it, resulting in children who are less likely to pay attention to life's slower offerings; in other words, children who need entertaining. These children are the antithesis of Natalie's "easier children."

A Systems Approach Revisited

As argued earlier in this book, family systems theory, with its emphasis on the interrelation between family attitudes and beliefs, family norms and individual members' behavior, may also offer insight into why nonviewing families may have, or at least perceive themselves as having, "easier" children. According to the family systems perspective, beliefs held by family members are an active part of family life. In other words, beliefs about how the family functions or how it should function affect actual family behaviors.

In this section, I will discuss two relevant aspects of the systems perspective as they relate to perceived convenience in homes without television: the *social environment* of the family affects family functioning; and family *beliefs* about an issue affect family functioning, apart from the reality of the situation about which those beliefs are held. Therefore, television exists in the home as both an environmental feature and as a social phenomenon, and television exists in the home as part of the family belief system, replete with family myths and mores about it.

First, I will address television as part of the social environment. Television occupies a unique space in the social environment of the home. According to Alexander (2001), "Television is more than an object of perception, but not quite another—not an object of social cognition. Occupying an uneasy space between the two, television occupies what might be termed in the cultural tradition a *contested space*" (original emphasis, p. 285). In other words, Linda Hoffman, the mother in a viewing household discussed earlier, may be upset about television precisely because it is not an object of perception, like a painting on the wall or a plant in the corner; nor is it a social being. In fact, the family tension that arises over television may in fact be *because* Linda would like television to be treated like an object. However, her children (and her husband, according to Linda) treat it with more attention, like a social actor. In this case, *contested space* becomes an apt metaphor, as the family struggles with how to treat it, how much attention to pay to it, and conversely, how much to pay to each other. In this uneasy space between object and being, Linda and her family are not certain how the television should be treated or what the role of television should be in the household.

Conversely, imagine a visitor sitting down with one of Linda's children. It is unlikely that it would make Linda upset that the child was absorbed in the interaction. One mother put it this way: "When my child is reading, we go through all of the same hooplah. 'One more paragraph, one more page!' Or I ask something and she just doesn't hear me. But it is different than if she were doing that with TV. Somehow, I don't mind as much. It doesn't drive me nuts." Perhaps this is because the mother thinks that, compared to the television, a book is more of an object of social cognition, deserving of the attention that the child is paying it. The difference is in the way one family member (the parent) thinks the other family member (the child) should respond to a particular object or person. Given these perceptions, television, or its absence, is a social phenomenon, a part of the social environment that may affect the functioning of the family, both because it affects the flow of family life and because it is seen, at times, as an unwelcome visitor whose presence is more than it should be. It affects social functioning because of the way it is *perceived*. For those without television, television was seen to intrude too much on the social environment, to be *part* of the social environment. Therefore, any convenience of having it was outweighed by its excessive presence.

The second way that systems theory applies to the notion of perceived convenience is that for most families I talked to, living without it comes with a set of firmly held beliefs. Natalie and Mike believe that the effect of television on attention span is what necessitates their avoidance of it. They also believe strongly that their children are better behaved as a result but it is difficult to know if this is true. Would Rachel and Levi have been "easier" children had they grown up with television? Or is it some other element of parenting that the Carlsons are doing—concomitantly with not having television—that make Rachel and Levi "easier"? Although the design of this study cannot answer that question, the point here is that the parents *believe* that living without television has made their children easier. This belief provides support for them in their continued decision not to have television, a point that was echoed in many of the interviews with families who did not own one. In short, their beliefs about the negative effects of owning television helped sustain their family decisions and may have also been responsible for their entire interaction style. One reason that Rachel and Levi were easier may have been because the Carlsons structured their lives to help make them so. Recall that Natalie said, "I always had a craft set up while I cooked dinner." At least two thoughts were relevant in that statement. First, the statement was about Natalie and her family's lack of television. Second, and perhaps more importantly, Natalie provided an alternative—in fact, structured her parenting—to make her children "easier." In this case, lack of television may not have been the only factor that made Rachel and Levi play quietly while Natalie cooked.

Rebecca Tanner, who has three children, said that if she used television as a babysitter, she would not actually be socializing her children. "If we don't want them to bother us," she says, "we have to teach them not to bother us. If I put them in front of television, they would be quiet, but I would not have taught them not to bother us. I have to give them something else to do." Clearly, she also believes that the long-term benefits of having what she thinks of as well-socialized children are outweighed by the short-term benefits of having television. However, other than simply eliminating television, Rebecca believes she must provide alternatives for her children and teach them not to interrupt her when she is busy. These ideas, too, are part of the belief system. Other families often echoed this notion. "You can't just take away TV. You have to take it away and replace it with other things," said Ted Randolph, a father of two children who are now grown.

Therefore, part of the system includes beliefs about the negative impact of television, but part also includes what occurs when television is removed. Nonviewers often argued strongly that living without television had made their children easier, ignoring the fact that the activities that filled the void left by television may have had an impact as well. In the end, Rebecca's children may be easier because the family has no television, or they may be easier because they have been taught to be so. Therefore, filling the television void with other activities may affect nonviewing children, but parents' beliefs about television set the causal linkages in motion.

A second family belief that may affect children is that nonviewing households often had specific beliefs about how their households should operate. They believed that the home should be a calm place or a peaceful one. They would then cite the lack of television as the sole, or at least primary, source of peace in their home. Jane Hart, mother of 8-year-old Pearl, 6-year-old Sena, and 3-year-old Jack, believes that living without television has made her children "calm." She talks with animation about each of them and about how they interact as a group. She claims:

> They get along much better when they do not watch television than when they do sit in front of the television. They communicate better with each other, there's less arguing, and there's more inventive communication, less bickering and we have noticed a distinct change from the summer when we were more lenient with them and they were allowed to watch videos, and then going cold turkey when school started and it's such a breath of fresh air and they are more in control of their emotions somehow.

It is clear from Jane's comment that she perceives that living without television causes her children to be calmer and more communicative with one another. However, another belief—that her home *should* be calm—is also likely to set the tone for family interactions.

Overall, Rebecca and Jane, like Natalie and Mike, believe that television strongly affects their children in a number of ways. Although it may be true that these particular children are easier without television, it is also true that the parents' belief systems about parenting, about how their families *should* operate, affect family behavior. In this way, living without television may serve two purposes: it may improve the family atmosphere, as so many families commented, but it may also allow families to see, and perhaps create, an atmosphere in their home that is calm. Therefore, living without television is not only an action that may create an outcome, such as peace in the home or autonomous children, but an outcome in and of itself, resulting from the belief that television shortens attention spans or creates disquiet in the home. Together, these beliefs and behaviors about television, and behaviors regarding it, make up the family system that results in a particular family.

Ultimately, then, nonviewing children are likely to be autonomous or "easy" under several interrelated conditions. First, television may have a negative affect on the attention span of children, making it possible that nonviewing children are more able to sustain attention. Second, families without television *believe* that television has negative effects on children's attention span. This belief causes them to not only live without television, but they consciously promote longer attention spans in their children by structuring their home environments to foster this skill. From a family systems approach, all of these factors—beliefs about television and its effects, the decision to live without it, the structure of the home environment and the attention spans of the children—are related. One single variable (e.g., nonviewing) does not exclusively cause an outcome (e.g., longer attention spans in children). Rather, longer attention spans and more autonomous children are likely to flourish in homes where these qualities are valued. In many homes without television, a high premium is placed on peace. In the end, does living without television create easier children? The answer may well be yes, but lack of exposure to the screen does not appear to be the sole cause.

Chapter 10

Time Use

In this chapter, I report on findings from the survey portion and the time-use diaries of the study. Because Americans report having approximately 5 hours of free time per day, and the average American watches 3 hours of television daily, it stands to reason that nonviewers have more time to do other things than viewers do. This chapter finds that nonviewing adults and children spend more time reading and more time doing chores; however, they do not spend more time on computers than their television viewing counterparts. In addition, nonviewers report wanting more time to do various activities than viewers do, leading to the conclusion that nonviewers avoid television because they want to be engaged in many activities, and not vice versa. In this chapter, I also discuss uses and gratifications, arguing that television is displaced by activities that are functionally similar to it. In other words, going on a walk with a friend can replace television when television is fulfilling a social need.

The average American adult has about 5 hours and 15 minutes a day of free time. Free time is typically defined as time that is spent neither working (paid or unpaid) nor sleeping. Men have about half an hour more than this; women about half an hour less (Mattingly & Bianchi, 2003). Other differences exist as well, of course. For example, married women have less free time than married men and less than unmarried women. Those with children have less free time than those without and those who spend more hours in paid employment generally have less. Children, even those of school age, have the most free time of all. The concept of free time is central to this chapter: how it is used, and how television—as a potentially continuous medium—is perceived to interrupt, interfere with, or waste time. Of the 120 nonviewers interviewed, only two adults and five children (6%) did not spontaneously mention time use, either that they had given up television in order to have more time, that watching television took too much time, or that watching television was not the way they wanted to spend their time. In interviews with those who did watch television, time use was mentioned by 75%. Specifically, they mentioned that television was a waste of either their own time or the time of others who watched it (e.g., a spouse). In this chapter, the defining feature of television is its potentially ongoing and omnipresent nature.

Americans and Time Use

The time that Americans have for leisure is actually on the rise (Aguiar & Hurst, 2006), despite the popular belief that we have less time than ever. What is it that Americans are doing with this time? On average, half of our leisure time is spent watching television. Adults spend about three hours per day watching television; children, with their greater amount of free time, watch somewhat more. Preschool-aged children watch three hours each day and gradually increase their viewing time until it peaks around age 12, usually at approximately four hours per day. Once children hit adolescence, however, their time spent watching television declines somewhat, perhaps due to increases in other time demands such as schoolwork and socializing. By the age of 18, hours in front of a television are at their adult levels. In short, for adults and children, leisure time is taken up by quite a bit of television viewing (Comstock & Sharrer, 2001). It is perhaps not surprising, then, that among nonviewers, having more time to do other things was a common reason cited for living without television. Although nonviewers were often more zealous about *other* reasons for forgoing television and more adamant about other objections to it, time use was mentioned by nearly every person interviewed. Time use was the most frequently mentioned factor, with 94% of all nonviewers mentioning it.

Research on leisure time is fraught with methodological disputes. (See, for example, Mattingly & Bianchi, 2003.) Generally, there are three methods of tracking free time. First is the questionnaire method, in which individuals are asked how much time they spend doing a number of given activities in a time interval, such as a week. Second, the diary approach, for which a respondent is asked to record what s/he was doing in a diary broken up into blocks of time. All blocks are reviewed until 24 hours are accounted for. Third, in the random paging method, participants are given a beeper and asked to record what they are doing when the beeper goes off. Overall, reports from questionnaires give somewhat different results (and tend to show less leisure time overall) than diary methods, which in turn provide somewhat different results from random paging.

In this study, I utilized questionnaires and diaries. Although the diary sample is somewhat small, making generalizations for some less common activities (e.g., volunteering) impossible because they occurred infrequently, diaries do provide a richness of detail to supplement and help interpret the questionnaire data. The questionnaire data, on the other hand, include a larger sample and allow me to report on specific questions. In this chapter, I use the questionnaire results and diaries together to describe viewers' and nonviewers' time use and their attitudes towards it. I also utilize the displacement hypothesis and uses and gratifications, both discussed at length in chapter 3.

What Do Nonviewers Do With Their Time?

Adults

Attitudes Toward Time Use

The survey and diary portions of the study paint a revealing picture of time use among viewers and nonviewers. In designing the study, I originally wanted to see if viewers were more pressed for time than nonviewers, feeling perhaps that they did not have enough time for other activities due to their television viewing, a notion consistent with the displacement hypothesis. I asked if they thought they spent enough time in specific activities and I asked about their desire to spend more time devoted to these activities. I expected that viewers would agree more strongly with statements such as "I'd like to spend more time exercising," or "I'd like to spend more time reading" because they had less time to do them. After all, they were spending time watching television, which might preclude time spent in other activities. Instead, the significant differences that emerged, taken together with the time diaries, suggest a different pattern, rather the opposite of what I had expected.

Overall, when I asked viewers and nonviewers if they spent *enough* time in various activities—time on the job, time spent sleeping—most answers were close to 4.0, or neutral on a 7-point scale. Generally, viewers and nonviewers felt similarly about spending enough time doing various activities. There were some differences, of course. Specifically, nonviewers agreed more strongly than viewers that they spent enough time doing chores, exercising and watching television. Given that both viewers and nonviewers felt they spent *enough* time in various activities (with some variance around the neutral point) would we not expect that they would also think they did not want more time for these activities? However, surprisingly, this was not the case. Instead, *nonviewers,* as compared to viewers, were more apt to agree that they wanted *more* time. This was true despite the fact that, by not watching television, we would expect nonviewers to have more time on their hands. However, nonviewers reported wanting more time to read than viewers, despite the fact that diaries indicate that they spend more time reading than viewers do. Nonviewers also wanted more time to spend with their spouses than viewers did, and nonviewers wanted to spend more time in their paid employment than viewers. They also wanted more free time (see Figure 10.1). Generally, then, it was the nonviewers who seemed to desire more time for various activities, despite the fact that by not watching television, they had more free time to spend in other activities than viewers did.

Why would this be the case? Perhaps television does not cause viewers to decrease their time spent in other activities. That is, the displacement hypothesis is not substantiated. Rather, television may be the default activity for those who watch it out of a perception that there is no alternative. In fact, as early as 1958, Himmelweit et al. suggested that television may be a habit that people fell back on when they had nothing better to do. Conversely, nonviewing may not cause individuals to seek out alternative activities. Instead, nonviewers may have interests beyond television viewing that cause them to seek out many various activities and forego television. Recall that the uses and gratifications approach (Rubin, 1981) argues that at least some television viewing is motivated by a desire to pass time or is a habit. From this perspective, television viewers may simply spend their free time watching television because they perceive no functional alternatives. They have time to fill and television may offer a readily available means of doing so. This notion would offer a solid explanation for the data showing that viewers felt they had enough time to do the things they wanted to do but nonviewers wanted more. Simply put, perhaps viewers watched television, at least some of the time, when they really have nothing else to do. Nonviewers, because of personality type or family demands, may never feel that they have extra time.

Another explanation may be that television, with its sizeable cast of characters and range of settings both exotic and mundane, can offer viewers many vicarious experiences. In chapter 12, we will meet the Tanners, who claim that they do not watch television because they do not want vicarious experiences to take the place of actual ones. If the Tanners and others like them are correct, then television, as a vicarious experience, may offer alternatives to similar, but real, experiences. Whether this vicarious experience is perceived as positive or negative may vary from individual to individual. The data may simply suggest that viewers want to spend less time in specific activities because their needs are met vicariously through television. Nonviewers, on the other hand, want to meet their needs (for social interaction or entertainment, for example) with activities that take more time than a 30-minute or 1-hour time block. In either case, nonviewers appear to want more time to fulfill their needs as compared to their television-watching counterparts. Nonviewers may want more time because they have more needs to begin with, or because they are missing

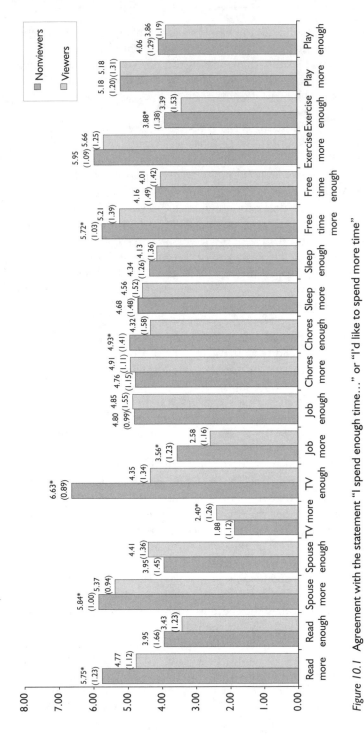

Figure 10.1 Agreement with the statement "I spend enough time..." or "I'd like to spend more time"

Note: (*) indicates independent sample t-tests are significantly different at $p < 0.05$

out on the vicarious experiences that television, in relatively short order, has to offer.

Household Chores and Childcare

Although I did not initially consider household chores and childcare to be related to the ideas about television viewing, interviews with both nonviewers and viewers suggested that notions of childcare, household chores and television viewing are intertwined. Perhaps because all three activities can occupy the time we spend at home, these concepts are intimate, personal and related to one another. For example, parents in television-viewing households mentioned that they needed a television to baby-sit young children while they performed household tasks, or they said that watching television caused them or their spouses to neglect work at home. In nonviewing households, parents often spoke wistfully about having 15 minutes to do some laundry, if only they had a television to occupy a toddler. Many nonviewers also mentioned that they spent their extra free time doing more housework. Therefore, in the surveys and time-use diaries, I explored the idea of household chores as they related to television viewing.

For each individual, I coded an activity as a chore or childcare if it was clearly identifiable as cooking (e.g., making dinner), cleaning (e.g., sweeping the garage), outdoor work (e.g., chopping wood) or childcare (e.g., bathing a toddler). Although disputes exist in the literature on definitions of chores and childcare (Mattingly & Bianchi, 2003), the coding I employed is consistent with several studies on time use. I also coded other fairly broad categories such as self-care (e.g., eating, sleeping, bathing), paid employment, sports/exercise and hobbies.

Overall, time-use diaries suggest that nonviewing adults do spend more time than viewers in chores and childcare. Indeed, among those who live without television, many cited increased free time as a reason for not having television. However, during the interviews, many nonviewers also mentioned chores and household functioning as a way that they spend their free time, suggesting that nonviewers are not necessarily spending all of their "extra" time in hobbies or play. For example, the 50 adult nonviewers who kept diaries spent approximately 95 minutes ($SD=52.16$) on chores daily. Viewers spent slightly less than this, approximately 86 minutes ($M=86.01$, $SD=47.21$). Therefore, it appears that there may be some truth in one nonviewing adult's contention that: "Our house runs better without television. I think I get more done."

For example, Charlotte Ford, the home-schooling mother of 10, mentioned chores within the first three minutes of our initial interview. But this comes as no surprise. "How can people fit it [TV] in? Even the videos? All of my time is jam packed with home-school, projects, cleaning, gardening, laundry, oh, the wash, and cooking..." She trailed off, probably tired simply contemplating it all. But even those with smaller households mentioned that their homes ran more smoothly without television. Another parent, a mother of two preschoolers, noted that instead of watching television after dinner, she did housework. She said, "In the evening after they're in bed, I start in on chores. I clean or do laundry. I don't know how I'd do it otherwise so I think our house probably runs better without TV."

Leisure Time

Despite the assumption that homes without television experience more free time, many nonviewers did not feel that they had additional time at their leisure. For example, at some point during the formal interview I asked people how they spent their free time. I would usually mention that since the average American watches 2–3 hours of television per day, they had an extra 2–3 hours. "What," I'd ask, "do you do with your extra 2–3 hours?" The most common answer was simply, "What extra time?" Most felt busy enough and typically wondered aloud how anyone had time to watch television. But then, because I had asked, they would gamely rattle off their list of activities. During the interviews, the most commonly mentioned activities reported by nonviewers were reading (70%), talking on the phone (15%) or to others in the household (64%), going on walks (20%), taking bike rides (10%), playing outside (52%), playing board games (18%) or playing a sport or exercising (67%).

The diaries also supported the idea that there was a great range of activities, especially among the nonviewers. To support this claim, I examined the range of leisure activities for each person. Across a two-day period, I counted the number of *different* leisure activities engaged in by each person. Repeat activities (e.g., reading on two separate occasions), were counted only once. Interestingly, the most common repeat activity among nonviewing adults was reading; among viewing adults the most common repeat activity was watching television. In addition, among the 63 nonviewers, across two different days, there was an average of 2.2 ($SD=1.10$) *different* leisure activities listed for a given person; among viewers, the average was somewhat smaller: 1.5 ($SD=0.97$). Therefore, it does appear that nonviewers engage in a greater variety of leisure activities. Recall, too, that the survey data suggested that nonviewers wanted more time than viewers to do a variety of specific activities. Taken together, it seems possible that nonviewers' greater interest in a wide variety of activities may be partly the *cause* of their nonviewing, and not only the outcome.

Although the sample of diaries was somewhat small, making it difficult to compare activities between viewers and nonviewers, I was able to compare two frequently mentioned leisure activities: reading and watching television. I coded an activity as reading if it met two criteria: first, the adult needed to be reading to himself and not to a child (the latter was coded as "playing with/caring for children"), and second, the medium was paper. Reading online was coded as computer use in order to assess questions regarding computer use that will be addressed in the next section. An activity was coded as television watching regardless if the source of the material was broadcast or recorded. Among adults reading to themselves, nonviewers spent an average of 42.17 minutes ($SD=16.18$) reading per day; viewers spent 18.62 minutes ($SD=18.71$). Conversely, adults in viewing households spent 63.07 ($SD=27.15$) minutes watching television daily (as either a primary or secondary activity); adults in nonviewing households spent 4.80 minutes ($SD=23.75$). This result occurred because in nonviewing homes, 2 of 50 participants watched a 2-hour rented movie.

Are Computers Replacing Television?

When we consider life without television, it is inevitable to ask if television time is simply being replaced by computer time for nonviewers—not for work, but for entertainment, news, passing time, and social facilitation. That is, are nonviewers merely heavy computer users? Are nonviewers merely using their free time with one medium instead of another? It appears that some functions of television, specifically, its ability to deliver news, are replaced by the Internet. But other functions, such as entertainment, are not.

The 125 adults who completed the survey answered questions about their own and their children's use of computers. In both cases, I was interested in their use of computers outside of work or school. Overall, nonviewing adults reported spending an average of half an hour ($M=26.03$, $SD=28.79$ minutes) on the computer per day, excluding time they spent using it for their jobs. Those in viewing households spent an approximately equal amount of time on a computer ($M=31.13$, $SD=31.13$ minutes). However, for both viewers and nonviewers, there were those who spent no time on a computer at all. Among viewers, 14% ($n=9$) did not use a computer outside of work. Among nonviewers, 36% ($n=23$) did not use one, suggesting that at least some nonviewers have no screen time at all. Therefore, I also wanted to look solely at those who used computers. In general, there was little difference among these nonviewers ($M=43.00$, $SD=26.24$) and viewers ($M=40.41$, $SD=24.93$). Therefore, it appears that viewers and nonviewers spend an equal amount of time in front of a computer, suggesting that nonviewers are not simply heavy computer users.

In terms of what they did with that time on the computer, nonviewers who used computers reported spending approximately 23 minutes reading the news, about 13 minutes e-mailing, chatting, and using instant messenger, and about seven minutes using a computer to play games or surf the Internet. Viewers use their computer time somewhat differently. Although they generally spend the same amount of time as nonviewers e-mailing and chatting, they spend somewhat less time reading the news online and somewhat more time in game play and surfing. Specifically, viewers who use computers spend approximately 15 minutes communicating online, 12 minutes reading the news online, and 13 minutes playing games or surfing. Therefore, nonviewers are not spending more time using a computer overall, but they do spend more time reading the news online. Furthermore, nonviewers spend about as much time as viewers on e-mail and online chat.

Perhaps the reason for this pattern of findings is once again related to uses and gratifications. We use media to fulfill certain needs: informational, social, or purely entertainment. In the case of communicating online, viewers and nonviewers may use computers equally because communication is the very thing that a computer can do that television cannot. Both nonviewers and viewers perceive the value of computers as a means of social facilitation. Furthermore, television is unlikely to fulfill this function of computers for either group. It is not surprising, therefore, that their usage patterns regarding e-mail and chat are similar.

In the survey portion of the study, I also asked participants a series of questions about their attitudes towards computer use for themselves and for their children. When I asked participants if they thought computers were a good means of communicating, both viewers and nonviewers agreed equally that they were. Generally, then, viewers and nonviewers spend approximately the same amount of time using computers and the Internet for communication purposes because they both approve of them for this purpose. Consider, however, viewers' and nonviewers' use of computers for other purposes, such as game play and surfing (i.e., entertainment) and news access. Although adults do not generally report spending much time in these activities, nonviewers report an average of 7 minutes daily; viewers report 13. A fairly straightforward reason for this is that viewers were significantly more likely than nonviewers to agree that computers adequately fulfilled their entertainment needs (see Figure 10.2). As Katz, Blumler and Gurevitch (1974) argued, all individuals have entertainment needs. Television, and presumably computers, provide merely one way of meeting those needs. Nonviewers may simply seek out non-mediated activities to fulfill a desire for entertainment.

Lastly, viewers and nonviewers have somewhat differing attitudes about the use of the computer for news access. Whereas both agree that the Internet

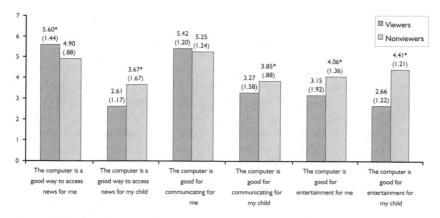

Figure 10.2 Attitudes towards computer use among viewing and nonviewing adults for themselves and their children

Note: (*) indicates independent sample t-tests are significantly different at p <0.05
Participants responded to Likert items, responses ranged from 1 (*strongly disagree*) to 7 (*strongly agree*); 4 indicates neutral.

is a good source of news for themselves, nonviewing adults agree more strongly. Therefore, from a uses and gratifications perspective, computers may be replacing some of the functions of television for nonviewers, such as the informational and social uses, but they do not fill their entertainment needs. As I will describe later in this chapter, nonviewers engage in a wide variety of activities to meet their entertainment needs.

Overall, then, computers do not seem to be filling the time gap left by television. Why is this the case? Nonviewers and viewers both agree that the Internet is a good communication tool. Indeed, they spend a near-identical amount of time using it to fulfill this need. However, nonviewers are less likely to value the Internet as an entertainment medium and consequently may spend less time using it this way. The final function, news access and information gain, is actually valued more by nonviewers than by viewers, and their use patterns also reflect this.

The simple fact that nonviewers are more likely to agree that computers provide an effective way of accessing the news might lead us to expect that they would spend more time using it, perhaps even closing the gap in screen time between those who watch television and those who do not. However, there are two reasons why this would not be the case. First, recall that many nonviewers argued that the Internet provided more in-depth news and did so more quickly and efficiently than television. As a result, nonviewers may access news, but spend less time with it. After all, as they argue, their time is not spent listening to news anchors banter or watching commercials. Second, whereas viewers spend some time with television for information and news access purposes, time is also spent for other reasons, such as entertainment, passing time or habit. It appears that nonviewers are somewhat less likely to use computers and the Internet to fulfill these needs. Certainly they spend some of their free time with a computer screen for entertainment, but not enough to close the screen-time gap between themselves and viewers.

Ultimately, the uses and gratifications theory suggests that a medium will be used during free time only if it meets certain psychological needs. When needs are not met, functional alternatives will be chosen. In the case of nonviewers, they have chosen the Internet to meet informational/news needs and to meet some social and communicative needs. However, their entertainment needs are not completely met by either television or the computer. Of course, the psychological need to be entertained can mean many different things. For some, as I argued earlier in this chapter, vicarious experiences, had via television, can be exciting and fulfilling. For others, as we will discuss in chapter 12, vicarious experiences are empty and vaguely dissatisfying. What constitutes entertainment for one person—whether a situation comedy, a trip to the opera, or a hike up a mountain—may constitute mind-numbing boredom to another. For nonviewers, it appears that their entertainment needs are satisfyingly filled by many activities; however, television is not one of them.

Children

Children generally spend more time than adults watching television. Time spent watching television peeks at about age 12, when the average child spends approximately four hours in front of a screen (Comstock & Sharrer, 2001). Compared to viewing children and to adults, nonviewing children have even more unstructured time. With generally fewer responsibilities, greater access to the commodity of time, and four more free hours than their viewing counterparts, what do nonviewing children do with their time? First, I will examine whether they simply replace television time with computer time. Then I will investigate time-use diaries to look more generally at the way they spend their free time.

Computer Use

On average, American children between the ages of 8 and 18 spend 62 minutes on a computer every day (Roberts, Foehr, & Rideout, 2005). While some of that time is spent on schoolwork, most of it is not. In other words, children are spending their free time with computers. Unlike most of their parents, who grew up before the Internet was readily available, most children now have ready access to computers and the Internet, as well as to television. With their greater amount of free time and their increased technological savvy, are nonviewing children spending their free time with a computer screen rather than a television screen? To answer this question, I asked parents to report on their children's use of the computer.[1] Because parents were reporting on all of their children, the children included in this sample are both greater in number and younger on average than those who participated in the self-report survey. A total of 157 viewing and nonviewing children are included in the questionnaire portion.

In general, preschoolers used the computer very little, and when they did, it was almost solely to play games. (See Figure 10.3 for computer-based activities for children of different ages.) Older children use computers for communicating and reading the news. Overall, however, children from viewing households tended to spend more time in various computer-based activities than children from nonviewing households. For example, viewing children aged 6–10 years spent more time on a computer than nonviewing children in the same age group. Among children aged 11–15, viewers also played computer games more frequently than nonviewers. In addition, it is telling that among preschoolers who watched television, 40% spent at least some time playing computer games; however, among nonviewing preschoolers, only 15% had any computer time. Similarly, in television households, all children aged 6–10 spent at least some time on a computer; however, only 57% of their nonviewing counterparts did. But, as nonviewing children aged, more gained access to computers. For example, by age 11, only 8% spent no time on computers, but among the oldest children, all spent at least some time on a computer. As one mother of a nonviewing teen reported, "He usually looks at the news and then e-mails some friends when we're at the library," she said. "He likes that and I think it's fine." Like their parents, children from nonviewing households are not replacing time in front of a television screen with time in front of a computer screen.

One reason for this circumstance may be that parents in nonviewing households do not always approve of computer use for their children. When asked if computers were a good way for their children to be entertained, 46% said no; only 7% of parents from viewing households said this. Generally, parents in households with television were somewhat more supportive of computer use for their children as a tool for communication and as a medium for entertainment. (See Figure 10.4.) Therefore, as much as nonviewing families think that television is not a good use of leisure time, they seem to feel similarly regarding computer use as a leisure activity. If it were up to them, leisure time would not be spent in front of any screen. What, then, do children in nonviewing households do with their time?

---

1 Although diary information was available, instances of computer use were not prevalent enough to draw valid conclusions.

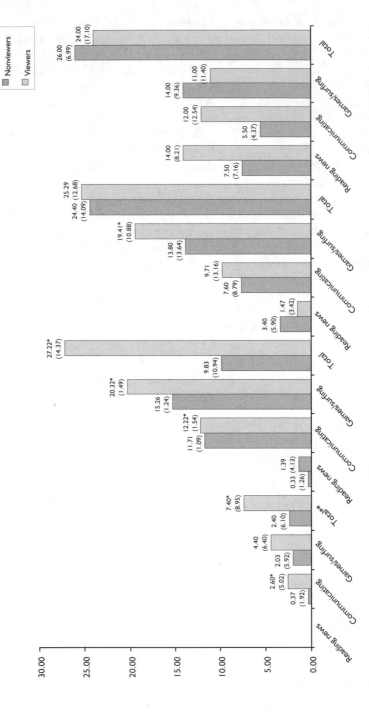

Figure 10.3 Average time in minutes spent in computer-based activites for viewing and nonviewing children, based on parent reports

Note: (*) indicates independent sample t-tests are significantly different at p <0.05; (**) indicates parents were asked to report on their children's total computer time in a separate question. For some respondents, the amount of time reported for various computer activities, when totaled, actually surpassed their response for total time

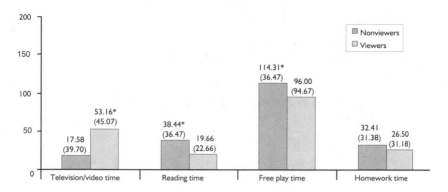

Figure 10.4 Mean time (in minutes) spent in activities for viewing and nonviewing children

Note: (*) indicates independent sample t-tests are significantly different at p <0.05

Leisure Time

Children spend their free time in a range of activities—from sports and hobbies to free play and reading. To assess children's time use, I coded the diaries that they kept. Entries were coded into seven fairly broad categories: sleeping, self-care (e.g., eating, bathing, getting dressed), free play (e.g., playing outside, dressing up, crafts, drawing), screen use (e.g., television, video, computer games), school, homework, and reading. In many cases, children used broad categories to describe their own activities (e.g., playing, homework, school), making coding a mostly simple process. In the survey portion of the study, I also asked them to respond to several Likert items concerning how they *like* to spend their time. Specifically, using a 5-point Likert scale, I asked them how much they enjoyed each of 11 activities.

The interviews, the diaries and the surveys converged on some fairly straightforward findings about children who do not watch television as compared to their viewing counterparts. Children in nonviewing households spend more time in free play and more time reading or being read to. They do not spend more time on homework (see Figures 10.4 and 10.5.) or sleeping. Interestingly, nonviewing children report enjoying watching television less and enjoying reading more than children in viewing households, but there are no differences in their reported enjoyment of playing pretend, playing outside, playing board games, homework, sleep, playing video games, spending time with friends, doing chores, going to school, or spending time with their parents. In fact, both viewing and nonviewing children generally reported enjoying all of the activities listed in the survey. Even homework and chores, items designed to provide a

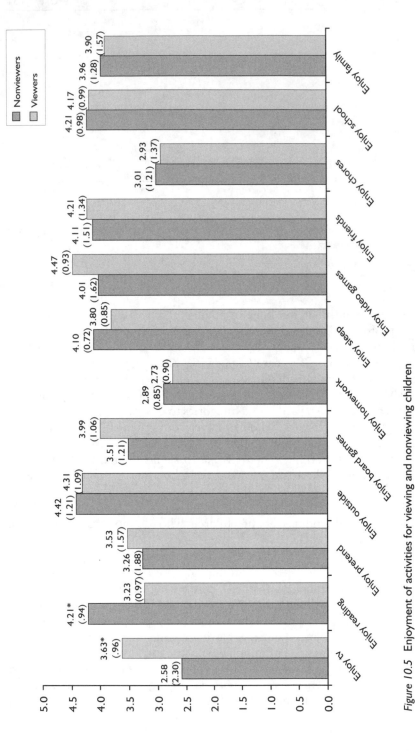

Figure 10.5 Enjoyment of activities for viewing and nonviewing children

Note: (*) indicates independent sample t-tests are significantly different at p <0.05. Times taken from children's diary entries (N=45) and enjoyment data taken from surveys (n=59). Participants responded to Likert items, responses ranged from 1 (strongly disagree) to 5 (strongley agree).

contrast for the young respondents, garnered approximately a neutral on the Likert scale. (See Figures 10.4 and 10.5.) Therefore, it is possible that within certain reasonable parameters, children enjoy the experiences to which they have been exposed.

As we discussed in chapter 4, children in nonviewing households do not seem to pine for television or miss having it. Rather, they have adapted by enjoying other activities, such as reading and free play, to a greater degree than children from viewing households. Perhaps, here, uses and gratifications theory again offers some insight. For all children, psychological needs exist: the need to be entertained, to escape, to pass time, to learn, and to socialize. And for most children a variety of activities are available to fulfill their needs. For children in viewing households, television is certainly one available form of entertainment, providing a means to pass time, to learn or to fulfill other momentary or ongoing needs. Furthermore, television is readily available, and its continuous availability makes it an easy option. However, television as a means to fulfill needs has many functional alternatives. The diaries reveal that nonviewing children simply fill television's void with other activities, from fencing and playing "dragon school" to coloring or riding a bike. These activities also serve to pass time or to provide escapism.

Therefore, in understanding how children from viewing and nonviewing households differ in their use of free time, it is perhaps *not* surprising to say that they watch television less and read or play more. What is interesting, however, is that they enjoy these activities as much as, or even more than viewing children enjoy television. As discussed earlier, children may enjoy television to some extent because it is familiar. Without it, children in nonviewing households find other activities equally familiar, comfortable, and enjoyable. Nonviewing children may spend their free time reading or learning to play musical instruments, but they too have a need to escape or pass time. Therefore, their activities may also serve those needs, such as the boy who spent an hour taking his chicken for a walk.

Overall, both nonviewing children and nonviewing adults engage in a wide variety of activities. Although individuals from viewing households often mentioned unusual hobbies or engaged in a variety of activities and diversions, those from nonviewing households did so with greater frequency, mentioning a wider variety of activities compared to their viewing counterparts. In addition, adult nonviewers responded to the survey items by reporting that they wanted to spend more time in several of the activities listed. Similarly, nonviewing children often mentioned during their interviews that without television, they had more time to play or to read. In other words, nonviewers are active people. In fact, as I will discuss in the next section, nonviewers may simply have an aversion to what they perceive as "wasting time." They often mentioned the concept of "television addiction," an idea that was brought up repeatedly by nonviewers but rarely by viewers. This concept reveals an attitude toward television viewing that may ultimately also address questions about core differences between viewers and nonviewers.

Television, The Power of Addiction, and Time Use

In their study comparing heavy viewers and nonviewers, Foss and Alexander (1996) found that both talked about television in terms of an addiction. Among nonviewers in the present study, one theme that often emerged was also that of addiction. The addiction metaphor came up even in interviews with people who had not watched television in 20 years. When I then asked if they themselves had ever felt addicted and they assured me that no, they had not, the addiction metaphor remained. Some nonviewers did not watch because they were convinced that addiction was a possibility, and if television was not quite a drug pusher, getting the unsuspecting hooked, then at least it was a thief.

Mark Armstrong does not appear to be addicted to television. In fact, when he did own a television, "it basically held up a big fern." But now, 10 years later, he feels that television is somewhat dangerous because, "it could get its hooks into me." He argues that "Time zooms ahead and personally, if I find myself in front of the screen, I could spend all night there." So despite the fact that he has no television, and despite the fact that when he did, it was used primarily as a plant stand, Mark is convinced that television has power, a theme that I addressed in earlier chapters. Nonviewers seem to perceive television as having power over their time and even over their social interactions. Kyle Neff argues that "A group of people can go to a bar to hang out and talk and then the TV is there and then there's no conversation. They fall into a catatonic state." In the cases of Mark and Kyle, perhaps they see television as having power in order to justify a need to eliminate it entirely. After all, a mere appliance need not be controlled. But something with power must be, and what controls better than total elimination?

A similar story comes from Elaine Sloan, who has not watched television in almost 20 years, although when she talks about it, the feelings associated with television and its use of time, are vivid. "I hate feeling like it tricked me and cheated me of time...It's like a drug and I don't want to give myself over to it," she says. "But it wasn't because it was boring. It was more the pull of it as well as the worthlessness." Does television actually have that kind of power? Although research on television as an addiction typically finds that television is not similar to, say, cigarettes in its addictive quality, even nonviewers report that they have gotten pulled in. One television viewer reported that "I sit down to watch 30 minutes and then three hours go by like nothing."

So perhaps television can pull viewers in and then promote inertia. After all, it keeps providing stimulus until the viewer actively turns it off. But it is not truly addictive. What matters, however, is that nonviewers *perceive* it as addictive. It is that perception that affects their decision to live without it. As Rick Drabman argues, "I don't have television because *I* want to be in control, not it." So among nonviewers, time, and how it is used, is a valuable commodity. To gain control of time, they live without television, and with this found time they are free to use their time productively in chores or, as one called it, "worthwhile pursuits," or in activities that are "not that far ahead in terms of being enlightening." Once again, the theme of personal power emerges. Nonviewers feel that it is important to "control" their time.

If television "steals time" or "cheats you of time" it obviously has a power that, if not addictive, is almost anthropomorphic. As Alexander (2001) has argued, it exists in contested space, as neither an object of perception nor of social cognition. It is not still and powerless, like a table or a picture on the wall; nor is it interactive and requiring attention like a needy toddler. To nonviewers, it seems that television exists more as an object of social cognition than of perception. Because of this view, they simultaneously grant it power and feel its power to draw them in. Like several nonviewers, Rebecca Tanner, a nonviewer whom we will meet in chapter 12, complained that when she visited the home of viewers, they left their televisions on during the visit. "I just want to turn it off but they leave it on and they don't even seem to notice it. But I hate that so much." Perhaps, then, nonviewers feel that television is powerful because they themselves feel that it is an object of social cognition. Nonviewers may find it easier to relegate the television to the realm of perception. This feeling that television has power may leave nonviewers feeling vulnerable. In the end, their desire to retain control over their time use, coupled with their aversion to wasting time or having it spent in the "worthless" pursuit of television viewing has led them to regain power by living without the screen.

Uses and Gratifications, and Time Use

As discussed in chapter 3, early research on the uses of television (Rubin, 1981) argued that we might better understand the effects of television if we consider how people use the medium. This research identified various uses of television including entertainment needs, such as escapism or enjoyment; social facilitation needs, such as talking about a program or talking during a program; and informational needs, such as news access. Furthermore, uses and gratifications argues that media use can be goal-directed and purposeful, which is referred to as instrumental use; or it can be less goal-directed and perhaps habitual, as in the case of ritualized use. Media researchers have found that among television viewers, instrumental use is associated with more exposure to television news, and ritualized use is related to greater exposure to entertainment, such as comedy (Rubin, 1984).

Applications of this approach to Internet research assumes that users see the Internet as a functional alternative to television. For example, Lin (1999) found that when people use the Internet for entertainment, it can act as a substitute for television. However, additional uses, such as online shopping or searching for information, typically resulted in more screen time overall—that is, both more Internet use and more television use. Apparently, if the Internet fulfills entertainment needs, then television is no longer useful. However, if users surf the Web to fulfill other needs, such as e-mail to fulfill social needs, users may still look to television to fulfill their entertainment needs (Papacharissi & Rubin, 2000).

How would uses and gratifications' interpretations of television and Internet research translate into research on nonviewers? First, nearly unanimously, nonviewers do not feel that television adequately fulfills their needs—neither entertainment, information, nor social needs. It does not, as a whole, entertain them, as argued by nonviewer Sean Greene, who called television "formulaic," "predictable," and "boring." They also do not feel that their news and information needs are adequately addressed by television, as I discuss in chapter 8. And they generally feel that television hinders, not assists, their social needs. Many nonviewers do, however, have computers. Although I argued above that computer time does not completely replace television time, if we consider the uses and gratifications approach, we get a better understanding of why this is the case.

First, recall that a significant majority agreed or strongly agreed that the Internet was a good way of accessing news. We might argue, therefore, that for nonviewers, computers replace television news because they feel it meets information needs well; however, computers can do so more thoroughly and more efficiently. Therefore, if we imagine a hypothetical viewer sitting down to watch 30 minutes of television news to fulfill their information needs, a hypothetical nonviewer may seek out news online; however, as I discuss in chapter 8, it may take less time to access news online than it takes to watch television news. Second, a majority of nonviewers also agreed or strongly agreed that the Internet provided a good means of communicating. During the interviews, they often cite face-to-face communication as their preferred mode, but they see the

Internet as adequately complementing this. Therefore, their needs for social interaction are met by face-to-face communication and by e-mailing and Internet chat on a computer. Again, these nonviewers may spend some time on a computer to meet their social needs, but many of their social needs are met in other ways. Third, many nonviewers generally felt that the Internet did not adequately meet their entertainment needs. Therefore, time that viewers might spend meeting their entertainment needs by watching television, was spent by nonviewers in other entertaining activities. Therefore, nonviewers do not seem to replace their television time with computer time. Generally, nonviewers may use computers to meet information needs; they may use computers to complement their communication needs. However, for entertainment, nonviewers seek out other sources.

Overall, then, nonviewers are not simply heavy computer users. Adult nonviewers spend their nonviewing time in a wide variety of activities; in fact, engaging in more varied activities than viewers. Both adult and child nonviewers spend a lot of time reading and neither group seems to miss having television in their lives. They seem to read and play and spend time with others because they prefer it, not because they need to fill up the hours left empty by television. The data paint a picture of nonviewers who choose to be active, not nonviewers pining away for television. Similar to other findings regarding nonviewing, living without television is not merely an independent variable with a cascade of effects. Instead, living without television is a choice that is intimately related to other decisions, attitudes and modes of being. Although it plays some role in time use for both adults and children, nonviewing is ultimately one factor in a complex set of variables that determine lifestyle.

Chapter 11

Encouraging Creativity

This chapter introduces the concept of creativity in children. Parents of nonviewing children often claim that their children are creative or imaginative and they attribute this to their children's nonviewing. In this chapter, I begin by defining creativity. I then discuss three possible explanations for the creativity perceived in nonviewing children. First, I introduce the idea of flow, or the state in which a child is so involved in an activity that s/he loses track of time and seems unaware of other things going on. I argue that the "creativity" that parents perceive in their children may arise in part from their children's greater opportunity to achieve flow states when a television is not present. Simply put, with more uninterrupted free time available to them, children fill that time with activities that they ultimately enjoy, making flow possible. Second, the empirical literature suggests that television may cause interference with children's ability to create novel visualizations by providing them ready-made visualizations. The result may be that nonviewing increases creativity. Third, using family systems theory, I argue that creativity may be increased among nonviewing children due to the value placed on creativity in nonviewing homes and by parents expectations that their children be creative.

Grace is 9 years old. Like any 9 year old she is simultaneously earnest and goofy. Grace grew up without television. When I ask her what it would be like to have television, she thinks a moment and then responds, "It would be like the games I play with my stuffed animals except I wouldn't get to decide what happens. The show would. I have shows going on in my head all the time but I decide what happens." Grace is commenting on her own creativity, her ability to decide the course of actions she imagines. This type of creativity, sometimes referred to as creative imagination (Valkenburg, 2001), is one form of creativity that parents often referred to when discussing their nonviewing children.

Parents in these households often use the terms creative or imaginative to refer to their children, and they credit their children's creativity or imaginativeness to the fact that they do not watch television. However, parents generally do not think that particular programs interfere with creativity. Rather, they believe that television as a medium has the ability to take time away from free play or to interfere with spontaneously generated imaginative play. Of the 63 nonviewing parents interviewed, 92% (n=58) spontaneously mentioned television's negative effect on creativity, imaginative play or imagination, either as a factor in their decision to get rid of television, or as a benefit of not watching it. None of the parents in television-viewing households spontaneously mentioned creativity as a benefit or drawback to television viewing.

An extensive review of the literature on the effect of television exposure on children's creativity and imagination (Valkenburg & van der Voort, 1994; Valkenburg, 2001) suggested that television does have some short-term effect on children's creativity, although it depends on how creativity and imagination are defined and to what kinds of programs children are exposed. For example, exposure to television does seem to affect creative imagination. In research on creativity, creative imagination refers to the ability to generate many novel or unusual ideas, many possible solutions to a single problem, or many novel uses of a single object. A related term, imagination, has also been studied in relation to children's television viewing; however, television exposure does not really seem to have a universally negative effect on imagination. When imagination is operationalized (i.e., defined and measured) as daydreaming, it has been found that television viewing actually increases the amount of daydreaming children do; however, the content of programming affects the kind of fantasies that occur. Children who watch a lot of violent cartoons, for example, experience more aggressive and heroic fantasies. So to simply say that children who watch no television are more creative than viewing children may or may not be true. It depends partly on how creativity is defined. Furthermore, longitudinal data that attempts to look at the long-term effects of television viewing on creativity are not available because such research has not been published.

However, what does appear consistent is that parents in nonviewing homes believe their children to be creative, largely as a result of their nonviewing. In this chapter I will explore definitions of creativity, both in the research literature and as described by parents, and I will discuss nonviewing families' perceptions of creativity in their own children. I will also briefly discuss the research on television viewing and creativity, and I will examine possible explanations for those relationships.

Creative Imagination

What do parents mean by creative with regard to their children? In talking to them about this issue, parents mean many things, although their ideas seem to cluster around several related concepts. The first and most common idea that emerges is that they believe that, due to lack of TV exposure, their children can spontaneously generate many ways to entertain themselves. This meaning of creative seems similar to researchers' use of the term *creative imagination*. As mentioned earlier, creative imagination is operationalized as the ability to generate many novel solutions to a single problem or the ability to go beyond the information that has been readily provided in the problem's presentation. When parents of nonviewing children discuss their children's creativity, what they seem to mean is that when faced with a problem—in this case, how to fill unstructured free time—they believe their children solve this problem in many novel ways. As one parent said, "Without TV, they might get bored. But boredom is good. Boredom helps you find new things to do. And I'm shocked by the range of things they come up with." Therefore, when parents say that their nonviewing children are creative, they often mean that they are creatively imaginative.

Danielle Long is the mother of one child. When she talks about giving up television, she talks about creativity not just for her daughter but also for herself and her husband. With the extra time they have found by not watching television, she admitted that, at first, she and her husband were a bit unsure of what to do. But as they grew accustomed to it, they also found benefits. She argued that "pushing the boundaries of comfort is good. When we're bored this pushes us to explore how we use our time, and that boundary pushing is good. That causes growth."

In other words, the time that may otherwise be occupied by television is amorphous. Children, as well as adults can spend that time doing productive things that some parents mentioned, like learning to play a musical instrument, or it can be filled simply by idling away that time. However, rather than seeing this as a waste of time, quite a few families mentioned that idle time provided the entire family with opportunities to explore. For example, Lily Dawson and her husband, who decided to raise their 2-year-old daughter without television, cite the value of play as one thing that fills the space. When Lily talks about what her daughter does, she does not talk, like some parents do, about reading or complex puzzles or educational pursuits that her daughter can follow. Instead, she talks about play, which she also values as a form of creativity. Lily argues that, "I'm glad that she's doing exactly what kids want to do. Our 5-year-old neighbor came over and he asked if he could watch TV and I said we didn't have one. He was pretty surprised, and asked what Amanda did all day. Then he answered himself and said, 'Oh, does she just play?' And I thought, 'he gets it.' So now I think to myself, 'Yes, she just plays.'"

A related definition of creativity was introduced by several parents of nonviewing children. Some discussed their children's ability to extend their imaginative play or their conversations beyond specific things they had seen on television or even read in a book. This ability to go beyond the information given is also consistent with the term *creative imagination*. For example, Rebecca Tanner, who will be discussed in depth in chapter 12, was a teacher before her children were born. Her insights into television come from not just her own family life but also from her experiences with her young students. She claims that creativity is the ability to draw on experiences other than television, and she notes that she always valued it when her students made connections in the classroom between things that they had seen or heard and some piece of information she was trying to teach. However, she recalled the following from her teaching experience:

> Kids who watched TV in the morning, they needed to be decompressed before sitting down to work. In the kids without TV, they had a lot of variety in what they talked about. And the TV kids seemed to talk about everything in terms of what they saw on TV; almost were not able to get beyond that.

Several empirical studies offer insight into Rebecca's observation. Researchers interested in the effect of television exposure on children's creativity tested what is generally known as the "visualization hypothesis." The basic premise of the hypothesis is that the negative effect of television can be attributed to its visual nature. As a result of the ready-made images, children exposed to television are less likely to generate their own images. In other words, they generate fewer ideas, and these ideas tend not to stray from the audio-visual presentation. Rather, they fall back on the images that have been prepared for them. In a typical study used to test this hypothesis, children are presented a problem or told a story either on video, via radio or in print. These studies have found that video presentations lead children to generate fewer novel ideas than audio-only or print presentations (Valkenburg, 2001). In fact, children in the video conditions tended to rely heavily on what they had seen, and were, as Rebecca Tanner argued, "almost...not able to get beyond that." Therefore, whether we define creative imagination as the ability to generate a novel solution to a problem, or as the ability to generate many novel games and play experiences, empirical research tends to support the notion that television can interfere with creativity. In part, due to its visual nature, television images supplant children's own creative visualization and interfere with their tendency to generate novel ones.

Inner Direction and the Flow Experience

The second idea that parents bring up in relation to creativity and imagination is what one mother aptly called *inner direction*. Andrea Haggerty has two sons, both preschoolers. Like many parents, she mentioned that her sons have the ability to fill their free time in many different ways; however, she relates this ability to an idea, one that was also discussed by quite a few parents in nonviewing households. She believes that the experience of creativity manifests itself in the ability to "look inward," as she called it, or the ability to "spend time in her own world," as another parent mentioned. The idea of inner directedness that many parents discussed seems somewhat related to the notion of imagination, or a child's ability to build play experiences inside of the mind. For example, Andrea says of her own sons:

> They both have a very long attention span. When he [one son] was 18 months he could literally sit for over an hour with a book. They can look at the pictures forever...When he plays, he has his own little world. He is more inner directed.

Another parent of a 9-year-old girl and an 11-year-old boy claimed, "I never bought the little kitchen or the super hero characters. Everything they did was with stuff we had. And they'd make these elaborate games. And sometimes I'd walk through the room and I'd swear I was invisible, they were so absorbed in their minds' play."

This concept is not a new one. When a child sits and plays for hours, what Andrea refers to as being "inner directed" or "in his own little world," Mihaly Csikszentmihalyi (1990) refers to as *flow*. Csikszentmihalyi has spent over two decades studying the concept of happiness asking essentially, in what situations are people happy? What causes happiness and how can it be achieved? By looking at people's moods and the activities they are engaged in at those times, he has been able to understand when people are happy. He has concluded that people are happiest when they are experiencing flow, or "The state in which people are so involved in an activity that nothing else seems to matter; the experience itself is so enjoyable that people will do it even at great cost for the sheer sake of doing it." Importantly, it is achieved when there exists a perfect balance of challenge and skill. Most of us recognize flow experiences. We lose track of time; we continue to do the activity for hours at a time. We may even become less aware of our surroundings, focusing instead on the activity in which we are involved. Flow for adults can be experienced doing some rewarding sport, such as skiing or hiking, or another activity, such as painting or playing music. Flow can be achieved through rewarding work or through some volunteer task. What causes flow varies from person to person, of course. However, flow is most likely to occur when the task has intrinsic rewards and when the level of difficulty is at or slightly beyond our level of skill. Flow tasks offer challenge.

In addition to the familiarity of the flow experience, many of us are also familiar with the experience of watching children play. They may become so absorbed in some imaginary world or project that adults who are not involved in the game cease to be present, as described by the mother earlier. For children, imaginary play is a cognitive skill. As they age, the imaginary play they engage in goes from simple single instances of "pretend," such as the 2 year old who uses a spoon as a phone, to the elaborate games of make-believe engaged in by older children. Importantly, the skill level is elevated as they age, keeping cognitive skill and challenge in balance. At some point, cognitive skill is advanced enough that imaginative play is no longer satisfying. But until that point, play seems to have the potential to provide children with an exceptionally satisfying flow experience.

Obviously, play is a flow experience for most children, not just those who live without television. Furthermore, there is no published research that suggests that exposure to television limits children's ability to achieve flow during play. But what may be different, and what parents in nonviewing homes noted, is that children without television have more time for play and more time to achieve flow. Consider the experience of flow. Important qualities of flow are total absorption and loss of a sense of time. To achieve flow, an individual must have an intrinsically rewarding pastime, and, importantly, time to reach the flow phase. It also seems to be important, although not crucial, to be uninterrupted in order to achieve true flow (Csikszentmihalyi, 1990). There are two ways that television may interfere with children's flow experiences during play. First, as most parents noted, children who do not have access to television simply have more unstructured free time than children who do watch television. As the results from the time-use diaries in chapter 10 indicated, children in nonviewing homes spend more time in free play than do children in viewing homes. Second, although children in viewing homes often play in front of a television, engaging in early multitasking (Anderson, Field, Collins & Lorch, 1985), it is likely that their play is interrupted by what they are viewing. Therefore, children in nonviewing homes seem to have two important criteria that would make flow possible: free time and uninterrupted time. In other words, they have the opportunity to achieve total absorption in their play activities.

In the case of creativity, then, when Andrea Haggerty refers to her sons as being "inner directed," perhaps what she perceives is flow. Therefore, to parents in nonviewing homes, creativity means several things. It is similar to researchers' use of the term creative imagination, with children filling free time with many novel activities. It also parallels the notion of imagination. Lastly, creativity seems to be similar to an ability to achieve flow. In all of these cases, parents attribute these outcomes to children's nonviewing, the benefits of which include the greater amount of free time it affords, greater uninterrupted time, and the lack of ready-made images and conversational topics—what researchers have referred to as *visualization*. In this last case, imagination and creativity must step into the void in the absence of those provided by television.

Explaining links between nonviewing and creativity

Most of those interviewed, both parents and adults without children, felt that the relationship between creativity and television was causal. Television, the argument seemed to go, dampens creativity because it provides readymade stories, interfering with children's ability to come up with their own stories. Furthermore, television takes time, removing opportunities for boredom which ultimately may generate novel play ideas. It is possible, as well, that television interferes with children's ability to achieve flow when they are engaged in play. All of these explanations are at least partially supported by the available data and extant literature. However, it is possible that the connection is not quite so clear. After all, in a family without television, other ingredients are likely to encourage creativity—or encourage parents to perceive a unique creativity in their children. So what is the cause of creativity in these nonviewing homes? The answer is probably three-fold.

Creativity in children may be encouraged by, first, the greater time children spend in uninterrupted free play and the greater likelihood that, uninterrupted by television, children will achieve flow in their play experiences. Second, as suggested by the empirical literature and mentioned by some parents, television may cause interference with children's ability to create novel visualizations by providing them ready-made visualizations. Ultimately, this may hamper creativity. However, there exists a third possibility that has not been explored in the empirical literature, nor was it voiced by the parents interviewed. In homes without television, there may be value placed on creativity and heavy emphasis placed on those activities that foster it (e.g., playing a musical instrument, building a model of the Empire State Building). This argument is consistent with family systems theory presented in earlier chapters.

It seems apparent from the interviews with nonviewers that many of these parents value creativity. Certainly parents in general value this trait. However, recall that 92% of nonviewing parents mentioned creativity; whereas no parents from viewing homes did. Although it is impossible to generalize from this relatively small sample, the trend is interesting. Why is value placed on creativity in nonviewing households? Perhaps because parents who live without television are, by definition, unusual. They have chosen to actively reject a fairly common and universal practice. For them, being different is part of a lifestyle and, as I will discuss in chapter 13, for many, being different is valuable. It is no surprise, then, that value is placed on this cousin of difference—creativity. Therefore, creativity as a value may spur on other behaviors that then encourage creativity in children. This argument would suggest that nonviewing is partly spuriously related to creativity. Although the experimental research cited in this chapter suggests that television viewing is also causally related to creativity, it is worth exploring family attitudes and behaviors as an additional contributing factor.

When parents value a particular behavior—athleticism, for example— it is possible that they perceive greater athleticism in their children. Similarly, parents who value creativity may have expressed their children's creativity to me not because it was somehow greater or more developed than that of other children, but simply because the parents wanted to see it that way. However, bias aside, parents who value creativity are likely to do other things to foster it, apart from eliminating television from their homes. For example, one mother reported that when she initially got rid of television, one of the first things she did was go out and buy craft supplies for her children. "And I mean lots of supplies," she said. "I think I spent almost 200 bucks on stuff for them to make things." Sam Steinberg, who we will discuss in chapter 13, is helping his young son build a replica of the Empire State Building in their basement, and one father reported that his son liked to make up stories, and he lent him his own tape recorder so the child, who was a bit too young to write, could record his creations. Clearly these behaviors serve to foster creativity, or at least serve to convey to young children that their parents value it.

In sum, it seems likely that there are some negative effects of television viewing on creativity. After all, it displaces free play (Singer & Singer, 1990), inhibits children's creativity due to its visual nature (Greenfield & Beagles-Roos, 1988), encourages children to use it as a reference point for play, story-telling and conversation, and may inhibit flow. However, ultimately, it is likely that creativity arises from many sources. Fertile ground is needed, including, perhaps, a home free of television, but also one replete with other sources that nurture creativity, whether those sources are music lessons, art supplies, books or an empty back yard. In addition to the sources of creativity, there must also be a value placed on that commodity. Creativity is likely to flourish in homes where creativity is itself valued. Lastly, creativity is likely to be perceived by parents who want their children to be creative. Not only will they encourage it, but they will see it. Therefore, creativity, like many of the other family beliefs mentioned in earlier chapters, is part of a family system. It is possible, therefore, that in homes without television, creativity flourishes as part of the system. Ultimately, creativity may indeed go hand-in-hand with growing up in a nonviewing household, but nonviewing itself may be the cause of creativity, or it may be linked to creativity in a more complex way than experimental designs have tested for.

Chapter 12

Engaging in Real Life

In this chapter, I explore the idea of real life, as mentioned by many nonviewers. These nonviewers frequently believe that television distances viewers from their daily lives by presenting a false reality and by separating viewers from other members of their family or community. To understand this notion, I first draw from the uses and gratifications perspective, specifically its notion of television as a form of escapism. As such, it may be possible that, as nonviewers argue, not watching television may encourage a greater connection with on-going, everyday life. Second, I bring in cultivation theory, which predicts (and finds) that those who watch more television, as opposed to light or nonviewers, hold a view of the world that more closely matches the television world. Third, I address ideas discussed by Adorno (1974), who argues that learning can only come from actual life experiences and, when we watch television, we cannot be said to be experiencing the things we see, only watching them. Last, I review literature on infants' understanding of television in order to posit that television is not real to babies and, therefore, lacks some inherent reality that we must learn to give it.

As we have considered in previous chapters, the presence of television is perceived in family life in many ways. According to 35% of the adult nonviewers in my study, television influences either their perceptions of "real life" or, more inscrutably, it interferes with their real lives. At least one-third of the adults who do not watch television believe that there is a "real" life, separate from television viewing, that must be embraced, and that living with television distances us from that real life. Although some nonviewers who expressed concern over this potential effect of television worried that television *content* could affect their perceptions of their real lives, they were more often worried that the mere presence of television could keep them disconnected from what they considered to be their "real" lives. In this chapter, television is viewed as both content and medium; however, among nonviewers, the concept of medium was mentioned more frequently in relation to their concerns over *engaging in real life*.

Eric and Rebecca Tanner

The catalog for the Nova Natural Toy Company shows angelic looking children playing with beautiful toys in idyllic settings. Two little boys crouch on a rock, floating a wooden boat down a small stream; a young boy and girl sort wooden produce in front of a wooden cash register. "But" says Eric Tanner, who works as the warehouse manager for Nova Natural Toys, "We don't really think children need toys. They need to experience life." Not a very hard sell, there. "We're thinking of having an article in the next catalog called: 'Don't buy this toy.'" Eric explains, "We think kids need their parents and freedom to explore but not a lot of toys." He goes on to say that parents will probably always buy toys for their children, so the goal of Nova is to get parents to buy good toys, toys that will help children use their imaginations and play creatively. Here his wife Rebecca interrupts: "But probably the best toy for children's imagination is no toy." Eric nods. They agree on this point. They agree that children do not need toys, do not need TV, and do not need fancy or designer label clothes. Rather, they believe that what children need, what we all need, is to experience "real life" and watching television gets in the way of that.

Eric, Rebecca and their three children moved from Texas to Vermont just seven months prior to our conversation. According to them, they had discussed moving many times. They even talked about moving with another family, perhaps doing it together so they would know someone when they got to a brand new town. The other family moved, and then came back to Texas, and still Eric and Rebecca stayed. Then, Rebecca was looking online one day, checking out a gift for one of their children, and she noticed a posting for a job at Nova Toys. "We'd been customers and so when I saw the job, all the way in Vermont, we figured we'd just try it." Eric recalled that Rebecca showed him the job posting in early August and he sent a resume at the end of the month. By the end of September, the family had loaded a U-Haul and started the long drive from Texas to northern Vermont.

For both of them, the move seems to have been symbolic. Although they lived without television before their move, both agree that in the last few months they have started living in a way that suits them more so than ever before. Living without television is part of their belief system, the one that sets the parameters for a good family life. But it goes beyond that. Rebecca reports that, "We realize that the work that we do, all of it, not just the paid work but all that we choose to do with our lives, that is also our entertainment. We see it as a whole. We're not trying to get through our paid work to get to our entertainment. It's all just life."

How is this belief connected to life without television? Rebecca says, "Everything we do becomes part of who we are and I just think real life is so much more important than a screen and any time you sit in front of a screen, you're not having a life." In other words, Rebecca and Eric believe that time spent with television interferes with, or, as they say, "distances" them from life's everyday experiences. Eric goes on to argue that he thinks television "disconnects us from our real lives that we have right here. I can be not engaged with my spouse or child and it's never-ending. It's 24-7. And then you could just have this false connection that distances you from your real life." In other words, the Tanners, and other nonviewers, reject the escapism that television offers.

Recall that the uses and gratifications approach delineates nine motives for television exposure, including relaxation, companionship, habit, passing time, entertainment, social facilitation, information gain, arousal, and escapism (Rubin, 1983). Escapism through television allows viewers to briefly experience an existence other than their own and potentially to forget about their own lives. Particular programs allow us to experience other lives, real and imaginary. This effect may be seen as a benefit to viewers but as a drawback to nonviewers. However, according to the Tanners, it is not just a given program that may offer escapism. Rather, all viewing is somehow escapist. For example, Eric argued that "There's a way in which the scheduling demands of television work beyond the TV. Even as a favorite program approaches, and we're talking, I'm not totally present because there's something else calling." So for Eric, a television show—as it approaches, when it's on, even afterwards, after the set is off—demands attention, and that attention is taken away from what he repeatedly called "real life." Like others who perceive television primarily as a medium, the Tanners argue that television is omnipresent. Even when it is off, the possibility of it remains. So television not only offers escapism when it is on, but also lures us with the possibility of escapism when it is off. Like other nonviewers, the Tanners recognize the same uses of television that viewers do; however, they either reject television as a means of gratifying the need, or reject the need entirely. In the case of escapism, many nonviewers believe that escapism itself is problematic. Over and over again, they talked about the importance of engaging in *real life*.

Although the entire family is active—Rebecca sews and knits and plays the guitar; Eric plays the banjo and gardens; their 6 year old plays the violin—engaging in "real life" goes beyond their hobbies. It is more a matter of how they approach living more generally. Their home, for example, is a tumble of activity. They live in a first-floor apartment, a maze of rooms in an old house. No one room seems to serve a single purpose: sewing things are spread across the dining room table, games sit on Rebecca and Eric's bed and on the children's futon. In the living room, there are guitars and a banjo and books and a bicycle. A wooden horse swing hangs in the doorway between the hall and the living room. Life seems to proceed from room to room with no delineation of what activity should occur in a particular space. "We try a lot of things," Eric explains. "We're experimenters." For the Tanners, and other nonviewers, living without television is not just a way of capturing more hours in the day to do other things, but it also causes life to proceed in a qualitatively different way. Activities occur, life is lived without interruption, and importantly, without any vicarious experiences. As one nonviewer stated, "Television is a drug. It numbs you and then your real life is less sharp. You're less aware. I don't want anything to get between me and my real experiences."

So if "real life" cannot be had via the television screen, and if watching television somehow interrupts real life, what is *real life*? Given that the Tanners believe that television is omnipresent and robs attention from family life, it is safe to assume that for them, television is not synonymous with content. Rather, it is a potentially ever-present source of incoming stimuli. Like other nonviewers, the Tanners are concerned with television as a *medium*. But the Tanners, and others like them, seem to mean something very specific when they argue that television distracts them from "real life."

Experiences and "Real Life"

Cultivation theory (Gerbner, 1969), one of the most frequently cited theories in mass media effects research, argues that the more television we watch, the more our conception of reality matches the reality that is presented on television. In doing so, cultivation theory assumes a clear distinction between television reality and the real world. In the former, there are proportionately more police and law enforcement officials; more crime; more beautiful, thin people; more white collar professionals; and fewer African Americans than there are in the "real world," by which cultivation researchers typically mean the United States (Gerbner, Gross, Morgan, Signorielli & Shanahan, 2002). Cultivation theory goes on to demonstrate that the more television we watch, the more we begin to think that the world of television accurately represents the real world. Our estimate of the number of crimes in our society, for example, begins to rise, mirroring more closely the number that appear in the world of television rather than the actual number that exist in the world around us.

Despite strong support for cultivation theory over the past several decades, the theory itself does not describe what is meant by the difference between television and the real world. On the face of it, perhaps this difference needs no explanation. Under the rubric of cultivation theory, television reality is that which happens on the screen, and the real world happens off of it—in the space outside of the screen. It's that simple. But the Tanners and other nonviewers are not talking about what is on television, as cultivation theory is; they are talking about the act of sitting down to watch it. Their distinction, as I will describe more thoroughly below, seems to have more to do with real action and real experiences juxtaposed with those actions and experiences that we watch. They compare real experiences with vicarious ones.

It is worth trying to understand, in this case, why the action of sitting down to watch television does not constitute the real world to nonviewers. When we talk about people watching television, what distinguishes between television and the real world? After all, television viewing *is* an experience. And if it is an experience, why is it not a *real* experience? Here, we will explore the answer from two markedly divergent sources: first, a critical–theoretical perspective and second, a logico-empiricist one. Both argue that the real world and learning from it derive from actual physical interaction with the tangible world, including people and objects, leaving television, a non-interactive, *watched* experience as less real.

The Medium of Experience

What distinguishes television from the real world? The first way that nonviewers seem to perceive television as unreal is that it deals with people, stories and ideas that are not part of our everyday life experiences. In other words, to nonviewers, the real world is one where we interact; the television world is one where we simply observe. To them, real life comes from experiences or, as Adorno (1974), argues, "comes to us through a network of prejudices, opinions, innervations, self corrections, presuppositions and exaggerations, in short, through the dense, firmly founded but by no means uniformly transparent medium of experience" (p. 80). How is this distinct from television? Although we bring all these factors to the viewing experience—prejudices and opinions, innervations and presuppositions—we cannot be said to be *experiencing* these things, only *watching* them. When we watch an educational nature program, no matter how well produced the show is, no matter how vivid the cinematography, we are not in nature. When we watch a situational comedy, no matter how humorous the material, we are not really interacting with nutty neighbors and wise-cracking family members. The experience is once removed.

Joanne Colton describes the difference between television and reality as one in which television is removed from everyday life. She does not refer to escapism, per se, but rather to the notion of getting involved in the lives of people who are far removed from one's own life. She said:

> I remember distinctly, I was at the grocery store and there was this couple and they were on every magazine cover and they were from a reality TV show who just got married. And it seemed so bizarre. But to everyone reading it, it was completely normal...I get the impression that some people and their TVs are in a virtual community and they really care about these characters. But they could be cartoons and yet they seem to take a role in their lives. But I'd rather have a relationship with our neighbors and with real people. I want to invest my effort in them and not in fictional people.

Similarly, Tanis McElrone, a college librarian living in Indiana, said, "To be so involved, I don't know. To hear people talk, you'd think it was real life."

Therefore, for Joanne and for Tanis, it is the emotional investment in fictionalized characters that represents *un*reality, especially when it happens on a large scale, or, as Joanne says, when it is, "something that everyone is paying attention to." Unlike a character in a book, who may exist for a given person at a given time while the book is being read, Joanne objects to the ubiquity of those people who are not real, the way audiences care about them and are involved in a "virtual community" with them. Unlike adolescents who, as we discussed in chapter 4, want some connection to television's characters so they can have social collateral, Joanne, the Tanners, and other nonviewers do not want it. They want to reject television characters and the discussion of these characters because they think that gets in the way of talking to real neighbors about real people. Similarly, Eric Tanner thinks that watching television interferes with his willingness to engage with his spouse or other family members. In this way, relationships with television characters can take time and attention away from our relationships with real people.

For nonviewers who reject television because they want to engage in the real world, the real world is made up of people who are geographically close, such as neighbors, or people who can have an impact on their lives, such as family members. The television world, on the other hand, is made up of fictional, or at least pseudo-fictional characters (such as those on reality television programs) who might exist somewhere out in the world but who we are unlikely to meet any time soon. However, this circumstance puts television news on a shaky middle ground. Although those who carefully distinguished between television and the real world often talked about entertainment programming, the topic of news came up as well. Does news, for them, constitute the real world or does news also fall into the category of unreality? If their definition of reality includes people and things with which we can connect, then what is news? There seemed to be two distinct camps here. Some nonviewers believe that news and politics are so far removed from their own lives that they do not feel the need to follow it. Others felt that news is real because they are affected by, and can affect, the world around them, and therefore they need to be informed.

Consider again Rebecca Tanner. She and her husband avoid many forms of media. By her own account, they went a year without a radio. They do not get a newspaper and, although they do have a computer and Internet connection, she reports spending no time using it to access the news. Instead, she says, "I scan the headlines when I'm at the store to see if I need to know. But I have no control over it. So I wonder, do I need to know?" She also says that they have no newspaper because "The pictures are not something I want to have to explain to a child. We avoid the radio because what we call news is really so far out of our control." She continues, "My children have no computer time. I'm still trying to explain the postal system so I don't want to take on radio and e-mail." So for Rebecca, avoiding news is justifiable precisely because, to her, it is as removed from her real life as the fictional characters she avoids.

Other nonviewers have a similar take, like Mark Armstrong, who said, "If something big happens, someone will tell me" or Oregon resident, Joseph Tyson, who said, "I wonder if needing to know news is really just fascination with other people's pain. Really, why do I need to know that?" For nonviewers who see news as irrelevant to their lives, they are willing to lump it into the category of the television world. It is not, in any meaningful sense, "reality." They avoid it for the same reason they avoid entertainment. To them it is not real.

However, for some nonviewers, news *is* part of their reality. For those, they may dislike television news, but not news, per se. Some, by their own admission, are news junkies. Peter Westman, a single man living in Sommerville, Massachusetts, reads the news online, gets two daily papers, subscribes to *The Economist*, and listens to NPR. He says, "I like to keep up to date." And for some, such as Isabel Slanovich, news is real, precisely because she feels it *does* touch us. "Look," she states, "we have a responsibility. We're the richest country in the world so we have to help where we can. Charity or the way we vote. We have to. It's my obligation to know." Not surprisingly, Isabel describes fictional television as unreal ("It's weird to talk about people who are not real as if they were."), but she describes news as the real world. So even among nonviewers, news is both real and unreal. But what makes it real or unreal is the extent to which it is perceived as touching our lives or affecting us. Therefore, when the Tanners want to live their lives, not watch it, as Eric says, what he is referring to is engagement in that which immediately surrounds us. And when Isabel Slanovich reads or listens to news, it is because she believes it does touch her. Although they come to different conclusions about whether or not news is "real," these nonviewers use the same criteria for making the decision. Something is real if we can interact with it and if it affects our lives.

Like those who do not want television to steal their time, those who insist that television interrupts their engagement with the real world perceive television as a kind of trick, one that gets in the way of engagement with family or with activities that they enjoy. Mark Armstrong states that for him, television might take time away from his kids. "And then," he says, "you spend your whole night waiting for something to happen and it never does. You have three hours with nothing to show for it and you haven't even spent good time with the people in your *real* life." Therefore, according to some nonviewers, television distances us from real life by taking time away from real activities and human interactions. Recall that Eric Tanner argued that the very scheduling of television requires that we think about television even when it is off.

Similarly, Adorno (1991) argues that television is, what he calls, a variety act. He states that:

> What really constitutes the variety act, the thing that strikes any child the first time he sees such a thing is the fact that on each occasion something happens and nothing happens at the same time. Every variety act, especially of the clown and the juggler, is really a kind of expectation. It subsequently transpires that waiting for the thing in question, which takes place precisely as long as the juggler manages to keep the balls going, is precisely the thing itself. (p. 70)

Nonviewers believe that while this waiting is occurring, they escape from everyday real life. Therefore, television removes us from real life, not only because it is non-representative in its content, but also because as a medium, its omnipresence distracts us from the immediate present. One way to define reality, then, according to both Adorno (1974) and to the nonviewers discussed above, is to identify the real, interactive experiences of life, that come to us through "the medium of experience" (Adorno, 1974, p. 70). To the extent that television distracts us from that, either because it is not an interactive experience, because it does not depict factual events or because it is omnipresent, television is not only unreal, it interferes with reality.

Television vs. Three-dimensional Space

A second way to identify reality is to consider the empirical research on television and social reality. Here, we will address cultivation theory and its assumptions about social reality, and examine research on very young children's understanding of television, given that they have relatively little experience with the television world and considerably more experience with the unmediated world.

Cultivation theory makes no claims about the *qualitative* differences between television and the real world. Instead, it assumes that the difference between the two has only to do with how closely one matches the other in terms of quantitative or numerical representation. That is, television becomes less real simply because it shows more police, more crime, and fewer African Americans than exist in the real world, not because of its quality as a medium or because it makes us talk to real people less frequently. Its lack of reality is due simply to its lack of representativeness.

Cultivation theory has garnered much research attention in the media effects literature for at least two reasons. First, it is parsimonious and fairly straightforward to test. Demonstrate a lack of statistical representation on television (of, say, solved crime), then measure viewers' estimates of that issue in the real world and measure their degree of exposure to television. Last, show that viewing is significantly correlated with our own perceptions of the televised issue. Although that description of cultivation theory is simplified, it does capture the most basic tenets, and its parsimony explains in part why so much research attention has been paid to it. Second, there are many possible cultivation effects as we consider how our perceptions of reality affect other potentially important outcomes such as our attitudes (e.g., Shrum, 2001) and our behavior (e.g., Nabi & Sullivan, 2001). With so much attention paid to it, it is not surprising that one of the ways that television is perceived as "unreal" is by virtue of this implicit definition of reality in cultivation theory. This definition does not rely on explaining what reality is or how watching television is somehow an unreal experience; rather it assumes a reality and then compares television to it. By watching television, we make our own perception of reality "less real." Empirically, tests of cultivation demonstrate that the more we watch, the greater our reality mirrors television and the less it mirrors the world outside of television.

However, other empirical tests have also shown that television lacks reality in ways that are not solely due to lack of representativeness. There appears to be something qualitatively different about two-dimensional representations of reality—even moving ones. One way of assessing the qualitative reality of television is to consider what sense very young children make of it. Because their experiences are unmediated and real from birth onward, it is interesting to ask how they interpret television in their very earliest encounters with it. Do they perceive it the same way they perceive the unmediated experiences they have had until that point? In other words, is television real to them?

Troseth (2003) asked precisely that question. Because of babies' relative lack of experience with the medium and because current research is unclear on what babies take away from it, she designed a study that explores their understanding of the medium. More broadly stated, she explored how very young children make sense of television's reality in comparison with the reality they have come to know in their everyday lives. The results of the study are intriguing.

The task was fairly straightforward. Two year olds were shown an adult hiding a colorful toy, and were subsequently asked to find the toy. When children watched the adult's activity through a window, most were able to find the toy. However, when children were shown the adult hiding the toy in the same room, but watched the activity via a video monitor, they were less likely to be able to find the toy when shown the real room. Even when efforts were made to teach the toddlers, by showing them the real event at the same time as the event appeared on the monitor, their performance did not improve in subsequent trials with only the video monitor. In short, most of the children did not seem to recognize the connection between reality and the video monitor. Television reality was not "real" reality as they knew it. They were not using the content they saw on the screen to guide their own actions in the real room. Similar research using slightly older children (30 months) provided the same results. Apparently, in our earliest years, the two-dimensional images on television do not seem to represent the reality that we know in our day-to-day experiences.

Troseth (2003) argues that these results are due to problems with dual representation. That is, to understand how to find the hidden toy, children must create a mental representation of the videotaped event—itself symbolic—and simultaneously create a mental model of the real event (the room, the activity of hiding the toy). Then, children have to assume that the former can map onto the latter and they must use their knowledge of the videotaped event to draw an inference about the outcome of the real event that they have not yet themselves experienced. For an older child and for an adult, these steps are seamless and unbelievably easy because we have grown accustomed to symbolic representation. We no longer need to struggle to map the concept of dog onto the furry thing itself. A dog *is* the furry thing. But for young children, reality is that which they do and touch and interact with, as Adorno (1974) argues, "through the medium of experience" (p. 80). So, like many nonviewers, toddlers might agree, had they the capacity to reflect on it and articulate it, that television is not a real experience. Television is something that toddlers need to *learn* to treat as real. Initially, they do not or cannot use it as a parallel to their real experiences. Therefore, television must have some inherent unreality in it, and, as we age, we begin to accept dual representation. One way that it is not real is that it interferes with real life. But another way that television is not real is that it has no inherent connection with experience.

So, overall, is television real? Certainly Eric and Rebecca Tanner would argue that it is not, as would Joanne Colton and many other nonviewers. In fact, the theme that television blocks our engagement with the real world came up in many interviews. On the simplest level, nonviewers argued that television interrupted or completely eliminated conversation. But for many, it went deeper than this. For them, it was not just that the audio and video of television interrupts life, but that its presence, even when it is off, gets in the way of life. Nonviewing women described how, free from the constant barrage of images of beautiful women, they felt released to be themselves without the need to look like a particular kind of woman. As Joanne Colton described, "The best thing for me is not being assaulted with cultural norms of how I should look or behave. My self-image is much better not having to look at beautiful women all the time. That's the biggest benefit, that you can be your own person. And your own person is okay." And free from what he called the "constant track going in your head," Eric Tanner felt he was able to engage in ways with his spouse that were chosen by himself, and not by the writer of some television program. He worries that with exposure to television programs, we learn their dialogue and their way of interacting rather than our own. He states that:

> There's more of a depth to relationships when you're not seeing these sitcoms that are just a caricature of life. So if I'm talking with my wife, I don't feel like I have to come back with a snappy comment or insult her because then people will laugh. You can engage in a much deeper way because you don't have this constant track going in your head.

So for nonviewers, a certain amount of reality is not just living without television in the moment, but also developing their own sense of what is right, good, and worth doing. Those values, they argue, should not come from television but should come from our own, nonmediated experiences.

For their children, parents also want what they perceive as real experiences. Lynne Selridge, who lived without television when she was a child, now says of her own young son: "It's so nice to see him outside stacking rocks. I remember as a child having so much time to play outside or to play Legos and I see a lot of that reflected in him." And Ted Randolph, whose children are now in their early twenties, says that without television, his children were able to live what he calls a "richer" life. A strong opponent of censorship, his main objection to television was not what his children would see when they watched it, but what they would not see and experience because they were watching it. Now, with his children grown, he is pleased with the results of their varied experiences. "My son is in a punk band now and he's creative," he says. "I didn't prohibit that. And I know he still rejects all of the standard stuff. But that's just for now. Who knows in the future? And my daughter, she could take it or leave it. But the best thing we did with our kids was to let them run like we did. They'd lose their shoes in a mud puddle and I was glad they did. They did all kinds of things."

To summarize: for nonviewers, television is not real for several reasons. First, television interferes with real life by taking time away from our real interactions with real people. It interferes with real experience by providing escapism that distracts us from our immediate environment. Nonviewers believe that television and its continuous nature comes between them and everyday life. Furthermore, it is the "constant track," or the thing that is calling even when it is off. Second, television interferes with reality because it is not representative. As cultivation theory argues, television and the real world are not similar and the former does not accurately represent the latter. The more television we watch, the more our own perception of reality is influenced by the images we see on television. Lastly, television may interfere with reality because, at some level, we do not recognize it as real—or at least we need to learn to do so. If very young children do not perceive television as real, it is possible that two-dimensional space is less real than what we experience every day. Therefore, for nonviewers, what constitutes reality and what keeps them in touch with reality is experiencing their immediate environment uninterrupted and undistorted by television.

Part IV
Television as Industry

In the final section of the book, I present chapters in which participants seem to see television as synonymous with the larger industry, referring to their use of television, or alternately their rejection of it, as a commentary on the entire industry of actors, directors, producers and advertisers. With this belief comes a particular approach to television. Rejecting the television industry seems to make nonviewers feel as if they are different from the broader culture that consumes it. In addition, it allows them to feel as if they are making some social or political statement that rejects not only the programs or the medium, but all of the industry, or sometimes even all of corporate America. With this broad definition of television, these participants reject TV in order to stand out, or to follow certain principles that they have set for themselves.

Chapter 13

Choosing to be Different

In this chapter, I begin by defining the concept of mainstream, a term that I used in a question and then explored with the participants. Interestingly, more than half of the nonviewers believed themselves to be out of the mainstream; whereas a minority of the viewers felt they were mainstream or "regular." To understand this difference between viewers and nonviewers, I introduce the notion of mass culture and the culture industry (Adorno, 1974). In the voices of the participants, I explore their belief that television delivers and creates a culture of similarity which many viewers buy into and I explore how nonviewers believe that by avoiding television, they are living somehow outside of that culture. Next, I draw on cultivation theory and its finding that there exists a shared conception of reality among otherwise diverse audiences (Gerbner, Gross, Morgan, Signorielli & Shanahan, 2002). Lastly, I bring in themes from the literature on family communication and argue that by emphasizing their difference from others, individuals are really creating a sense of similarity and hence cohesion among members of their own family.

During the first interview, I asked individuals if they felt that they were in the mainstream (which I define presently). I asked children if they felt they were pretty similar to other kids. Of the 120 nonviewing individuals who responded, 54% (n=65) said that they were different from others who they knew (e.g., "Our families think we're so strange. So no, not mainstream."). Only half of these (n=33) said that this difference was directly due to not having television. Some 30% of all nonviewers said that they were both different from and similar to others (e.g., "In some ways I'm non-mainstream and in some ways I'm pretty conventional."). The remaining 16% said they were not different in any real or meaningful way (e.g., "Maybe the reason people are surprised [that we don't have television] is because we're so regular.") However, a large majority (84%) perceived themselves to be at least somewhat unusual, and not having television was at least one reason for that.

Among the television viewers interviewed, only 1 (5%), reported that she was not "mainstream."

In this chapter, the concept of mainstream culture is explored. For many nonviewers, what they think of as "mainstream culture" is generated by the television industry: the producers, actors, advertisers, and the corporations who advertise. By eliminating television, many nonviewers believe they are choosing to be different from others in the mainstream, and they believe they are keeping the television industry out of their lives. I will discuss the role of nonviewing as a marker of difference in the lives of nonviewers. In addition, I will discuss the role of television in establishing mainstream culture and, conversely, how nonviewing is associated with keeping the television industry at bay. For individuals in this and the following chapter, television is synonymous with the television industry.

Sam Steinberg, Mary Peters, and Jeremy Steinberg-Peters

Sam Steinberg contacted me by e-mail. He had seen a small sign I had hung at the local food co-op. The sign simply said, "TV-Free? I am interested in interviewing people who live without television," and included my e-mail address. Somehow, among the postings for yoga retreats, guitar lessons, child-care swaps, and free-range chickens for sale, he had found my flyer. I was online when Sam first e-mailed, so I e-mailed him right back. And then he responded, and so did I. I described the interview, told him more about what I did, got his address and some additional information about the location of his house, and scheduled the interview all in a matter of minutes. In one message he mentioned, perhaps unnecessarily, that he was online "all the time." Clearly this was not someone who was eschewing technology entirely—just television.

We had scheduled the interview for a Saturday afternoon, and it had snowed quite heavily a couple of days prior. The main roads were plowed, though, so I did not mind driving. Sam had mentioned a couple of times that he and his family lived "way out" so I left a bit early for our first visit and ended up getting there late anyway. The directions included things like: "steep hill and then you'll see a river and the dam to your right," and "after the third sharp bend in the road..." Sam and his family had chosen to live in a spot that was more secluded than most of the homes in the area.

When I rang the doorbell, Mary, Sam's wife, opened the front door and said hello. Jeremy, their exuberant 7 year old, slid to the door on his socks, a mode of transportation that, as it turned out, he seemed to prefer. He also greeted me briefly but their focus was clearly on something else. Mary motioned me to the couch, then quickly sat back down on the floor where she was playing Crazy Eights with Jeremy. Sam was in the back of the house, in the kitchen, eating his lunch. The living room was spare with a couch, a couple of chairs, a coffee table and a very small Christmas tree in the corner. Then, central to the entire room was a large wood stove surrounded by a sturdy, wrought iron gate. No one was going to get accidentally burned on that stove.

When Sam ambled in, he introduced himself. Both Sam and Mary are psychologists. Mary works in the school system and Sam works as a therapist. He also does some freelance journalism "on the side," as he says. Sam is 48 with a graying ponytail. During our initial interaction, he was quick to claim that "TV is crap!" In fact, much of what he said reflected his notion of himself as a bit outrageous, as a radical. He seemed generally fond of sweeping statements. Somewhat later he claimed this about television, "I'd rather have second-hand smoke blown in my face!" Eventually, he would get around to explaining what he meant in more specific ways. Still, when asked what his main objection was to television, he reiterated that it is, all of it, just a lot of "crap." "It's the biggest waste of time on the planet," he claimed, waving his hand dismissively.

Despite this strong objection to television, Sam and Mary found themselves living without television in a more circumstantial way than you would expect, given their mutual aversion to it. They got rid of television for, what we called in chapter 3, environmental reasons. "See," said Sam, leaning forward animatedly:

> We built this house. And when we built it, we built it on the side of this rock. And we couldn't get the cable in. It would have cost a lot of money to get the cable in. Or we'd need to have a satellite. And really, neither of us cared a lot about television. So it wasn't a big deal, a big decision. It was easy.

So, like many people who I interviewed, Sam and Mary did not choose to throw their television out; they did not get fed up with the content and toss it in the trash; they simply found themselves in a situation where they were without it. "But then," remarked Mary, "we found we liked it. We liked living without it."

I began then asking Sam and Mary questions about what went on *inside* the walls of their home, without cable television. I asked about their relationship, about their interactions with Jeremy, about their use of time. Although they certainly answered my questions, what struck me was that they gave briefer responses than other families I had interviewed. When asked to think about how living without television affected their life as a couple, their life as a family, neither Mary nor Sam had too much to say. But they had not been particularly quiet people, throughout the interview or during our other interactions. For example, when I ask Mary about television and married couples, she said she did not think that television had affected her relationship with Sam. "It's pretty much like before," she said. "When we lived in the other house [before giving up television], we watched movies and sometimes baseball. And that Kennedy trial. But really not much has changed."

Sam agreed with Mary about how living without television had affected their relationship. When I asked, he answered, "We're Netflix customers." When I expressed confusion over how this circumstance addressed the issue of their relationship, he went on. "Well, we just about get our money's worth. We'll get a movie twice a month, watch them on the laptop. Mary and I might watch them together or not. So it's the same as before." So television, or its absence in this case, does not affect their interactions, or at least their perceptions of their interactions with each other. They both agree that life has proceeded as before. And in fact, they were not very engaged in questions about themselves as a couple or about television and the family overall. When we talked about this topic, the original idea that "it's all crap!" had toned down or slid out of focus.

Certainly, Mary claims that, "Oh yes, living without television means we have more of a family life…We spend more time parenting Jeremy… We don't have the option of using it as a babysitter." But when I asked what they did instead, they were both curiously muted. It seemed to me that they saw all of these questions, about them as a couple, and about their interactions with Jeremy, as somewhat irrelevant. What possibly, they seemed to ask, could this have to do with television?

And then, I asked this: "Do you think of yourself as living outside of the mainstream?" Sam leaned forward and Mary looked up from watching Jeremy, who was on the floor playing with a small car. "Oh, yeah," said Sam, at the same time that Mary started her sentence. "I felt outside of the cultural mainstream before giving up television," she said. And they began talking about their jobs, about others with whom they had interacted and about their beliefs about their role as Jeremy's parents. In the case of Sam and Mary, television seemed not so much about what goes on inside of the house, but how the home relates to the outside world, the world that they perceive as representing American culture.

When I asked about the home, *inside*, without a television, the question itself seemed odd to them. Unlike other families who talked at length about their family life inside of the home, Mary and Sam seemed to think of television as an entirely different thing—not some thing that interrupted the everyday ebb and flow of family life and family interaction, but some cultural representative. Television was the conduit, bringing the outside in. To them, television was the mainstream and they were voluntarily living outside of it. It is their difference that marks them and avoiding television both identifies their difference and sustains it. In the next section, I will discuss how television is synonymous with the broader culture in the minds of some viewers and why it is valuable to them to reject this notion of culture.

Television as Culture

Many nonviewers readily accept the notion that there *is* a cultural mainstream and that not watching television is an effective way of keeping it out, or at least of keeping themselves outside of it. In other words, television is somehow seen as synonymous with culture or, more specifically, with popular culture. For some nonviewers, they believe that with television exposure, you can be part of American culture; without it, you are removed from it. Therefore, television, and the television industry itself is seen as the thing that either delivers culture or actually *is* the culture.

An important question must be addressed before we can understand why Sam and Mary feel they have separated themselves from popular culture and what that has to do with television. Later, I will discuss what is meant by popular culture and how that is related to television. With this defined, I can then try to understand how living without television keeps Sam and Mary, and other families like them, free of popular culture and importantly, why they see their difference as a valuable outcome.

Although no single definition of culture exists, one classic definition refers to it as, "The system of shared beliefs, values, customs, behaviors, and artifacts that the members of society use to cope with their world and with one another, and that are transmitted from generation to generation" (Ember & Ember, 2002, p. 4). From this perspective, culture is shared beliefs and behaviors which might arise from the common experience of television but might also be related to other common experiences, such as schooling or language. However, when nonviewers talked about culture, they often referred to culture and television in the same breath, as in, "the culture of television," or they equated culture with "pop culture." In this way, they seemed to be referring to what Adorno (1991) called *mass culture*. According to Adorno, mass culture, of which media are a major part, encourages—in fact dictates—that everyone, every viewer, strive to be similar to the images and to share the ideas produced by the mass media. For example, he argues that:

> The totality of mass culture culminates in the demand that no one can be any different from itself...Today, anyone who is incapable of talking in the prescribed fashion, that is of effortlessly reproducing the formulas, conventions, and judgments of mass culture as if they were his own is threatened in his very existence. (p. 92)

Therefore, mass culture is that content that first presents, and then dictates how to speak, what to buy, how to look, and how to behave. It is this notion that many nonviewers seem to be referring to and like Adorno, a fierce critic of mass culture and the culture industry, some nonviewers believe that television is responsible for commodifying and standardizing everything in its reach.

According to Adorno mass culture does this through its omnipresence. It cannot be escaped because it is everywhere. In fact, in the first line of his classic essay *The Schema of Mass Culture*, Adorno (1991) states that the "…commercial character of culture causes the difference between culture and practical life to disappear…On all sides, the borderline between culture and empirical reality becomes more and more indistinct" (p. 61). In other words, commercial culture, because it is so readily available, standardized, produced for and bought by everyone, has become more and more synonymous with—or at least indistinguishable from—other aspects of culture, such as those noted in the traditional definition. Members of a culture can have, buy, and experience similar stimuli, largely because of the *mass* aspects of culture. Mass culture becomes synonymous, then, with "shared beliefs, values, customs, behaviors, and artifacts." Television may not always be the genesis of these beliefs, values, customs, behaviors, and artifacts, but it can effectively and efficiently transmit a standardized version of them to many people. It is perhaps for this reason that when those who live without television use the term culture, they see it as the same as mass culture. For example, in trying to explain his perception of culture, Sam offered, "I guess what I mean by that is mediated culture. The thing that is delivered to your home by the major media and that's mostly television. Because it gets into the most homes. So television is mass culture." Therefore, television and mass culture itself are nearly synonymous.

In fact, one nonviewer described how he had grown up without television for the most part. First, he did not watch any until he was 12 because his family, a Swiss mother and American father, lived in Japan. The language barrier made television unappealing. When he came to college in the United States, he said, "I watched a tremendous amount of television. It was a big part of becoming American." Why is it that television is such a big part of becoming American? Perhaps because it is such a shared experience, providing a shared lexicon and shared semantics to its audience. Because television reaches 99% of American homes, it is a central experience, regardless of where in the U.S. you grew up, who your parents were, where you attended school or any number of features that might otherwise separate Americans. Therefore, the knowledge gained from television is a shared experience that delivers culture, but through its ubiquity, may in fact *be* culture. Or, as Adorno (1991) calls it, "an organized mania for connecting everything to everything else, a totality of public secrets" (p. 83).

When Sam talks about television, he rarely refers to particular content. Rather, he uses the term television as a shorthand for culture: "There's this whole vocabulary out there. It's television vocabulary but it's the culture's vocabulary." He continues, "I'm a therapist and people will say, well, you know, 'did you see such and such?' They identify with a particular character or TV show. It's actually part of their lives." Similar to the nonviewer who believes he "became American" by watching television, Sam recognizes that television offers an opportunity to share in the cultural lexicon of his clients, to share in what Adorno calls "the totality of public secrets." But he actively chooses not to experience it.

Sam is also a freelance journalist. Although the family gets news from the Internet, and receives several newspapers, there are times when his editors feel he may not have the knowledge to tackle a certain story because he does not have television. In fact, he tries not to let them know. After all, Sam reports, he recognizes that as much as he wants to avoid television, a certain amount of knowledge about pop culture might serve him well as a journalist. He describes it this way, "I really have to keep up with what's going on and I try not to let people know that I don't have TV," he says. "We have high speed Internet access and I use it to actually keep up some with what's going on on TV. So I read all over the place that Tom Cruise jumped up and down on a couch and then I went to see the clip on the Internet."

Interestingly, Sam and other nonviewers often persisted in thinking of themselves as living outside of the mainstream, despite the fact that many, like Sam, took measures to follow some aspects of television culture. Many were also politically active, got their news from the Internet and read one or more newspapers per day. They talked to neighbors and listed among their activities everything from playing music in a local band to contra dancing to delivering meals to shut-ins. In other words, they did things that kept them in touch with both their immediate and broader world. Nevertheless, to them, these things did not count as mainstream culture. Instead, mainstream culture was consistently associated with television. That leads us to ask to what extent mainstream culture *is* synonymous with television.

The Mainstream and Mass Culture

George Gerbner (1969) and his colleagues, pioneers of cultivation theory, are philosophically aligned with the Chicago school. Adorno's (1991) work on mass culture, on the other hand, emerged directly from the Frankfurt school and critical theory. The philosophical roots of the two are vastly different and yet their ideas about mass culture share common themes. As was discussed in the previous chapter, cultivation theory (Gerbner) argues, most broadly, that the more television individuals watch, the more their social reality matches the one presented on television. Like Adorno, Gerbner argues that what is shown on television serves to minimize individual differences among viewers, specifically by affecting viewers' perceptions of social reality. One effect of greater viewing is what Gerbner refers to as "mainstreaming." Although Gerbner and Adorno differ markedly in their philosophical roots, assumptions and methods, the resulting assertions are similar. "Exposure to the total pattern rather than to specific genres or programs is therefore what accounts for the historically distinct consequences of living with television: the cultivation of *shared conceptions of reality among otherwise diverse publics*" (Gerbner, Gross, Morgan, Signorielli & Shanahan, 2002, p. 44, emphasis added) shares much in common with Adorno's (1991) idea that "mass culture culminates in the demand that no one can be any different from itself" (Adorno, p. 92). In fact, within the broader theory of cultivation, Gerbner talks specifically about the concept of mainstreaming, an idea alluded to not only by Sam and Mary and many other nonviewers, but by Adorno's work on mass culture.

In addressing the issue of what, precisely, is meant by mainstream culture, Gerbner and his colleagues (Gerbner et al., 2002) state that:

> Most modern cultures consist of many diverse currents but in the context of a dominant structure of attitudes, beliefs, values, and practices. This dominant current is not simply the sum total of all the crosscurrents and subcurrents. Rather, it is the most general, functional and stable mainstream, representing the broadest dimensions of shared meanings and assumptions. It is that which ultimately defines all the other crosscurrents and subcurrents. (p. 51)

They go on to argue that television's central role in our culture is to be what Gerbner (1969, 1972) calls in some of his earlier work, the *dominant storyteller*. This makes television the primary channel of the mainstream of our culture. Mainstreaming, then, according to Gerbner and his colleagues, is the process by which heavy viewers come to adopt this dominant worldview that is shown on television. Differences in perspective are blurred and more neutral, middle-of-the-road attitudes, ideas and beliefs are adopted. Gerbner and colleagues (2002) say specifically:

> ...differences that are usually associated with the varied cultural, social, and political characteristics of [these] groups, are diminished in the

responses of heavy viewers in these same groups. For example, regional differences, political ideology and socioeconomic differences are much less influential on the attitudes and beliefs of heavy viewers. (p. 51)

Although the theoretical idea of mainstreaming was referred to by those who live without television—a belief that they are outside of the mainstream at least in part because they are not exposed to the mainstream culture portrayed on television—there is also some empirical support for this idea. For example, heavy viewers are more moderate in their political beliefs than light viewers (Gerbner, Gross, Morgan & Signorielli, 1984), regional diversity, such as political attitudes, that might otherwise result from geographic differences are less extreme among heavy viewers (Morgan, 1986) and sex role attitudes are somewhat more traditional among them (Morgan, 1987).

In fact, several nonviewers, although they did not mention cultivation theory per se, were very clear and articulate in their beliefs about mainstreaming. Daniel Coleman, a public school teacher in Michigan and the father of five children stated that, "TV has the function…through the media to have a homogenizing effect. You don't have provincial differences as much as you used to. Advertising influences what's popular and acceptable." In other words, like Gerbner, he believed in the mainstreaming effect of television.

The Value of Difference

There seemed to be three main themes that emerged when nonviewers talked about their uniqueness as it related to nonviewing. First, they believed that nonviewing was simply *part* of their difference, not necessarily the cause of it. Second, they valued the perceived uniqueness that came from living without television. They thought of themselves as bucking a cultural norm. Third, some even saw their nonviewing as a form of active resistance against that norm, over which they bonded with their nonviewing family members and sometimes other nonviewing families, and nonviewing friends. Ultimately, these factors added value to their nonviewing that went beyond the benefits of rejecting television as a medium and the content it delivered.

First, many nonviewers believe that rejecting television is a way of cultivating difference; however, they recognize that they may be different in other ways as well. As a result, nonviewing is simply a part of a system of difference. People who lived without television often identified their politics as being either more conservative or more liberal than their perceptions of their TV viewing peers. They saw their ideas as being unusual. They pointed to ways their lives were different: "We're vegetarian," or "I don't own a car or a cell phone," or "I hate shopping," as one woman remarked. One 15-year-old boy, after the idea of being mainstream came up with his family, had this to add: "Well, there aren't very many people who have chickens. And we have plenty of them." So living without television is part of a larger difference that many feel and identify with. Other nonviewers felt similarly, noting that they were not like other people they knew or even others who they did not know but assumed lived out there, in that thing called mainstream America. Compared to television viewers, most of whom said they were pretty much like other people, nonviewers felt outside of the mainstream. They feel, as many put it, culturally isolated or different, but often, by choice.

Although living without television is a part of that feeling of cultural isolation, it is not the whole story for many of them. Living without television is partly the cause of their uniqueness, but, to them, symptomatic of it as well. An unemployed single man living in Massachusetts said:

> I've often said that I live in a bubble. I don't think I live in the mainstream and I think TV has partly to do with that, but I would also say I'm not mainstream American—whatever that is. I'm on the periphery. I'm not out of it because I can actually keep up with things by reading about TV in *The New York Times*. But I definitely feel like I live on the periphery of the mainstream.

Second, nonviewers feel that they are, by definition, different from the vast majority of Americans simply because they do not watch. When Daniel Coleman said that television has a homogenizing effect that makes everything bland, an idea that he associated with the mainstream, what he seemed to be saying was that television makes everything common. For him, and for other nonviewers, inherent in the mainstream is not only the commonality of shared knowledge that Adorno talked about, but also the commonality of shared attitudes, ideas, even modes of dress. If the mainstream is common, then the periphery must be less common. To many nonviewers, less common seemed to be more valuable. Like an uncommon resource or an unusual product (e.g., diamonds), the value increased in their eyes because of its uniqueness. Therefore, rareness, or the perception of uniqueness, is valuable. The trick, of course, is where you find your exclusivity. In the case of nonviewers, they seem to find value and uniqueness in their nonviewing precisely because they reject what they perceive as the commonness of the mainstream. As one nonviewer, an owner of a painting company and a part-time Emergency Medical Technician, said, "Sure, I'm out of touch with society." But he went on to say, "I don't have a problem with that. I don't want to be in touch with them. I'm not mad at them. I just don't want to be like them." Therefore, living without television seems to allow some nonviewers to feel a sense of individuality. As Mark Armstrong, said, "I've always been a smidgen on the edge of the stream. I guess I prefer it that way, to not be just like everyone."

Third, some nonviewers saw their nonviewing as an active resistance against mass culture. By sharing that resistance with their nonviewing friends, or with a spouse, their difference not only set them apart from others, but united them with each other. For example, Mary and Sam chose to live in a somewhat geographically isolated place but they also stressed their differences in the stories they told. One story in particular seemed important to both of them. As they conveyed it to me, it became clear that this was a part of their shared past that had been discussed and mulled over before. For Sam and Mary, on one hand, not owning a television was an act of resistance against outsiders, and on the other hand, living without television united them.

At the time, Mary recalled, Jeremy was in a preschool that was near a post office that had gotten a letter with anthrax in it. She had heard the gossip at the preschool and wanted to find out more about it, perhaps out of concern for Jeremy who spent part of his day in the vicinity of the post office. Calling the police department, she was connected through to a sergeant. "He told me," said Mary, "to watch the six o'clock news. And I said, 'We can't. We don't have TV.' And he said "What!? What kind of person doesn't have TV? What did you say your name was?' And he was very angry and intimidating." Turning to Sam she said, "Remember that? Remember when that happened?" Sam nodded emphatically. "They thought it was weird and that must mean we were worth checking into. It was like we were criminals." "Exactly!" responded Mary.

This is a point of agreement between them: they were odd for living without television, but at least they shared their ideals with each other, despite the fact that these ideals differed markedly from what they perceive as the cultural norm. First, their nonviewing is an act of resistance. Even the police seemed to think it was strange. Why else, Mary reasoned, would he ask for her name? Second, both rejected television which made them similar to each other, but different from their peers. Ultimately, this thing that they perceived as an oddity, united them.

The idea of a shared sense of purpose that emerged from living without television came up with other nonviewers as well. Nonviewing was something that joined them together. For both parents and children, nonviewing was often spoken of as a point of pride. Somehow, what made them different from other families also cemented the idea that family members were similar to each other. This similarity made them feel more like a family or more like a couple. For example, a retired Coast Guard captain with two children, both now older and in college, commented that having grown up without television makes his children feel unique. "It's a badge of honor for them, too." Other nonviewers mentioned that they had friends who were also nonviewers. These similarities also served to bond them together, identifying in-group characteristics, in contrast with viewers who were, at least on this point, the out-group. Living without television, then, is something that sets individuals apart. It sets them outside of the mainstream and even as it isolates them from what they think of as the larger culture, it bonds them together, as a couple, as a family or even as a friendship unit.

A 30-year-old mother of one living in the Midwest described how living without television had brought her and her husband closer, not because they spent more time talking with each other, but because they had this common idea over which they agreed. When asked about the decision to live without television and then their rationale to remain this way, she said:

> At first it was something we weren't sure we wanted to do. I wanted to more than him but we kept talking about it and then we agreed. He started to see what I meant and then we had our daughter. And now, when we're somewhere with a TV, or someone brings up a TV reference, we just shoot each other this look. And we say, oh, I get it. It's the two of us over on this side, saying "it's a great thing. See, we're doing this great thing for ourselves and for Megan." And the rest of everyone is over there saying, "you guys are nuts." And I kind of like it because it's this thing that bonds us.

Similarly, parents and their children felt that living without television was something that identified their family as unique, and in that way, acted as a bond that kept them together. Their difference from everyone else was at the same time their similarity to others in their family. Although the parents were generally more articulate, describing how their family identified itself as a TV-free family or mentioning their agreement over it as a point of cohesion, children mentioned it as well, albeit more indirectly. Children would say things like: "We just don't watch TV in our family," or "The other kids in my class watch it, but we don't." In this case, the "we" identified the child as part of a family that did something differently from friends' families. In other words, cultural isolation is not simply a matter of keeping aspects of mainstream culture out, it is also about unification within the family.

In the case of Mary and Sam, keeping television, and conversely mainstream culture out becomes an integral part of identifying their family *as* a family. At one point, Sam said:

In ways, implicitly and explicitly, we feel like it's our job to protect him [Jeremy] from the mainstream culture. Sure, there's a certain amount of calluses that he'll get. And it's an obnoxious enough culture that it will affect him at some point. Eventually society is going to be out there so we don't want to protect him from it. Probably like everyone else, he'll be affected by it. But why now. Why start now? We're his family now so we should be responsible.

Mass Culture and the Mainstream vs. Family

From these many ideas relating to mass culture, mainstreaming and American television, several related ideas emerge as families reflect on what it means to *be* mainstream and how television is related to that. First, those without television feel somewhat culturally isolated. They often use terms to describe themselves as "out of the loop," "living in a bubble," or "on the periphery." Inherent in this idea is the belief that television *is* American culture. That Tom Cruise jumped on a couch during his interview with Oprah Winfrey becomes culture. Indeed, Tom Cruise and Oprah Winfrey, knowing who they are, what they do, and something about the lives they lead is seen as culture—one that nonviewers go without, or sometimes actively eschew. Second, this cultural isolation is something they seem to feel proud of. Although some children, usually those in middle childhood and early adolescence may feel left out and ostracized by this cultural isolation, a topic addressed in chapter 4, most adults seem to want it. They devalue Tom Cruise and what he stands for and choose to ignore it. They perceive mainstream as being common and themselves, at the periphery, as being unique. Third, those living without television seem to believe, whether explicitly or implicitly, that television would bring them toward the cultural center, an idea consistent with the construct of mainstreaming in cultivation theory (Gerbner, 1972). To bring this full circle, they feel isolated and out of the cultural loop but because they devalue what they think middle America takes as culture, they are happy to avoid it because they prefer their cultural difference as an identity marker. In this way, living without television *makes* them what they are and stands as a signifier for who they are. As one woman living in California said, "I am not mainstream, whatever that means."

Perhaps the cultural segregation that Mary Peters and Sam Steinberg strive for, one that they try to garner for Jeremy as well, is one that keeps television out of their home to keep mainstream culture at bay. Many families talked about the sex and violence on television but that is somehow apart from the mainstream aspect of television. What these families seemed to want is a kind of difference, one that marked them as politically more liberal or politically more conservative. A difference that staked their claim to oddness and kept them and their families away from what they generally perceived as American culture, writ large. Mary Peters "want[s] the isolation" and the EMT from the Midwest is "not mad at them," he just does not want to be like them. And Sam Steinberg wears his difference like a badge in his profession, his choice of clothing, and his grand, sweeping statements about America and its politics. For all of them, it seems, difference is something of which to be proud.

Chapter 14

Battling the Industry

In this chapter, I discuss those participants who understand television to be not just the content of television or the medium, but the entire industry. They perceive television content as merely the end result of an entire empire made up of actors, editors, directors, producers, and advertisers. By avoiding television, they believe they are rejecting the industry. Interestingly, this notion of the television industry as immoral or unethical is held by those who consider themselves ultra liberal and those who label themselves ultra conservative. In addition, some "nonviewers" watch prerecorded content. They believe that by controlling when they watch it, how much they see and whether or not to watch commercials, they are taking the power away from the industry and regaining power in their homes.

Anika Bradinski is a Polish immigrant. It is how she refers to herself and often, in conversation, she refers to her Polish identity, her language, to Poland itself, and to the communist government which she left behind when she migrated to the United States 15 years ago. The communist government came up often in her speech, as in, "This American television. It's propaganda. It's worse than the communists!" And then she laughs, which accompanies much of what she says. She laughs as she states her strong opinions, as if you both should and should not take her seriously. For example, when I ask what she dislikes about television, she responds, "They give only an American perspective and I cannot stand their primitive, manipulative way of treating the audience! Only a moron would believe it!" And she laughs again.

To Anika, television is clearly more than content. The "they" she talks about is the industry. It is the industry that is stupid and manipulative. As we will explore later, it is the industry with which Anika, and others who share her viewpoint, believe they are wrestling. In this chapter, I will discuss how those who watch some rented programs but screen out most of television can still consider themselves nonviewers. I will consider how the acts of choosing some and, importantly, rejecting most of television, allows individuals to gain some power over the industry and I will discuss what, precisely, they are screening out. Interestingly, in many cases they are not attempting to screen out the content that is commonly censored: sex and violence.

Anika lives with her husband, Kevin, their 8-year-old daughter, Danielka, and Anika's 19-year-old son, Milan. Their house is a small, yellow farmhouse set on a hill. They have been working on an addition to their house for quite some time, and in the small, New England town where they live, the progress of their addition has been a topic of conversation—how far they had gotten, the color of the paint chosen. Because of the addition, and perhaps for other reasons as well, their house does have the feel of a construction site: a hammer sits on the counter next to the teapot, and a pile of house plans balances on top of a stack of books, most of them novels.

Beside Danielka, with her stuffed animals and Legos scattered on the floor, the three older residents sit at the table and talk, disagreeing, discussing, talking at once, debating in a lively, engaged way. But there is no apparent animosity. They just agree, or alternately disagree. When Anika throws herself into an answer, providing detail, depth, and some tangents that Kevin thinks are too far removed from the original question, he reminds her to stay on track. Both Kevin and Milan laugh at Anika's hyperbole, especially when communism comes up. The three of them correct each other, argue and talk over each other. Often, when I let myself out the front door, the conversation started up again and one of the three is up, making more tea. In fact, my interviews seem more an excuse for the three of them to share their opinions with each other than for them to showcase them for me.

Anika got rid of television herself about 15 years ago. The decision was made suddenly. She recalls, "In my previous marriage, I had a TV. Milan was 4 and I felt as if television was insulting and distracting. They [the industry] just think we buy whatever they put on there. I was a graduate student when I moved out and I said we weren't taking the TV...so we didn't have one at my new place." Like many individuals discussed in chapter 3, Anika first stopped watching television largely due to environmental reasons. An event occurred—in this case, leaving a home she shared with her then-husband—and it did not seem essential to replace the television. But why not replace it now, 15 years later? Why do Anika, Kevin, Milan and the ever-quiet Danielka live without television? They are not, by their own admission, concerned about the sex and violence that concerned the Fords, although Anika does mention, just once and in passing, that television has too much sex and violence. Nor does the language bother her. After all, their favorite DVD to rent as a family is *South Park*, a program with a TVMA (for Mature Audiences) rating due in part to the language it contains.

Instead, Anika seems more concerned with the assumptions that television, or television producers and directors, make about audiences than she is with specific aspects of the content. She worries that, "They think we're a bunch of idiots to believe it." She worries that we are all buying into what television has to offer and this, too, she finds offensive. "It's the worst. The level of commercial presence is unacceptable. [I dislike] the stupidity and propaganda, communist propaganda," she says. "Image is everything and people buy into it."

In other words, Anika imagines the producers and directors behind the programs. She imagines them thinking about the American public, including herself. She is insulted by their perceptions of her that might enable them to produce the programs that they do. To Anika, and others who share her beliefs that television is synonymous with the television industry, they object not to the content or television's intrusion into their home, but to the industry. Among this group of nonviewers, they object to particular content only insofar as it represents the industry's beliefs and attitudes. As Anika says, "They think we're a bunch of idiots." In the course of our early conversations, Anika mentioned that she likes movies. She also said her family had gotten DVDs of several seasons of *South Park*. Is this ironic, that a family who perceives themselves as living without television rents episodes of *South Park*? The show typically presents programs that reflect current events, but it does so bluntly—through parody and black humor. The show is frequently offensive, sometimes provocative, and its material often draws protests from various groups. The program is known for many things, including breaking the swearing record by saying the word "shit" a total of 162 times in one 22-minute episode. That is an average of once every 8 seconds. Even the program's network, Comedy Central, and its producers note that the show only airs during nighttime hours and never during the day, when children would be more likely to see it. Clearly, Anika and her family are not trying to screen out content that other families might find offensive.

However, despite the fact that many individuals might find programs such as *South Park* problematic, Anika and her family are not alone in enjoying these controversial shows. Over the course of this research, I often asked nonviewing individuals and families if there were any shows that they had liked, or that they would be willing to watch if they had a television now. Although many of the families found this difficult to answer because they were so unfamiliar with television shows from the last 15 or even 20 years (for example, the Fulvios of Connecticut cited the original *Star Trek* and *M*A*S*H* as shows that they had last enjoyed), those who did have an answer did not mention educational shows like

Sesame Street or PBS programs such as *Masterpiece Theatre*. It was not the traditionally "good" shows that drew people in, at least not those shows that are often mentioned as a knee-jerk reaction to what constitutes good. No one mentioned the History Channel or *Dora the Explorer*. In fact, parents without television often questioned the value of educational shows and stated that their children got at least as much out of books. Instead, families like Anika's mentioned *South Park*. Or, nonviewer Jen Eveland, who lives with her husband outside of Boston, sometimes misses *The Simpsons*, another animated program with often irreverent and satiric content. Mark Armstrong of North Carolina had a recent "near miss with *The Sopranos*," by which he meant he had seen it at a friend's house and had started to get drawn in. In cases such as these, nonviewers want to control what comes into their home, but it does not appear to be the violence, sex, or offensive language that they are trying to keep out.

There are two related questions here. First, if they are watching some programs, albeit just one or two, how do they retain a belief that they are nonviewers? After all, they feel that they avoid television and yet at the same time, they choose some of it. How then do all of these individuals retain self identities as nonviewers? Second, if it is not the violence and sex they are trying to keep out, then what is it? Among those who do watch some programs, they appear to be watching programs that are not sanitized. These two questions, "Why do they consider themselves nonviewers?" and "What are they keeping out?" may at first seem unrelated. However, on further analysis, these questions are closely tied.

Retaining the Identity of a Nonviewer

Although some of the individuals I discuss in this chapter live entirely without television, there are those who have a set to watch movies or rented television programs. Why do they consider themselves nonviewers? There are three possible answers, and each is related to the way that an individual perceives television. The first way in which they can identify themselves as nonviewers is that they create categories for television: juxtaposing television/propaganda/trash with *art*. And art is not television (which I will discuss in the next section). Second, they believe that they get something out of a particular television show that is different from what others get and therefore they are not like most television viewers. Instead, they get the subtle message that the program offers. Third, some individuals reject most of what television has to offer but carefully select a program or two that they find acceptable. By choosing one or two programs, but rejecting everything else, they regain control from the television *industry* and that act removes them from the category of "television watcher" because they are not participating in the industry. By regaining control of the industry, they are able to reclassify what they do when they watch a program. This third idea, utilizing choice and thereby gaining control from the industry, is also tied to the question "What are nonviewers keeping out if not the sex and violence?" In the next sections, television as art, getting the subtle message, and regaining control from the industry are discussed in greater detail.

Television as Television vs. Television as Art

It is relatively common for those who are active television viewers to choose certain kinds of programs over others and then, after the fact, to create categories for them to explain their preferences. A viewer may prefer news and then refer to everything else as "blaring noise," thereby creating her own categories for what is acceptable television and what is not acceptable (Morley, 1986, p. 57). Therefore, it is not surprising that when those who consider themselves nonviewers *do* choose to watch a television program (at a friend's house, say, or by renting it), they assign a specific classification to the program to maintain their identity as nonviewers—a classification that they find acceptable. They may categorize television as everything they do not watch and a particular program that they do watch as something else, something other than TV. Initially, this explanation sounds like a perfect tautology: I do not watch television because television is junk, but I watch this show because this show is not junk and therefore cannot be television. Recognizing and understanding this logic helps to answer our first question: how can nonviewers think of themselves as nonviewers when they watch a television program?

Traube (1996) offers some insight when she argues:

> The primary axis constructs a mass produced low culture as "other" to a high culture that supposedly transcends commodity production. On this axis, the standardized goods produced in the culture industry and governed by the "external" demands of profit realization are opposed to *art*, which derives a critical potential from an "internal" aesthetic process. (p. 131)

Anika made this point clearly when she juxtaposed television in general with a particular program, in this case *South Park*. She argues that, "When we choose something and there are no commercials, you can view it as a piece of art, which it is." What seems to make it art for Anika is the combination of lack of commercials and the ability to choose what constitutes good programming to her. Again, consistent with Traube's (1996) argument, Anika sees television as low culture or "standardized goods"; whereas what she chooses, with its "critical potential," stands in stark contrast to television. It is art. And when it is art, it is worth viewing. And when it is worth viewing, it is not television.

Other nonviewers also distinguished between television, which they often described as "junk," "crap," or "garbage," and "good" or worthwhile programs. Nonviewers such as Kyle Neff commended HBO, saying that some of what the cable network had to offer was "good, in-depth news," but added "TV is really just garbage." Here, he contrasts good news programming with TV, which is garbage. Anthony Fulvio said the following of television: "It's a waste. With a movie, you might recommend it to a friend but you'd never turn off the TV and say, 'That was good.' That was a great use of my time." He continues, "Maybe there are some good things. We used to watch *M*A*S*H*, but now it's junk." Others, like Mark Armstrong, simply said, "If there's something worth seeing, I'd be able to get hold of it." So in some cases, what defined television was its low quality. To these individuals, avoiding the low-quality content qualified them as nonviewers. And if they occasionally watched something due to its high quality, it was not really television. A tautology? Perhaps, but one that helped maintain nonviewers' sense of themselves, of television and of their relationship to it.

Getting the Subtle Message

But why are some programs okay? And why are they okay for Jen Eveland and her family, and for Anika Bradinski and her family? For example, it is unlikely that the Fords or, in fact, many other families I interviewed, would think of *The Simpsons* or *South Park* as "intelligent and of good quality," as Jen Eveland described, or as "art," as articulated by Anika. How is it that a family that rejects television might still choose to watch certain programs specifically because they are "of good quality"?

In his article, "Difficult Viewing: The Pleasures of Complex Screen Narratives," Chisholm (1991) argues that, for some viewers, television is not escape. Rather, people watch to "revitalize thoughts." He argues that a simple story can present subtle plot lines or perhaps bold satire. For some viewers, these additional plot lines provide pleasure, especially when viewers believe they understand the underlying intent. Although Chisholm uses *The Simpsons* as a classic example of this, *South Park*, too, falls into this category. Both are cartoons with a fair amount of juvenile humor; however, they also attempt to offer political commentary.

Viewers of these programs may feel that *South Park* or *The Simpsons* carry some subtle messages that only they can understand. With their understanding comes the knowledge that they are not only able to comprehend the message or social satire but they also are among those who share the joke created by the writer. They are not only able to view the programs as crass and caustic cartoons but also as savvy political and social commentary. The very act of understanding the message is a pleasure beyond the act of viewing the storyline and the plot. By understanding the subtle intended message, they are able to identify themselves as different from "average" television viewers. So, a second way that viewers are able to watch a program, or "choose" what to watch, but still consider themselves nonviewers, is by identifying themselves as different from others who might view to escape or to be entertained. Rather, some take pleasure in what they perceive as a more complex screen narrative. They are not providing an oppositional reading of a common program. Instead, they believe they are getting a subtlety that others might be missing. As a result, in providing subtle and complex messages to those viewers who can understand them, the program is raised to an art form and removed from the realm of television.

Rejecting the Television Industry

The third point, discussed earlier in chapter 5, is that some individuals think of television as the entire industry. When television is perceived as an industry, we can answer the questions of audience members as "nonviewers" and of what they are screening out if they are watching programs that contain sex and violence. It is here that we see the connection between the two questions. If television is thought of as an entire industry, then I can watch a single program without becoming tied to the whole industry. In exercising my power to choose, and importantly, my power to reject, I assert my power over the industry. And with power over the industry, I am no longer a passive viewer. In fact, I can be no viewer at all. This argument, however, requires a more detailed analysis.

That some individuals equate television with the industry can be seen in the way they talk about television. For example, although commercials and consumerism was brought up by approximately 4 out of 5 nonviewers I interviewed (see chapter 7), commercials are seen by some nonviewers as a simple 30-second segment that they would rather their children not see; whereas for others, commercials are an indicator of something larger. Jane Hart, mother of three children, worries that her children will be, "Too culturally sophisticated. I'd rather the marketers not get their claws into them too early." Compare this with Janine Jones who says, "I don't want my kids to see commercials because then they want everything they see at the grocery store." In Janine's case, commercials cause her children to want things, but she does not clearly connect this with a larger marketing industry. Jane, on the other hand, sees commercials as a "claw" of the marketer. She perceives commercials in much the same way that

Anika thinks of propaganda. Jane Hart does not want the industry to be in control of the culture that her children absorb. As she says, "I prefer that I be in control, not them [the industry]."

Others also perceive television as an industry. For example, Jen Eveland says:

> I don't know when it started happening but it seemed like television transformed into something else. There really wasn't anything entertaining but not totally stupid. So much of what is on now is just trash basically and I don't know if I'm part of that school of conspiracy theory: "numb their minds and we can take over everything."

Here, she pauses and laughs, "but I do think it a little bit." Jen clearly demonstrates here that she perceives television as having a set of goals and motives and a group of people behind it who have "transformed [it] into something else." To Jen, the industry is to blame for the downfall of television and not just for its moral decline but its intellectual one. Furthermore, she believes that, to some extent, the industry works intentionally, trying to "numb us" and then "take over everything."

The belief that the media industry is responsible for creating and disseminating mass culture is consistent with the one forwarded by the Frankfurt school and Theodore Adorno (1991) in particular, who had originally coined the phrase "mass culture" to describe the Nazi propaganda machine. In its earliest inception, the culture industry was compared to a factory, made up of all those who create the end product, in this case, mass culture (Adorno & Horkheimer, 1944). They later discarded the term mass culture and adopted "culture industry," a term that is still used commonly today to refer to the production and output of popular culture (Adorno and Horkheimer, 1944). Adorno and Horkheimer argue that:

> While the mechanism is to all appearances planned by those who serve up the data of experience, that is, by the culture industry, it is in fact forced upon the latter by the power of society, which remains irrational, however we may try to rationalize it; and this inescapable force is processed by commercial agencies so that they give an artificial impression of being in command. (p. 127)

That is, these standardized cultural goods, of which television is one example, are made to seem as if we want them, but that want, that desire is in fact created by marketers. Programming is merely a vehicle to deliver commercials.

Adorno and Horkheimer also argued that "The American culture industry had transformed culture from a potentially liberating process of self creation into an instrument of social control, a manipulative force that blocked class consciousness, stifled or deformed individuality, and assimilated passive receivers to the homogenous mass" (Traube, 1996, p. 131). In other words, "numb their minds and we can take over everything." To nonviewers who adhere to this idea, the industry—not just the producers, but the marketers and the advertisers—have control. They use that control to keep viewers passive, and, above all, to keep them purchasing. Furthermore, nonviewers believe that it is their responsibility to take back control. Although these ideas are tied to notions of commercialism and the rejection of commercials themselves, nonviewers who reject the industry want to reject the entire intentional machine, not merely the resulting programs and commercials.

"It's more a matter of selection"

However, the desire to keep the "propaganda" out and to regain control does not necessarily mean keeping out all of the content that television has to offer. In fact, to some nonviewers, choosing some material may garner more control for us than total rejection. For example, Lance Vincent, a 34-year-old pastor and father with one daughter, has lived without television for nearly five years. But he easily discusses his love of technology and his interest in politics and world affairs. Unlike Sam Steinberg and Mary Peters, who claim to desire the isolation brought on by living without television, Vince does not. Instead, he says, "It's more a matter of selection than a desire to live with my head in the sand." Similarly, Anika and her family do watch content from television so it is not isolation they seek. Anika explains, "Danielka watches movies with bad words if these serve as a social or political satire. At her level it is explained as what is wrong with some of the ways people treat each other or the planet. We explain to her that words are not bad, but violence is, so she doesn't watch violence."

Other nonviewers also express the desire to be selective rather than to tune out all media entirely. Jane Hart goes on to argue that:

> It has occurred to me this year, now that Pearl is in third grade, to try and upgrade. A lot of things like the Harry Potter movies she has never seen and this year all of her friends have seen it. So I feel like it is my duty to introduce her to some of the cultural icons so that she can have the choice on whether or not she wants to be in on a Harry Potter conversation. If she doesn't ever know what it is, no exposure, how will she know what kind of choices she wants to make?

Therefore, avoiding television is not a means of marking their difference, like it is for Sam Steinberg and Mary Peters, or keeping out the sex and violence like it is for the Fords, but rather a method of controlling what does and does not come into the home in very specific ways. In particular, some nonviewers perceive the things that they do watch to be a critique of the things they do not. As described by Anika, if television is ever a social critic, they will watch it, but when it is "propaganda" or "an arm of the companies," as Anika also called it, then it is screened out. By making this choice, they reject the industry of television, even if they choose to watch one or two programs produced by that industry. It is *choice* that allows them to feel that they control the television industry, rather than the industry controlling them.

Rejecting as Power

How does choice, or more specifically, the decision to reject most of television, create a sense of power in nonviewers? If, as argued earlier, popular culture and mass media use entertainment as a form of social control (Adorno & Horkheimer, 1944), then turning off the television or drastically controlling what is watched wrests control from the industry back into the hands of the viewer. The greater the rejection, the greater the sense of control. Several viewers argued that in rejecting most of what aired on television, they were able to send a message to the industry that they did not like what was offered. "Really," argued Jen Eveland, "in the kind of TV we have here [in the United States], turning it off is the only way to go. It's the only way to say that we think it's horrible."

Jane Hart argued that she is:

> ...very happy that we don't have television, *very* happy, and mostly because I am in control of their [her children's] cultural awareness. I can control how much my children watch—there is such a thing as being too culturally sophisticated in children, particularly in girls and I think in fashion and where their values lie and if you see so much commercialism in television, they start to think that what they see is what they have to be. They have to be the pretty princess girl or the tough boy, the boy who plays with trucks. There's too much of that sexual stereotyping going on in television ... I do want my children to have choices and I want them to be exposed, but I think I want them be exposed only to the good parts of media. I want to choose the aspects of our culture. I don't want them to be bombarded with messages that they are too young to understand.

Therefore, nonviewers see control and rejection of content as a means of gaining power in their homes. As one nonviewing parent argued, "It's my home. I get to decide."

Overall, then, Anika Bradinski and others like her, who choose very specific media content, yet call themselves nonviewers, are able to do so because they believe that their choices allow them the opportunity to reject the television industry. By rejecting the industry, they gain power in their homes. Nonviewers are nonviewers not only because they do not watch television but because the choices they make allow them to reject the industry they decry.

Chapter 15

Conclusion

In this chapter, I summarize some of the main findings of the book. I also draw conclusions based on these results. First, I argue that nonviewers, as compared to viewers, have very strong opinions not only about television but also about issues they see as being associated with television, such as politics. Second, nonviewers are zealous and idealistic. Third, nonviewers seem to be more highly protective parents. Fourth, they strongly express that one of their guiding philosophies is that they feel engaged in their lives. Last, they believe themselves and their families to be iconoclastic.

I started this book with several questions; others emerged over the course of the research. For example, I started out asking how family life is affected by living without television; however, as my research progressed, I realized that other issues also needed to be addressed. For example, what television *is* differs from family to family. Furthermore, this difference is related to why they gave up television in the first place. What television *is* to a family also affects how that family functions. In this chapter, I will begin by summarizing some of the broader findings of this research. Next, I will consider what these findings say more generally about families without television. I will discuss some of the similarities between families and draw conclusions that go beyond those themes that were discussed in earlier chapters. Finally, I will consider the role of television in the American family in today's media-saturated world.

A Triadic Definition of Television

Because television is consumed predominantly in the home and can affect time use and family interactions (Lull, 1980), its role in the family is perhaps greater than other media such as the radio or the newspaper (see Jordan, 2002 for a discussion of the growing importance of the family computer in the home). Television has an intimate role in the family. It is the almost-member that can impact the pacing and rhythms of family life. As Alexander (2001) has argued, television exists in the home in contested space, halfway between object of perception and object of social cognition. In this contested space, television has power. Perhaps more accurately, nonviewers perceive television to have power. They believe it can steal time, can affect consumer behavior and can influence how autonomous children are.

However, the meaning of television to nonviewing families is not unidimensional. Furthermore, the meaning of television for a given individual or family may be related to why they gave it up in the first place, whether they own a set at all, and if they do, how they use the set in their homes. These definitions are not mutually exclusive for a given nonviewer; rather, individuals seem to hold multiple definitions. These definitions are then used as part of a broader framework that helps families explain why they gave up television, what they object to about it and how these ideas are related to family life and family functioning.

When nonviewers equate television with content, they describe how they gave it up because they worried about the effect that television messages can have on themselves and on their children. Their concern might be about the violence on television, the lack of depth in political coverage or the excessive focus of television content on commercials and consumption. In some cases, living without any television whatsoever is the only way to entirely shield oneself and one's children from the content that is delivered through the medium. Not all families who viewed television as content had no set at all, however. For those who objected most strongly to commercials and consumerism, watching movies might still be acceptable. However, for some families, especially those who identified themselves as conservative Christians, the main problem on television, or in the media in general, is its overemphasis on sex. When this is the case, removing television's input (i.e., cable, network access) will not solve the problem. Instead, access to movies, some magazines, and the Internet all contribute to the problem of sex and the media. Therefore, the actual television set and, sometimes, magazines, movies, and the Internet are removed as well. After all, the particular kind of content that families find objectionable varies from household to household, and screening out that content can be achieved by eliminating only the input, or eliminating the entire television set itself.

When television is defined as a medium, nonviewers described the potential impact that the continuous source of stimulus could have on their lives. Many of these nonviewers removed television from their home to regain control over family interactions. Whether they wanted to increase the frequency of marital interaction, to provide their children with more uninterrupted play time, to remove a distraction from their lives, or simply to have more time to do other things, nonviewers who think of television as a medium removed it to remove its ubiquity. However, to remove its ubiquity, families do not necessarily need to remove the screen—only the input. Many of these families own a television set that they occasionally use to watch movies. For these nonviewers, removing television's input is akin to removing television overall because in so doing, they regain control of family interactions. In this case, the medium *is* television.

The third definition of television equates it with the industry. For individuals who define it this way, television extends beyond what happens within the walls of the home. They believe that television represents the attitudes and beliefs of those outside of the home—the industry that creates television. Whereas *medium* and *content* are two ways of thinking about television that emphasize how it exists in the private sphere of home, television as *industry* emphasizes the relationship between the outside world and home. The industry is perceived as problematic because the very ideology that allows it to create its messages is seen as problematic. Some nonviewers (e.g., conservative Christians) perceive the industry as morally corrupt because it shows sex on television, others because they consider the industry to be beholden to the demands of corporations to keep itself afloat. Among these nonviewers, the content might be offensive but it is the industry that produces the content that ultimately defines television. Like those who believe television is synonymous with content, *industry* nonviewers may or may not own a television set. However, their choice, either to reject all television or to selectively watch one or two programs, is what allows them to feel as if they have gained power back from the industry. In the battle between individuals and the industry, *control* is paramount. These nonviewers believe that they win the battle when they maintain control of their home, rather than handing that control over to the television industry.

Uses and Gratifications of Television

I did not frame this research as a uses and gratifications study. After all, how could the absence of something (i.e., television) help understand its use? However, as themes emerged in the interviews, it became clear that nonviewers think about television in many of the same ways that viewers do. They have needs, both social and psychological, that can be met by any number of stimuli, including media stimuli. Like viewers, nonviewers want to be entertained, to pass time, to learn, to facilitate social interactions, and to fulfill other needs that could conceivably be met by television. They enumerated those needs and then described how, in the absence of television, they met them quite neatly. Most often, nonviewers chose not to watch television precisely because they wanted to meet those needs in ways that suited them better than television did. Although some nonviewers gave up television in order to kick a habit that they perceived as problematic, most gave up television to better and more thoroughly experience things that were not television. They preferred it that way. Both nonviewing adults and nonviewing children did not seem to miss television. Their time was filled with activities and interactions and events that they enjoyed. As the uses and gratifications approach has argued, we return to activities repeatedly only when they meet the needs we set out to satisfy. In the case of nonviewers, television did not meet their needs, so other activities filled in the gaps. Alternately, they were so busy filling their needs doing other things that little time, or indeed need, remained to be filled.

From a uses and gratifications perspective, then, nonviewers gave up television because it did not meet their needs or because other activities did so more fully. Another reason existed, as well: in some cases, other needs trumped the need to be entertained by television or informed by it. For example, for some individuals, the need to minimize consumerism or foster autonomy in their children may have been deemed more important than meeting the needs television might fulfill. Overall, then, for nonviewers, television not only failed to meet their needs, but it also interfered with other needs that they wanted to emphasize. Although these needs are not readily identified in the nine dimensions of uses and gratifications, the basic notion that we seek out stimuli and experiences that meet our needs is relevant as an explanatory tool here.

In the end, uses and gratifications theory, which has been applied to a variety of different media, can be thought of most broadly as an approach to time use. It examines the needs individuals have and considers the sources of stimulation they choose to meet those needs. Indeed, Katz, Blumler, and Gurevitch (1974) conceptualized it this way when they stressed that need satisfaction could derive from many different sources, of which television was merely one. Narrowly examining the uses and gratification of only one medium or one source of stimulation may limit our understanding of human activities. By studying nonviewing families, we see that when we think about the uses and gratifications of television— indeed, of any medium—we also need to consider why people and families do *not* seek out a certain medium. Doing so offers insight into media use and into family life.

In fact, concepts of the home, family and family life arose repeatedly in this examination of nonviewing. Individuals seemed unable to talk about viewing without talking about how they interacted with other family members or with friends. They talked about dinner time, time spent playing games with neighbors, or how a television in a bar affected their conversation with friends. Therefore, it is once again to systems theory that I turn my attention. It is here, in this analysis of the family system, that we are able to gain some insight into and draw some conclusions about families and individuals who live without television.

Family Systems and Nonviewing Families

Like an organic system, a family is a set of phenomena that are interdependent and exhibit coherent behavior. A family is open to and interacts with its environment. The parts of the system, however, are not only the individuals who make up the family but also the attitudes, beliefs, and behaviors present therein. Each phenomenon functions to affect the other, and changes in one result in either adaptive or nonadaptive adjustments in the others. As other scholars have also argued (e.g., Jordan, 2002; Lull, 1980; Morley, 1986), television, with its strong, almost social presence in the home, often becomes part of that system. Families use it to punctuate time, structure interactions and encourage or discourage interactions between family members. Given that a change in one aspect results in adjustments in other aspects of the system, it seems likely that nonviewing families differ in specific ways from viewing families—and not solely because they do not have a television. After all, attitudes and beliefs are aspects of the family system as well, and as I have argued earlier, the specific attitudes that nonviewing families have towards television, and the behaviors that result, also differ from those of viewing families.

One question I set out to answer in this research was whether there is such a thing as a prototypical *nonviewing family*. Are there similarities across all nonviewing families that might mark them as a group? In some ways, it appears that there are not. After all, nonviewing families can be markedly different from one another: rural or urban; single with no children or married with many children; socially and politically conservative or liberal. And yet, there is some overarching similarity, visible only by looking closely and thinking deeply about this idea of family.

Family Beliefs, Attitudes, and Behaviors

Each individual in a family comes to the system with a set of beliefs, attitudes, and behaviors. These are interconnected within the individual and interconnected between family members. Each belief, whether shared among members or specific to an individual, sets off a ripple of attitudes and behaviors in the family. In the case of nonviewing, there are many, many attitudes and beliefs that result in nonviewing behavior. For example, both the belief that violence on television is problematic and the belief that watching television detracts from time that could be spent with a spouse, might result in avoiding television. But inherent in these beliefs are assumptions: real violence is bad; spending time with a spouse is valuable. These assumptions are beliefs themselves that in turn lead to specific behaviors that may seem unrelated to television viewing. For example, these beliefs might lead to behaviors such as avoiding violent toys or structuring other activities to encourage shared time with a spouse. Although these behaviors may seem unrelated to nonviewing initially, from a systems perspective, anti-violence attitudes, avoidance of violent toys, nonviewing, and any resulting lowered aggression may all be intimately linked.

Whereas many families, viewing and nonviewing alike, may hold anti-violence attitudes, may avoid aggressive toys or may disparage television, it appears that in nonviewing homes there is enough strength behind these beliefs that they have made a choice to eliminate the medium of television—a medium that is fundamental for most Americans. Alternately, these beliefs may have encouraged other behaviors that have made television unimportant, allowing them to give it up without much thought. For example, parents who have strong anti-violence attitudes may also believe that they need to spend more time together as a family to encourage these attitudes in their children. This increase in family interaction might lead to a concomitant decrease in available time to watch television. In either case, the beliefs are at least as important as the nonviewing behavior in structuring the family system.

Throughout this research, nonviewing families talked about their beliefs about television on one hand, and ideals that they associated with it on the other. Families did not simply talk about their nonviewing in ways that isolated it from other beliefs. Nonviewers often believed that television encouraged consumerism. However, tied to this, they mentioned that they disliked consumerism, and avoided shopping. Alternately, they mentioned that television interrupted or interfered with family life. Then, in the same breath, they would mention how important time with family was and the ways in which they attempted to foster it, perhaps through having a family Scrabble night or taking a family walk after dinner. In the end, their beliefs caused anti-television attitudes and the rejection of television, but their beliefs also fostered other activities, actions, and modes of being that encouraged the opposite of whatever it was they decried. It is likely, then, that the web of influence extended beyond the effect of nonviewing on, say, family time. In addition, the Scrabble players might feel more involved with other family members, and, as a result, valued family time even more. In that way, specific beliefs are intimately related to entire family systems and result in what could broadly be called the family environment.

Family Systems and the Family Environment

Throughout this book, I discussed specific beliefs, such as anti-consumerism, that emerged in the interviews. However, with the exception of "time use," there was no belief that all nonviewers shared in common. This might lead to the conclusion that nonviewers do not constitute a single group. However, I will argue here that from a broad perspective, all nonviewers do share things in common, despite their differences in politics, religion, education, and socioeconomic status. In addition to the specific beliefs that some nonviewers shared, discussed throughout the book (e.g., television is too violent and must be eliminated to protect children), there is something broader and less concrete that nonviewing families tended to share. I first addressed this idea in chapter 4, when discussing general similarities between nonviewers. I suggested that subgroups of nonviewers tended to group around a similar religious ideology (e.g., conservative Christians), but that not all nonviewers shared this in common. Similarly, some nonviewers identified with certain political views that were shared among some—but not all—nonviewers. Despite these sub-groupings among nonviewers, there was, nevertheless, a broader similarity among nearly all of them. All nonviewers tended to share a very broad ideal, and this ideal set the tone and established the *environment* for family life. Ultimately, it is this environment that distinguishes viewing from nonviewing families. It makes the family system neither better nor worse; it simply differentiates a family from others who do not share this marker. Although the majority of this book focused on particular attitudes and themes that emerged in interviews with nonviewers, I will turn my attention now to more broad-based similarities that I noted between otherwise dissimilar nonviewing families. In doing so, I will argue that, despite political or social differences in nonviewing families, their similarities are noteworthy and suggest that perhaps there *is* such a thing as a nonviewing family. These broad-based similarities include the following observations:

- Nonviewers, as compared to viewers, have very strong opinions not only about television but also about those issues they saw as being associated with it (e.g., politics, couple-interaction). In other words, they are zealous and idealistic.
- Nonviewers seem to be more highly protective parents.
- They strongly express that one of their guiding philosophies is that they feel *engaged* in their lives.
- They believe themselves and their families to be iconoclastic.

Families Without Television Have Strongly Held Attitudes Towards It

Even those families who gave up television by attrition were quick to note their many objections to it, although some claimed to have become more zealous in their attitudes after having given it up. In interviews with families who watched television, they were often unsure of how to answer questions regarding television and were, in fact, somewhat bemused by my project. Often, they had thoughts about television, but rarely were their attitudes as strongly stated as those who lived without it. Furthermore, nonviewers seemed to have spent time developing their ideas and were able to articulate them and discuss them at length. So one way in which they differed is simply that nonviewers have stronger opinions about television.

The connection between these anti-television attitudes and nonviewers' broader sense of how the world *should* work, also differed between viewers and nonviewers. For example, nonviewing families often discussed at great length their various convictions that they saw as being associated with their nonviewing. Whether it was religion, politics, or beliefs about consumerism, nonviewers had strong attitudes. Although they were on average no more likely to attend church than viewing families, those nonviewers who were religious spoke about it more openly. It was perhaps this broader idealism that tended to permeate the environment of nonviewing households. Their beliefs were a major part of family life for nonviewers and seemed to affect the way they went about their lives whether those sentiments led them to attend an anti-gay marriage rally, as one nonviewing family did, or attend a gay marriage rights march as did another nonviewing family. Recall, also, that I interviewed many nonviewing families on several occasions, and on each occasion they could speak at length about various beliefs connected with their nonviewing. In viewing households, however, the interviews concluded more quickly. Overall, although *all* families have attitudes and beliefs that permeate the environment of the family, these beliefs seemed to be more idealistic and more zealously held in nonviewing homes. Furthermore, these ideas were connected to other aspects of family life in nonviewing families, such as the other ways that they spent their time.

Parents in Nonviewing Homes are Deeply Committed to Influencing Their Children's Lives

Various pieces of data in my research suggest that parents in nonviewing homes are highly engaged in influencing their children's lives. In many cases, this characteristic took the form of protective behaviors; however, calling these families protective may be too narrow. Instead, I will refer to them as directive because they desire to direct their children towards certain options. For example, even those who might scoff at being labeled protective, such as Anika, who allows her 8-year-old to watch *South Park*, or Ted Randolph, who claimed his children "lost their sneakers in mud puddles and I'm glad they did," wanted to influence and direct their children. Although many parents are directive in this way, shielding their children from perceived dangers or influencing their ideas, parents in nonviewing households did so adamantly. Several factors point to this conclusion. First, in other research on nonviewing families, 28% of the 250 nonviewers surveyed home-schooled their children (Brock, 2001). In my study, 16% of the families home-schooled. However, only 2% of the children are home-schooled nationwide (Institute of Education Services [IES], 2003). While parents home-school for many reasons, concern over the school environment is one of the top three most frequently cited reasons (IES, 2003). Therefore, nonviewing parents are more likely than average to take protective action against the school environment by keeping their children at home. Second, as we discussed in chapter 10 on time use, nonviewing children also spend less time with computers and on the Internet than viewing children do. The primary reason for this was that nonviewing parents do not approve of computers and the Internet as a form of entertainment for their children. Therefore, that medium is controlled as well. Third, Cantor and Wilson (2003) have found that the more concerned parents are about the effects of television on their children, the more likely they are to limit their children's viewing. If we extend this argument, it is likely that parents who eliminate television from their homes are very concerned about it, especially compared to those who have few restrictions on their children's viewing. Therefore, it seems that parents in nonviewing households are indeed highly protective, or directive, parents.

Nonviewing Individuals are Engaged in their Lives

Whereas Putnum (2000) blames television for the lack of civic engagement among Americans, I believe nonviewers reveal a picture that is somewhat more complex. Television does not merely cause disengagement. Putnum's thesis is that television, by keeping people indoors and entertained, removes people from the more social aspects of the human experience. He points to the fact that volunteering has declined in recent decades, voting has declined, and our communities are disconnected—neighbors unfamiliar with neighbors. Instead, this present study of nonviewers indicates that nonviewing is part of a family system, of which engagement is one variable, intricately linked to the others. Nonviewing in the family is not the sole cause of engagement. Rather, as I have argued throughout the book, it is more accurate to say that nonviewing is also an outcome of their greater engagement in other activities. Recall that nonviewers spend more time in a greater variety of activities, and importantly, want more time for these activities than their viewing counterparts.

Like the Tanners in chapter 12, several nonviewers talked about the importance of engaging in real life. Still others expressed their desire to spend their time wisely, engaging with family members or pursuing hobbies. As I discussed in chapter 10 on time use, these individuals are largely active. But in addition to being active themselves and active in their communities, nonviewing families are engaged with their families, or, in the case of single nonviewers, engaged with their friends. Recall Kyle Neff, the artist living in Boston who spoke at length about the importance of conversation and spending time talking with his peers. Other nonviewers also mentioned spending time with their spouses and children. Certainly many families are engaged with each other, regardless of their viewing status, but in nonviewing homes, there is a strong emphasis on attention to, and engagement with, other family members. Interestingly, when I interviewed in nonviewing households, families often chose to be interviewed together. Even phone interviews with nonviewing families were conducted with one spouse on the kitchen phone while the other took the one in the living room. In viewing families, I conducted all but one of the interviews with a single individual, although I always invited the entire family to participate.

Unlike Putnum (2000), I doubt television causes extreme disconnectedness and anomie that is suddenly reversed when television is removed from the home. However, I do believe that the absence of television allows for a greater connection with family members, friends and community. After all, given that television fulfills a social function in the lives of many viewers (Rubin, 1983), it stands to reason that its absence does not remove the social need. Rather, the need is filled by other stimuli. For nonviewing families, that stimulus is often (although not always) other family members. This circumstance, coupled with the belief that they *should* be engaged in their lives may result in a greater feeling of engagement among nonviewers. Of course, social needs might also be filled with time spent online, connecting with others on the Internet (Markham, 1998). If this is the case, and computer time simply replaces television time, then social connections may not necessarily emerge when the television is turned off. Therefore, for social connections to result, nonviewing must be coupled with the belief that social connections, and efforts to create them, are important. Again, a systems approach may explain when and under what conditions, nonviewing increases social connectedness.

Nonviewers See Themselves as Unconventional or Iconoclastic

Despite other differences between families, nonviewing individuals and families shared a belief that they were iconoclasts, and for the most part, they relished that role. Whereas some, like Sam Steinberg whom we met in chapter 13, relished their perceived radicalism, others denied it. For example, Charlotte Ford, the home-schooling mother of 10, claimed that she was "pretty regular"; however, she revealed her antiestablishment core by questioning the television industry and its assumption that all Americans agreed with the sentiments presented on their programs. Anika Bradinski, whose own family was unlike Charlotte's in many ways, shared her outrage at the industry because "they think we're a bunch of idiots." From those who were conservative nonviewers to those who identified themselves as liberal, from single adults to those with large families, from the rural dwellers to the urbanites, nonviewers tended to view themselves as iconoclasts, even when they claimed to be conventional. And although I did not explore whether nonviewers were unusual or iconoclastic (whatever that might mean), many *perceived* themselves as such. Often, they passed these views on to their children, who would note their own difference from their peers, either because of their nonviewing status or for other reasons. For children and adults, alike, there exists a certain amount of notoriety in rejecting something so common. Although their nonviewing may have been a symbol of their difference, nonviewers often saw their difference in other things as well—differences that they may not have noticed had they not an initial sense of distinctiveness by virtue of their nonviewing. But because they were nonviewers, they seemed more inclined to notice other differences that otherwise may have seemed inconsequential—things like owning chickens, or not owning a cell phone. Ironically, perceiving themselves as unusual was a similarity across nonviewers.

How did these broad-based similarities create environments that were similar from one nonviewing family to another? From a systems perspective, their strongly held beliefs about television and about other attitudes and behaviors associated with nonviewing, their engagement in life, their protectiveness of their children, and their perceived uniqueness created a family environment that was marked by a sense of exceptionalism. With both its positive connotations and its negative ones, these families believed they were unique and odd. Their exceptionalism created a family atmosphere with a strong sense of itself, and with a strong sense of connection between family members. Although I do not argue that these families are more connected to each other, or are more unique, they do have a strong sense of family personality that marks them as *believing* these things. They stressed their connection as a family and in some instances saw this connection as buffeting them and distinguishing them from the outside world. Ultimately, from a family systems perspective, *perceived* family exceptionalism, coupled with increased engagement and increased parental directedness, sets the tone for the family as much as any true exceptionalism might.

Television as Choice

Based on the interviews, the surveys and the time-use diaries, it appears that those who do not watch television not only reject television to keep sex, violence, shallow news coverage, and consumerism out of their lives, but also to encourage family interaction, their children's autonomy and creativity, and a constructive use of their time. They list the many benefits, and, as one nonviewer said, "I just want people to realize it is a choice." In fact, it is not only that viewing is a choice, but each episode, each day, and each hour is a choice. For those who *want* to eliminate television, or to minimize it, recognizing that viewing is a choice may be the simplest starting place. And choosing wisely may come with a cascade of benefits. As the research suggests, and as nonviewers believe, television content can affect sexual attitudes, aggression, consumerism, political attitudes, and creativity. Therefore, minimizing television may improve our children's, our families', and our own lives in many small but meaningful ways. If eliminating television can go hand-in-hand with a greater sense of engagement in life, or with more time spent with family members, or with greater autonomy for our children, then turning it off more often could enhance our homes.

Of course, it is entirely possible that, for a given family, the benefits of television, as a babysitter, as a source of information and of entertainment, outweigh any disadvantages. As a result, watching television makes sense, functionally. A systems approach would suggest that the attitudes, beliefs, and behaviors of this family are also consistent, adaptive and useful. Although research suggests that certain content may have negative effects for a given individual, from the point of view of this family, television watching is effective. Ultimately, it is the contradiction between attitudes, beliefs, and behaviors that seem to cause strife in the family. It is the mismatch between what a given family purports to want, what they actually desire, and how they enact both of those that create tension. Eliminating television, or minimizing it, is best achieved when these attitudes, beliefs and desires are in balance. In the end, recognizing that television is a choice can set a family on the road to minimizing or eliminating it from their lives; however, and quite simply, the belief that eliminating it will improve life and the desire to do so must be in place first.

Conclusion

I set out to write this book to describe and analyze an understudied group in the media effects literature: those who do not watch television. Now, more than ever, I believe that *not* watching television is at least as important as watching it. Paradoxically, studying nonviewers has taught me a lot about television viewing and about families. I have always believed that television viewing is an important phenomenon in the lives of American adults and children, but now I see it as vital. Understanding the relationship between individuals and the media they consume, or even more broadly, between families and their media environment, holds one key to understanding much about family life. Television is intimately related to the way families use and structure time and to their attitudes about family interaction. Television is related to a family's attitude toward their relationship with the world outside, beyond their own neighborhoods, one that might be delivered to them via media. Ultimately, television is so seamlessly interwoven into viewing homes that it is nearly a family member. As one nonviewer said: "Television is there, and there and there." Studying its absence had led me to understand the importance of its presence. Like the old truism of the sick man: You sure don't know what it's like to be healthy until you are sick.

As for giving up television, I see now that for most it is a gradual process. Yes, some kick the habit, but many more lose interest in or commitment to television before it actually leaves their lives. Their rejection of it is spurred on by their interest in other activities. Engaged in hobbies, volunteer work, or activities with friends and family, nonviewers give up television and then begin singing the praises of their choice. All along they have objected to television for many reasons, but with its removal, they become zealots. Even children, who initially might complain, adapt with ease and fill the spaces left by the absence of the screen. So, for those who want to give up television, for any of the many reasons listed by nonviewers, it may be easiest to engage in other activities, thus lowering the importance of television, making its removal nearly an afterthought.

In the end, giving up television *is* a choice, but it is one that is enacted by families whose beliefs, attitudes and behaviors are consistent with that choice. It is seamless and easy, as many nonviewing families suggested, because their family system was ready for it, their environment well suited to it and their principles in harmony with it. Rejecting its presence and its message is not really the first step in giving up television; it is merely one thread in the complex fabric of family life.

References

Adorno, T. W. (1974) *The culture industry* (pp. 61–131), New York: Routledge.

Adorno, T. W. (1991) *The culture industry: Selected essays on mass culture.* London: Routledge.

Adorno, T. W. & Horkheimer, M. (1944) The culture industry: Enlightenment as mass deception. In M. Horkheimer & T. Adorno (eds.), *The dialectic of enlightenment* (pp. 120–167). New York: Seabury Press.

Aguiar, M. & Hurst, E. (2006, January) Measuring trends in leisure: The allocation of time over five decades. Working Paper No. 06-2. Boston, MA: Federal Reserve Bank of Boston.

Alexander, A. (2001) The meaning of television in the American family. In J. Bryant & J.A. Bryant (eds.), *Television and the American family* (pp. 273–287),. Mahwah, NJ: Lawrence Erlbaum Associates.

Allen, M., D'Alessio, D., & Brezgel, K. (1995) A meta-analysis summarizing the effects of pornography II: Aggression after exposure. *Human Communication Research, 22* (2), 258–283.

Anderson, D. R., Field, D. E., Collins, P. A., & Lorch, P. E. (1985) Estimates of young children's time with television: A methodological comparison of parent reports with time-lapse video home observation. *Child Development, 56,* 1345–1357.

Anderson, D. R., Levin, S. R., & Lorch, E. P. (1977) The effects of TV program pacing on the behavior of preschool children. *Educational Communication & Technology, 25* (2), 159–166.

Andreasen, M. (2002) Evolution in the family's use of television: An overview. In J. Bryant & J.A. Bryant (eds.), *Television and the American family* (pp. 3–32). Mahwah, NJ: Lawrence Erlbaum Associates.

Babrow, A. S. (1989) An expectancy-value analysis of the student soap opera audience. *Communication Research, 16* (2), 155–178.

Bandura, A. (1986) *Social foundations of thought and action: A social cognitive theory.* Englewood Cliffs, NJ: Prentice-Hall.

Bandura, A. (2002) A social cognitive theory of mass communication. In J. Bryant & D. Zillmann (eds.), *Media effects: Advances in theory and research* (pp. 121–154). Mahwah, NJ: Lawrence Erlbaum Associates.

Bateson, G., Jackson, D. D., & Haley, J. (1956) Toward a theory of schizophrenia. *Behavioral Science, 1*, 251–264.

Bertalanffy, L. V. (1972) History and status of general systems theory. *The Academy of Management Journal, 15* (4), 407–426.

Bird, S. E. (2003) *The audience in everyday life: Living in a media world.* New York: Routledge.

Bochner, A. P. & Eisenberg, E. M. (1987) Family process: System perspectives. In C. R. Berger & S. H. Chaffee (eds.), *Handbook of communication science* (pp. 540–563). Newbury Park, CA: Sage Publications.

Bok, D. (2001) *The trouble with government.* Cambridge, MA: Harvard University Press.

Booth-Butterfield, M. & Sidelinger, R. (1998) The influence of family communication on the college-aged child: Openness, attitudes and actions about sex and alcohol. *Communication Quarterly, 46* (3), 295–308.

Bourdieu, P. (1996) *On television.* New York: The New Press.

Brock, B. J. (2001) TV free families: Are they lola granolas, normal joes or high and holy snots? *TV Turnoff Network.* Retrieved November 22, 2005 from http://www.tvturnoff.org/brock1.htm.

Brosius, H. B. & Kepplinger, H. M. (1990) The agenda-setting function of television news. *Communication Research, 17* (2), 183–211.

Brown, J. D. & Newcomer, S. F. (1991) Television viewing and adolescents' sexual behavior. *Journal of Homosexuality, 21*, 77–89.

Bryant, J. & Rockwell, S. C. (1994) Effects of massive exposure to sexually oriented prime-time television programming on adolescents moral judgment. In D. Zillmann, J. Bryant, & A.C. Huston (eds.), *Media, children and the family.* Hillsdale, NJ: Lawrence Erlbaum Associates.

Buijzen, M. & Valkenburg, P. M. (2003) The unintended effects of television advertising: A parent–child survey. *Communication Research, 30* (5), 483–503.

Bush, T., Curry, S. J., Hollis, J., & Grothaus, L. (2005) Preteen attitudes about smoking and parental factors associated with favorable attitudes. *American Journal of Health Promotion, 19* (6), 410–417.

Bushman, B. J. & Anderson, C. A. (2001) Media violence and the American public: Scientific facts versus media misinformation. *American Psychologist, 56*, 477–489.

Cantor, J. (2002) Fright reactions to mass media. In J. Bryant & D. Zillmann (eds.), *Media effects: Advances in theory and research.* Mahwah, NJ: Lawrence Erlbaum Associates.

Cantor, J. & Wilson, B. (2003) Media and violence: Intervention strategies for reducing aggression. *Media Psychology, 5*, 363–403.

Cappella, J. N. & Jamieson, K. H. (1997) *Spiral of Cynicism: The press and the public good.* Oxford: Oxford University Press.

Chisholm, B. (1991) Difficult viewing: The pleasure of complex screen narratives. *Critical Studies in Mass Communication, 8*, 389–403.

Christakis, D. A., Zimmerman, F. J., DiGiuseppe, D. L., & McCarty, C. A. (2004) Early television exposure and subsequent attentional problems in children. *Pediatrics, 113* (4), 708–713.

Comstock, G. & Sharrer, E. (1999) *Television: What's on, who's watching and what it means*. San Diego, CA: Academic Press.

Comstock, G. & Sharrer, E. (2001) Use of television and other film-related media. *Handbook of children and the media* (pp. 47–72). Thousand Oaks, CA: Sage.

Cook, D. (2001, August 10) Lunchbox hegemony: Kids and the marketplace, then and now. Retrieved April 6, 2006 from http://www.lipmagazine.org/articles/featcook_124.shtml.

Csikszentmihalyi, M. (1990) *Flow: The psychology of optimal experience*. New York: Harper Collins.

Daly, K. (2003) Family theory versus the theories families live by. *Journal of Marriage and Family, 65*, 771–784.

Dexter, H. R., Penrod, S., Linz, D., & Saunders, D. (1997) Attributing responsibility to female victims after exposure to sexually violent films. *Journal of Applied Social Psychology, 27* (24), 2149–2171.

Ember, C. R. & Ember, M. (2002) *Anthropology*. New Delhi: New Delhi Press.

Foss, K. A. & Alexander, A. F. (1996) Exploring the margins of television viewing. *Communication Reports, 9* (1), 61–67.

Gdalevich, M., Mimouni, D., & Mimouni, M. (2001) Breastfeeding and the risk of bronchial asthma in childhood: A systematic review and meta-analysis of prospective studies. *Journal of Pediatrics, 139* (2), 261–266.

Geist, E. A. & Gibson, M. (2000) The effects of network and public television programs on four and five year olds' ability to attend to an educational task. *Journal of Instructional Psychology, 27* (4), 250–261.

Gerbner, G. (1969) Dimensions of violence in television drama. In R. Baker & S. Bal (eds.), *Violence and the media* (pp. 311–340). Washington, DC: U.S. Government Printing Office.

Gerbner, G. (1972) Violence in television drama: Trends and symbolic functions. In J. P. Murray, G. A. Comstock, & E. A. Rubenstein (eds.), *Television and social behavior: Vol. 1. Media content and control* (pp. 28–187). Washington, DC: U.S. Government Printing Office.

Gerbner, G., Gross, L., Morgan, M., & Signorielli, N. (1984) Political correlations of television viewing. *Public Opinion Quarterly, 48*, 283–300.

Gerbner, G., Gross, L., Morgan, M., Signorielli, N., & Shanahan, J. (2002) Growing up with television: Cultivation processes. In J. Bryant & D. Zillmann (eds.), *Media effects: Advances in theory and research* (pp. 43–67). Mahwah, NJ: Lawrence Erlbaum Associates.

Greenfield, P. & Beagles-Roos, J. (1988) Radio vs. television: Their cognitive impact on children of different socioeconomic and ethnic groups. *Journal of Communication, 38* (2), 71–92.

Gunter, B. & Furnham, A. (1998) *Children as consumers*. London: Routledge.

Healey, J. (1990) *Endangered minds: Why our children don't think and what we can do about it*. New York: Touchstone.

Heusmann, L. R. (1986) Psychological processes promoting the relationship between exposure to media violence and aggressive behavior by the viewer. *Journal of Social Issues, 42* (3), 125–139.

Himmelweit, H. T., Oppenheim, A. N., & Vince, P. (1958) *Television and the child*. London: Oxford University Press.

Hooghe, M. (2003) Watching television and civic engagement: Disentangling the effects of time, programs, and stations. *Press/Politics, 7* (2), 84–104.

Hornik, R. C. (1981) Out-of-school television and schooling: Hypotheses and methods. *Review of Educational Research, 51,* 199–214.

Institute of Education Services (2003) Homeschooling in the United States: 2003. Retrieved April 18, 2008 from http://nces.ed.gov/pubs2006/homeschool/.

Ireland, D. (2005, March 24) Censor alert: Congress considers controls for cable TV and the Internet. Retrieved May 1, 2006 from http://www.laweekly.com/news/news/censor-alert/806/.

Jordan, A. (2002) A family systems approach to examining the use of the internet in the home. In S. L. Calvert, A. B. Jordan, & R. R. Cocking (eds.), *Children in the digital age: Influences of electronic media on development*. Westport, CT: Praeger.

Katz, E., Blumler, J. G., & Gurevitch, M. (1974) Utilization of mass communication by the individual. In J. G. Blumler & E. Katz (eds.), *The uses of mass communications: Current perspectives on gratifications research*. Thousand Oaks, CA: Sage Publications.

Klapper, J. T. (1960) *The effects of mass communication* (pp. 19–32). New York: Free Press.

Krafka, C., Linz, D., Donnerstein, E., & Penrod, S. (1997) Women's reactions to sexually aggressive mass media depictions. *Violence Against Women, 3* (2), 149–181.

Kunkel, D. & Ganz, W. (1992) Children's television advertising in the multi-channel environment. *Journal of Communication, 42* (3), 134–152.

Kunkel, D., Cope, K. M., Farinola, W. J. M., Biely, E., Rollin, E., & Donnerstein, E. (1999, February) Sex on TV: content and context [A biennial report to the Henry J. Kaiser Family Foundation]. Report N. 1458. Menlo Park, CA: The Henry J. Kaiser Foundation.

L'Abate, L. & Colondier, G. (1987) The emperor has no clothes! Long live the emperor! A critique of family systems thinking and a reductionistic proposal. *American Journal of Family Therapy, 15* (1), 19–33.

Lin, C. A. (1999) Online-service adoption likelihood. *Journal of Advertising Research, 39,* 79–89.

Lin, C. A. & Atkin, D. (1989) Parental mediation and rulemaking for adolescent use of television and VCRs. *Journal of Broadcasting and Electronic Media, 33* (1), 53–67.

Linz, D., Donnerstein, E., & Adams, S. M. (1989) Physiological desensitization and judgments about female victims of violence. *Human Communication Research 15* (4), 509–522.

Lippmann, W. (1922) *Public Opinion*. New York: Free Press.

Lull, J. (1980) The social uses of television. *Human Communication Research, 6* (3), 120–136.

Malamuth, N. M. & Impett, E. A. (2001) Research on sex in the media. In D. G. Singer & J. L. Singer (eds.), *Handbook of children and the media*. Thousand Oaks, CA: Sage Publications.

Markham. A. N. (1998) *Life online: Researching real experience in virtual space.* Walnut Creek, CA: AltaMyra Press.

Mattingly, M. J. & Bianchi, S. M. (2003) Gender differences in the quantity and quality of free time: The U.S. experience. *Social Forces, 81* (3), 999–1030.

McCombs, M. & Reynolds, A. (2002) News influence on our pictures of the world. In J. Bryant & D. Zillmann (eds.), *Media effects: Advances in theory and research.* Mahwah, NJ: Lawrence Erlbaum Associates.

McLeod, D. M., Daily, K., Guo, Z., Eveland, W. P., Jr., Bayer, J., Yang, S., & Wang, H. (1996) Community integration, local media use, and democratic processes. *Communication Research, 23* (2), 179–209.

McLeod, D. M., Kosicki, G. M., & McLeod, J. M. (2002) Resuming the boundaries of political communication effects. In J. Bryant & D. Zillmann (eds.), *Media effects: Advances in theory and research* (pp. 215–268). Mahwah, NJ: Lawrence Erlbaum Associates.

McNeal, J. U. (1992) *Kids as customers: A handbook of marketing to children.* New York: Lexington Books.

Morgan, M. (1986) Television and the erosion of regional diversity. *Journal of Broadcasting and Electronic Media, 30* (2), 123–139.

Morgan, M. (1987) Television, sex-role attitudes, and sex-role behavior. *Journal of Early Adolescence, 7* (3), 269–282.

Morley, D. (1986) *Family television: Culture power and domestic leisure.* London: Routledge.

Mutz, D. C., Roberts, D. F., & van Vuuren, D. P. (1993) Reconsidering the displacement hypothesis: Television's influence on children's time use. *Communication Research, 20,* 1, 51–75.

Nabi, R. L. & Sullivan, J. L. (2001) Does television viewing relate to engagement in protective behaviors against crime?: A cultivation analysis from a theory of reasoned action perspective. *Communication Research, 28* (6), 802–825.

National Institute of Mental Health (2008) *Attention Deficit and Hyperactivity Disorder.* Retrieved January 16, 2007 from http://www.nimh.nih.gov/publicat/adhd.cfm.

Paik, H. & Comstock, G. (1994) The effects of television violence on anti-social behavior: A meta-analysis. *Communication Research, 21* (4), 516–546.

Papacharissi, Z. & Rubin, A. M. (2000) Predictors of Internet use. *Journal of Broadcasting & Electronic Media, 44* (2), 175–196.

Perse, E. M. & Rubin, A. M. (1990) Chronic loneliness and television use. *Journal of Broadcasting and Electronic Media, 34* (1), 37–53.

Pew Research Center of the People and the Press (2005) Support for tougher indecency measures, but worries about government intrusiveness: New concerns about Internet and reality shows. [Press Release]. Retrieved July 29, 2006 from http://peoplepress.org/reports/display.php3?ReportID=241.

Postman, N. (1985) *Amusing ourselves to death: Public discourse in the age of show business.* New York: Penguin Books.

Potter, J. W. (2005) *Media literacy.* Thousand Oaks, CA: Sage Publications.

Putnam, R. (2000) *Bowling alone: The collapse and revival of American community.* New York: Simon and Schuster.

Quisenberry, N. I, & Klasek, C. B. (1977) Can watching television be good for children? *Audiovisual Instruction, 22* (3), 56–57.

Riesch, S. K., Bush, L., Nelson, C. J., Ohm, B. J., Portz, P. A., Abell, B., Wightman, M. R., & Jenkins, P. (2000, January-March) Topics of conflict between parents and young adolescents. *Journal of the Society of Pediatric Nurses, 5* (1), 27–40.

Roberts, D. F, Foehr, U. G., & Rideout, V. (2005) *Generation M: Media in the lives of 8–18 year-olds* [A Kaiser Family Foundation Study]. Menlo Park, CA: Kaiser Family Foundation.

Rosenthal, T. L. & Zimmerman, B. J. (1978) *Social learning and cognition*. New York: Academic Press.

Rubin, A. M. (1981) An examination of television viewing motivations. *Communication Research, 8*, 141–165.

Rubin, A. M. (1983) Television uses and gratifications: The interactions of viewing patterns and motivations. *Journal of Broadcasting, 27*, 37–51.

Rubin, A. M. (1984) Ritualized and instrumentalized television viewing. *Journal of Communication, 34* (3), 67–77.

Rubin, A. M. (2002) The uses-and-gratifications perspective of media effects. In J. Bryant & D. Zillmann (eds.), *Media effects: Advances in theory and research*. Mahwah, NJ: Erlbaum.

Shah, A. (2003) Children as consumers. Retrieved April 6, 2006 from http://www.globalissues.org/TradeRelated/Consumption/Children.asp.

Shah, D. (1998) Civic engagement, interpersonal trust, and television use: An individual-level assessment of social capital. *Political Psychology, 9* (3), 469–496.

Shannon, P. & Fernie, D. E. (1985) Print and television: Children's use of the medium is the message. *Elementary School Journal, 85* (5), 663–672.

Shrum, L. J. (2001) Processing strategy moderates the cultivation effect. *Human Communication Research, 27* (1), 94.

Silverstone, R. (1994) *Television and everyday life*. London: Routledge.

Singer, D. G. & Singer, J. L. (1990) *The house of make-believe: Children's play and the developing imagination*. Cambridge, MA: Harvard University Press.

Smith, S. L., & Donnerstein, E. (1998) Harmful effects of exposure to media violence: Learning of aggression, emotional desensitization, and fear. In R. G. Geen & E. Donnerstein (eds.), *Human aggression: Theories, research, and implications for social policy* (pp. 167–202). New York: Academic Press.

Sparks, G. G. & Sparks, C. W. (2002) Effects of media violence. In J. Bryant & D. Zillmann (eds.), *Media effects: Advances in theory and research* (pp. 269–286), Mahwah, NJ: Lawrence Erlbaum Associates.

Spring, J. (2003) *Educating the consumer citizen: A history of the marriage of schools, advertising and the media*. Mahwah, NJ: Lawrence Erlbaum Associates.

Tarrant, M., MacKenzie, L. & Hewitt, L. A. (2006) Friendship group identification, multidimensional self-concept, and experience of developmental tasks in adolescence. *Journal of Adolescence, 29* (4), 627–640.

Thomas, M. H., Horton, R. W., Lippincott, E. C., & Drabman, R. S. (1977) Desensitization to portrayals of real-life aggression as a function of exposure to television violence. *Journal of Personality and Social Psychology, 35* (6), 450–458.

Traube, E. G. (1996) "The popular" in American culture. *Annual Review of Anthropology, 25,* 127–151.

Troseth, G. L. (2003) Getting a clear picture: young children's understanding of a televised image. *Developmental Science, 6* (3), 243–253.

Valkenburg, P. M. (2001) The development of a child into a consumer. *Journal of Applied Developmental Psychology, 22* (1), 61–72.

Valkenburg, P. & Cantor, J. (2002) The development of a child into a consumer. In S. L. Calvert, A. B. Jordan, & R. R. Cocking (eds.), *Children in the digital age: Influences of electronic media on development.* Westport, CT: Praeger.

Valkenburg, P. M., & van der Voort, T. H. A. (1994) Influence of TV on daydreaming and creative imagination: A review of research. *Psychological Bulletin, 116* (2), 316–339.

Williams, T. M. (1985) Implications of a natural experiment in the developed world for research on *television* in the developing world. *Journal of Cross-Cultural Psychology, 16* (3), 263–287.

Wilson, B. J., Kunkel, D., Linz, D., Donnerstein, E., Smith, S., Blumenthal, E., & Gray, T. (1997) Television violence and its context. In Mediascope (ed.), *National Television Violence Study, Volume 1.* Newbury Park, CA: Sage Publications.

Winn, M. (1985) *The plug-in drug: Television, children, and the family.* New York: Penguin.

Zillmann, D. & Weaver, J. B., III (1999) Effects of prolonged exposure to gratuitous media violence on provoked and unprovoked hostile behavior. *Journal of Applied Social Psychology, 29* (1), 145–165.

Zinsmeister, K. (1997) TV-free: Real families describe life without the tube. *The American Enterprise, 8* (5), 63–72.

Index